HIERARCHIES, TARGETS AND CONTROLLERS
Agreements Patterns in Slavic

CROOM HELM LINGUISTICS SERIES
Edited by James R. Hurford and John A. Hawkins

Hierarchies, Targets and Controllers
Agreement Patterns in Slavic

GREVILLE G. CORBETT

CROOM HELM
London & Canberra

© 1983 Greville G. Corbett
Croom Helm, Provident House, Burrell Row,
Beckenham, Kent BR3 1AT

British Library Cataloguing in Publication Data
Corbett,Greville G.
Hierarchies, targets and controllers.
1. Slavic languages – Grammar
I. Title
491.8   PG89
ISBN 0-7099-0744-3

To Judith

Printed and bound in Great Britain
by Billing & Sons Limited, Worcester.

CONTENTS

Contents

EDITORIAL STATEMENT

CROOM HELM LTD are publishing a Linguistics Series under the joint editorship of James Hurford (University of Edinburgh) and John Hawkins (Max-Planck-Institut für Psycholinguistik). These editors wish to draw this series to the attention of scholars, who are invited to submit manuscripts to Jim Hurford or to John Hawkins. Following is a statement of editorial intent:

The series will not specialise in any one area of language study, nor will it limit itself to any one theoretical approach. Synchronic and diachronic descriptive studies, either syntactic, semantic, phonological or morphological, will be welcomed, as will more theoretical 'model-building' studies, and studies in sociolinguistics or psycholinguistics. The criterion for acceptance will be quality and potential contribution to the relevant field. All monographs published must advance our understanding of the nature of language in areas of substantial interest to major sectors of the linguistic research community. Traditional scholarly standards, such as clarity of presentation, factual and logical soundness of argumentation, and a thorough and reasoned orientation to other relevant work, must also be adhered to. Within these indispensible limitations we welcome the submission of creative and original contributions to the study of language.

James R. Hurford, Department of Linguistics, University of Edinburgh, Adam Ferguson Building, George Square, Edinburgh EH8 9LL. John A. Hawkins, Max-Planck-Institut für Psycholinguistik, Berg en Dalseweg 79, NL-6522 BC, Nijmegen, The Netherlands.

PREFACE

It is a pleasure to record my gratitude to John Anderson, Wayles Browne and Bernard Comrie, who made valuable comments on sections of this work, and especially to Roland Sussex, who gave his reactions to most of it. I am also grateful to Paul Cubberly, Zhanna Dolgopolova and Ljubomir Popović for reading individual chapters, to Judith Bridgeman and Carol Trumble for highly competent typing and to several other friends and colleagues for help of various kinds. A large part of the research was carried out during the tenure of a University Research Fellowship, for which I wish to thank the Council of the University of Melbourne. Two travel grants, which enabled me to visit the Universities of Belgrade and Leipzig and to check on certain data, were generously provided by the British Council.

ABBREVIATIONS

acc	—	accusative	masc	—	masculine
anim	—	animate	neut	—	neuter
Bg	—	Bulgarian	nom	—	nominative
BR	—	Belorussian	NP	—	noun phrase
Cz	—	Czech	OCS	—	Old Church Slavic
dat	—	dative	P	—	Polish
DR	—	dialectal Russian	pers	—	person(al)
fem	—	feminine	pl	—	plural
gen	—	genitive	R	—	Russian
inan	—	inanimate	SC	—	Serbo-Croat
inst	—	instrumental	SF	—	short-form
LF	—	long-form	sg	—	singular
loc	—	locative	Sk	—	Slovak
LR	—	literary Russian	Sn	—	Slovene
LS	—	Lower Sorbian	U	—	Ukrainian
M	—	Macedonian	US	—	Upper Sorbian

TRANSLITERATION

Language	Letter	Transliteration
	а	a
	б	b
	в	v
B M OCS R S	г	g
BR U	г	h
	д	d
S	ђ	đ
M	ѓ	ǵ
	е	e
BR R	ё	ë
U	є	je
	ж	ž
M OCS	ѕ	dz
	з	z
B M OCS R S	и	i
U	и	y
BR U	і	i
U	ї	ji
M S	ј	j
B BR R U	й	j
	к	k
	л	l
M S	љ	lj
	м	m
	н	n
M S	њ	nj
	о	o
	п	p
	р	r
	с	s
	т	t
S	ħ	ć
M	ќ	ḱ
OCS	оу	u

Transliteration

Language	Letter	Transliteration
B BR M R S U	у	u
BR	ў	ŭ
	ф	f
B BR M OCS R U	х	x
S	х	h
	ц	c
	ч	č
M S	ѕ	dž
	ш	š
R U	щ	šč
B	щ	št
OCS	ⱎⱅ	št
R	ъ	"
B	ъ	ă
OCS	ⰺ	ь
BR R	ы	y
OCS	ⰺⰻ	y
B BR R U	ь	'
OCS	ь	ь
OCS	ѣ	ě
BR R	э	è
B BR OCS R U	ю	ju
B BR R U	я	ja
OCS	ѭ.	ja
OCS	ѥ	je
OCS	ѧ	ę
OCS	ѫ	ǫ
OCS	ⱑⱔ	ję
OCS	ⱑⱘ	jǫ

Notes:

1. When the language column is blank, the character is found in all the alphabets in question – Bulgarian, Belorussian, Macedonian, Old Church Slavic, Russian, Serbian (indicated by 'S') and Ukrainian.

2. *ё* is frequently written *e*. It is transliterated as *ё* only when *ё* appears in the original and otherwise as *e*.

3. Certain rare graphemes, particularly in Old Church Slavic, which do not occur in any of our examples, are not included.

1   INTRODUCTION

Agreement is a notoriously difficult problem for linguistic theory. The phenomenon is particularly challenging in the Slavic languages, where it is widespread, complex and subject to considerable variation. In investigating agreement in Slavic our aim is to establish the patterns of variation, to make general claims which hold for the full range of data. While we will concentrate on data from one language family, our claims are of general significance: first, in that we demonstrate a type of analysis which is appropriate for linguistic data showing variation in several different dimensions; and second, many of the claims made specifically about Slavic languages are also put forward as universals.

1.1 Agreement and Variation

At first sight agreement appears straightforward: the agreeing forms are there on the surface and the basic facts are usually clear. We may say, for example, that in particular languages (French, Latin or Polish) adjectives agree with their head noun in number, with little fear of objection. However, if we ask how agreement operates, or why it occurs at all, then we find that our understanding is limited. One way forward is to look for situations in which the agreement system partially breaks down. Our approach is like that of the geologist, who can learn more from a geological fault than from many miles of unbroken terrain. The cracks in agreement systems are instances where more than one type of agreement is possible. For example, English permits both *the committee believes* and *the committee believe*. We shall investigate many constructions where such alternative forms are possible. Variation in the choice of form depends on a wide range of factors. We shall consider data showing that the choice of agreement form is affected by the age, education, socioeconomic background and even the sex of the speaker. There are examples of diachronic change, and of variation between the standard language, colloquial usage and dialects. And when we compare similar constructions in different languages, we discover yet another dimension of variation.

The initial impression is that we are confronted by endless flux. But patterns of agreement can be established which remain constant through the range of sociolinguistic variation. It is possible to identify certain factors whose presence always favours a particular type of agreement. We can also make implicational statements specifying that a language can permit one type of agreement in a given syntactic position (e.g. the predicate) only if it is also possible in a second defined position. And, as we shall see, implicational claims of this sort can be linked into chains, which have considerable predictive power. The set of syntactic positions about which these claims are made is called a 'hierarchy'. We can extend our predictions to cover not only the opposition between possible and impossible agreement forms, but also relations of relative frequency. By establishing patterns like these we can begin to understand how agreement works. They may also give us insights into the nature of linguistic variation.

1.2 The Slavic Family

If we are to investigate agreement by searching for patterns of variation, the Slavic languages provide an ideal area for study. Agreement is almost ubiquitous, and there are several different constructions which permit agreement options. The Slavic languages have rich inflectional morphology: typically, adjectives agree in gender, number and case with their head noun (sometimes too there are forms for agreement with animates or personals). Verbs mark person, number and, in the past tense, gender. Nouns are divided into three genders, for which agreeing elements have separate forms in the singular. In the plural, the three genders may again be distinguished (as in Serbo-Croat), or there may be only two forms available (Polish), or a single plural form (Russian). Most often there are six cases, as in Russian and Polish, but Serbo-Croat has seven, while Bulgarian and Macedonian have three. The relevant grammatical background will be given when examples require it, and literal glosses are provided throughout. Articles are added to the glosses to aid comprehension. The sole purpose of the glosses is to enable the reader to grasp the grammatical point being made; Slavists should ignore them.

The Slavic family is divided into three groups: West, South and East Slavic. The Western group consists of Czech, Slovak, Polish and Sorbian (also called Wendish or Lusatian). Sorbian exists in two variants: Upper and Lower Sorbian. In the Southern group we find Bulgarian, Macedonian, Old Church Slavic, Serbo-Croat and Slovene. Finally, the East Slavic group comprises Russian, Belorussian (White Russian) and

Ukrainian (Ruthenian).[1] Common Slavic, the parent language, split into these three groups around the eighth century AD, though authorities differ over the exact date. There is no direct written evidence of Common Slavic. There are, however, Old Church Slavic texts dating from the eleventh century, which reveal a language similar to the postulated Common Slavic but showing distinct South Slavic traits; this relationship is indicated in Table 1.1. All the West Slavic languages,

Table 1.1: The Slavic Language Family

and Slovene in the Southern group, are normally written in the Roman alphabet. The East Slavic languages, together with Bulgarian and Macedonian, use Cyrillic. Both alphabets can be found in the Serbo-Croat language area. This division of the Slavic family can be traced back to the Great Schism: the Orthodox East uses Cyrillic, and the Catholic West uses Roman. The transliteration used for the various forms of the Cyrillic alphabet is given on p. xiii.

1.3 Data and Scope

As pointed out above, agreement in Slavic provides many interesting types of variation. However, it might be thought somewhat narrow to limit our attention to Slavic languages, particularly if we wish to make claims about language universals. Such universals are usually supported with evidence from a wide range of languages of different types,[2] a logical first step in establishing universals. The proposed universals we will be dealing with have already passed this test. Practical considerations make it impossible to go on to check all the potentially relevant data in the languages of the world. However, it is feasible to attempt to test the proposed universals against all the data available in a limited area. Thus in concentrating on Slavic languages but attempting to cover all relevant data we are taking a new step forward, rather than arbitrarily restricting the scope of our study. Slavic is of course a limited field, but one sufficiently large and varied to make our results significant. A second new step is to demonstrate the interaction of the various universals which can be shown to restrict agreement possibilities. This demonstration involves very detailed analysis, which is another reason for restricting ourselves to a single language family at this stage.

From a slightly different point of view, taking the Slavic languages as the starting point, we may ask to what extent our universals cover the data. We will meet various phenomena which do not constitute counter-evidence to any of the universals, yet are not covered by them. These are instances where there is evidence for a rule which is more restrictive than any applicable universal. There is thus an interplay between universal requirements and rules specific to an individual language or language variety.

Our investigation of constructions which allow agreement options will reveal many cases where the presence or absence of a particular factor makes one agreement form more or less likely (rather than obligatory or impossible). This aspect of our study shows a different emphasis to previous work on universals, which has tended to be more concerned with what can or cannot occur, rather than with the relative frequency of alternative forms. Of course, establishing that one construction occurs more frequently than another is much more difficult than establishing simply that a particular construction occurs. The most reliable way in which to analyse linguistic phenomena of this type is to examine all the examples which occur in a corpus. In order to investigate variation in the different dimensions listed above, we shall need large sets of data. A number of relevant studies is available, some of them buried in obscure publications, but information is limited. Most data have been found for Polish, Serbo-Croat and particularly Russian. This is fortunate since these three languages represent the main branches of Slavic — West, South and East, described above. However, the data required to show the interrelation of the restrictions on agreement options were not previously available. This means that a large proportion of the data presented has been collected by the author. Scanning for examples takes a great deal of time, so it is important that the results should be available to subsequent investigators. Full details are given of each corpus, and the exact type of example included in the count is specified. The data serve as the basis on which extensive claims are made about the factors which determine agreement: however, they are presented in such a way as to be available to others who may take a different theoretical position.

1.4 Summary of the Book

One of the major difficulties with the problem we are tackling is the large number of variable factors. Our technique will be to restrict the number of factors which we allow to vary at any one time. We can distinguish two major types: those which relate to the agreeing element, and those which relate to the element agreed with. In the Russian phrase *dokumental'nye fil'my* 'documentary films', *dokumental'nye* is in the plural because it agrees with *fil'my*. We shall call *dokumental'nye* the agreement 'target'. The element which determines the agreement, *fil'my*, we term the agreement 'controller'. Agreement depends on both elements: thus controllers like *fil'my* have the category of number, otherwise there would be no agreement in number; but equally importantly, targets like *dokumental'nye* belong to a class of targets which can show agreement in number. Attributive modifiers represent one type of target, as in the Russian example just discussed; another target is the predicate, since predicates agree with subject noun phrases. We use 'agreement' in the wide sense to cover any instance where the form of one syntactic element is modified so as to match properties of another. Under this definition, pronouns can agree with their antecedents, and so they too are agreement targets.[3]

The first part of the book is devoted to targets. We find that these have a major influence on the agreement form which is used in cases where alternatives are possible. We analyse comparable examples in which the controller remains the same, but where different targets have different agreement possibilities. Sometimes a given target makes the use of one of the competing agreement forms obligatory, while in other cases a particular type of target makes one of the forms more likely to occur than it would be otherwise. For example, a given agreement form may be more likely to occur when the agreement target is a predicate rather than when it is an attributive modifier. The implicational statements we can make about such cases are linked into two hierarchies. The first, the Agreement Hierarchy, is presented in Chapter 2. It constrains the agreement possibilities of attributive modifiers, predicates and relative and personal pronouns. The second, the Predicate Hierarchy, distinguishes various syntactic positions within the predicate (Chapter 3). The status of these hierarchies and the type of predictions they make are discussed in Chapter 4. It is logical to attempt to combine the two hierarchies. A provisional solution is given in Chapter 5, but the connection cannot be demonstrated conclusively until the role of agreement controllers is understood.

The second part of the book (Chapters 6-8) is therefore devoted to controllers. In this part we restrict variation of the target in order to isolate the major controller factors which influence agreement. For example, if we restrict the target by considering only predicate agreement, then we can establish that agreement choices are influenced by the animacy of the controller. Thus in Russian, plural agreement is more likely with the animate controller *Ivan i Maša* 'Ivan and Masha' than it is with conjoined inanimate nouns like *teatr i kino* 'theatre and cinema'. Chapter 6 outlines the constructions where controller factors are problematic. It appears that the most promising construction for isolating controller factors is in fact predicate agreement with conjoined noun phrases, which is treated as a case study in Chapter 7. Here the major factors of animacy and word-order are identified, and these are shown to be of wider application in Chapter 8; they apply similarly to agreement with quantified expressions. With the major target and controller factors both isolated, we turn in Chapter 9 to an analysis of the ways in which the two types of factor interact, and we assess their influence relative to each other. We are then in a position to re-examine and confirm the relationship between the two target hierarchies. In Chapters 10 and 11 we return to controllers, and investigate the more complex controllers which were excluded earlier. The analysis covers conjoined noun phrases showing clashes in person, in number and – the most interesting type – in gender. Quantified subjects also reveal surprising variation in agreement, dependent on the actual quantifier involved. In the final chapter we review the types of variation we have found together with the patterns discovered; we then consider the adequacy of our analysis, discuss its implications beyond the Slavic languages and suggest possible motivations for the agreement universals.

Notes

1. For a grammatical outline of each of the Slavic languages see de Bray (1980 a, b, c); Sussex (forthcoming) gives an account of the notable features of the family as a whole.

2. This is the approach adopted by Joseph Greenberg, and numerous followers. The alternative method is to propose universals on the basis of a detailed study of a single language – the method of Noam Chomsky and those following his lead (see Comrie, 1981, 1-29).

3. Apresjan (1982) shows the inadequacy of traditional definitions of agreement and argues that an adequate definition is impossible until we have, among other things, a full description of the rules of agreement with all their conditions and nuances. This work is intended as a contribution to that description. The complexity of the rules of agreement has been particularly clearly demonstrated by Morgan (1972).

Variation in agreement depends on many factors. Of these, the two most important are the controller (or element agreed with) and the target (or agreeing element). Let us first consider their role in two English examples:

(1) The committee believes
(2) The committee believe

We might assume that the existence of the two possibilities depends solely on the controller: *committee* is one of the nouns which permit two agreement forms. However, for there to be a choice of agreements, there must also be a target which allows both options. Verbal predicates like *believe* permit singular and plural agreement with nouns of the *committee* type, and so we find alternatives like (1) and (2). While agreement in English is certainly complex, most of the options involve agreement in number. In Slavic languages there are also complications with person and especially gender. The range of agreement options is bewildering. If we are to make sense of them, it is important that we restrict the number of variables operating at any one time. Were we to attempt to describe agreement while allowing both target and controller to vary, the picture would be hopelessly confused. It would be like attempting to assess the relative skills of marksmen who were trying to shoot different moving objects while riding on different vehicles. At first, therefore, we shall limit the types of controller as narrowly as possible. In some cases we discuss individual lexical items, in other cases, we consider different lexical items from a restricted set, and thirdly, we discuss controllers which can be clearly defined according to their syntactic construction. Our basic strategy is to keep the controller as 'still' as possible, in order to obtain a clear picture of the role played by the target in agreement variation.

Restricting variation of the controller will enable us to establish a hierarchy of target types, based on examples where alternative agreements are possible. At this stage we shall limit the investigation to cases where there are only two possible agreement forms (an example where three different agreements occur is analysed in Chapter 5). For the present, therefore, we can maintain the traditional terms 'syntactic agreement' and 'semantic agreement'. 'Syntactic', 'strict' or 'grammatical' agreement is the normal form of agreement, the form one would predict according to the morphological properties of the element which controls the agreement. Thus returning to our English examples, singular agreement with the noun *committee*, as in (1), is an example of syntactic agreement. 'Semantic', 'loose' or 'logical' agreement means agreement according to meaning rather than form. *Committee* is singular in form but refers to more than one individual; plural agreement with it, as in (2), is therefore semantic agreement. It is important to realise that 'semantic agreement' is a useful label for a problem, rather than an explanation. If we simply say that *committee* can take agreements according to its form or its meaning, then it is difficult to explain why (3) is grammatical while (4) is not:

(3) This committee sat late
(4) *These committee sat late

These examples show that semantic agreement is in fact restricted by syntactic factors; in this particular case the target cannot be an attributive modifier. Had we considered only sentences like (3) and (4), we would not have found a problem.

Let us therefore establish all the possible syntactic tests we can apply to determine the gender and number of a noun whose gender and/or number are not self-evident. As an example consider the Russian word *junoša* 'a youth'. This has the appearance of a feminine noun (the majority of Slavic nouns which end in *-a* in the nominative singular are feminine) but it refers to a male. Its gender is potentially a problem. We can use four syntactic tests to establish both its gender and number. These are the agreement forms taken by the following elements when they agree with the element in question:

1. attributive modifier
2. predicate
3. relative pronoun
4. personal pronoun

We will apply each test in turn. We simply require phrases or sentences in which *junoša* is the agreement controller, and the four elements above function as targets.

(5) R: *interesnyj* (masc sg) *junoša*[1]
    an interesting   youth

The adjectival ending is unambiguously masculine singular. In Russian the past tense verb forms agree with the subject in gender and number, as in this sentence:

(6) R: *Junoša*   *stojal* (masc sg)
    The youth stood

The relative pronoun has the same agreement possibilities as an adjective:

(7) R: *Junoša,*   *kotoryj* (masc sg) *stojal* . . .
    The youth who   stood

Finally, the personal pronoun also agrees in gender and number with its antecedent:

(8) R: *Junoša*   *dolgo*   *stojal, potom on* (masc sg) . . .
    The youth a long time stood then he

The result of each test is the same — *junoša* is clearly masculine singular; it can therefore tell us nothing about different types of target. From now on, however, we shall consider elements for which different tests yield different results, or for which alternative agreement forms occur within one of the test positions. For example, the Russian word *vrač* 'doctor', when referring to a woman, is usually masculine by the first test, but feminine by the fourth.

It has been demonstrated (Corbett, 1979b), on the basis of data taken from both within and beyond the Slavic family, that the four agreement positions listed above can be arranged into a hierarchy, known as the Agreement Hierarchy, as shown in Table 2.1. For any controller that permits alternative agreement forms, as we move rightwards along the Agreement Hierarchy, the likelihood of semantic agreement will increase monotonically.[2] In absolute terms, if semantic

Table 2.1: The Agreement Hierarchy

attributive	—	predicate	—	relative pronoun	—	personal pronoun

agreement is possible in a given position in the hierarchy it will also be possible in all positions to the right. In relative terms, if alternative agreement forms are available in two positions, the likelihood of semantic agreement will be as great or greater in the position to the right than in that to the left. It is evident that this hierarchy has considerable predictive power, since it rules out a large number of theoretically possible agreement systems. We will return to the question of the predictions it makes in §4.1. First we must examine the relevant data. In §2.1 we consider evidence from different Slavic languages. This evidence is summarised in §2.2. Then we will analyse a particular instance of variation, for which there is a great deal of data showing several distinct factors at work (§2.3).

2.1. The Data

In this section we will review evidence for the Agreement Hierarchy. We start with examples where syntactic agreement is dominant, and then move on to those where semantic agreement has made greater inroads.

2.1.1 *Czech* děvče

The Czech word *děvče* 'girl' (colloquial) looks like a neuter singular noun. In the following example, attributive and predicate agreements are neuter singular:

> (9) Cz: *To* (neut) *děvče se vdalo* (neut)
>   That   girl   got married
>   (Vanek, 1970, 87)

Similarly the relative pronoun is neuter singular:

> (10) Cz: *Najmula jsem děvče, které* (neut) *přišlo včera* (informant)
>   Hired did girl which   came yesterday
>   (I hired the girl who came yesterday.)

(**která* (fem) *přišla* is unacceptable.) The personal pronoun may be neuter too, but the semantically expected feminine is also found:

> (11) Cz: *To* *děvče přišlo včera,*   *ale* *já jsem je* (neut)/*ji* (fem)
>   That girl came yesterday but I did it   her

> *nenajmula*
> not hire
> (Vanek, 1977, 88)

The examples show that syntactic (neuter) agreement is found in all four positions. Semantic (feminine) agreement occurs in one position only – the rightmost position on the hierarchy. This is a pattern which is in accord with the requirements of the hierarchy.

2.1.2 *Russian* para

The Russian word *para*, meaning 'couple, man and woman', has the appearance of a feminine singular noun; the agreement of attributive adjective, predicate and relative pronoun seem to confirm this:

(12) R: ...   *byla* (fem sg) *izjaščnaja* (fem sg) *vljublennaja* (fem sg)
              (there) was   an elegant   loving
              para,   za   kotoroj (fem sg) *vse s   ljubopytstvom*
              couple after which   all with curiosity
              sledili   i   kotoraja (fem sg) *ne   skryvala svoego*
              followed and which (did)   not hide   their
              sčast'ja: on *tanceval tol'ko s   nej, i   vse*
              happiness he danced   only with her and everything
              vyxodilo   u   nix   tak tonko,   očarovatel'no, čto
              turned out with them so delicately charmingly   that
              tol'ko odin komandir   znal, čto èta (fem sg) *para*
              only   alone the captain knew that this   couple (was)
              nanjata (fem sg) *Lloydom igrat'   v ljubov' za xorošie*
              engaged   by Lloyds to play at love   for good
              den'gi i   uže   davno   plavaet to na odnom,
              money and already a long time sails   now on one
              to   na drugom korable.
              now on another ship.
              (Bunin, *Gospodin iz San-Francisko*)

The attributive modifiers (*izjaščnaja, vljublennaja* and *èta*) are all feminine singular, as are the predicates (*byla, nanjata*) and the relative pronoun (*kotoroj* – instrumental case and *kotoraja* – nominative case). In the phrase *s nej*, 'with her', the feminine singular pronoun clearly refers only to the woman, not to the couple. The appropriate personal pronoun for *para* is *oni* 'they'. This pronoun is found in the following example with the derived form *paročka*:

(13) R: *Krome Mariny, avtobusa   dožidalas'* (fem sg)
      Besides Marina for the bus was waiting
      kakaja-to (fem sg) *paročka. Im* (pl),   *kak   vidno,*
      some   couple To them as (was) evident (it)
      bylo vse ravno   *– pridet   avtobus ili ne*
      was all the same (whether)   will come the bus or not
      pridet.
      come (i.e. whether the bus would come or not)
      (Laskin, *Kak togda*)

The plural form *im* (dative of *oni*) is an example of semantic agreement, as reference is to two individuals. With *para/paročka* we find semantic agreement in one position only, the personal pronoun, and this is fully in accord with the Agreement Hierarchy.[3] It differs from the previous case in that semantic agreement is obligatory (as opposed to optional with *děvče*) in this one position.

2.1.3 Serbo-Croat Dual Noun

In the next example, alternative agreement forms are possible within two different positions on the hierarchy. In Serbo-Croat the numerals 2, 3 and 4 require a special form of masculine nouns (a survival of the dual number), and the attributive adjective must agree with this form:

(14) SC: *dva dobra* (dual) *čoveka*
      two good   men

In the predicate, we find that both the dual form and the masculine plural form are possible:

(15) SC: *Ova   dva čoveka su dobra* (dual)/*dobri* (masc pl)
      These two men   are good

It is the masculine plural form which represents semantic agreement. (This claim will be justified in detail in §5.4 below, where we reanalyse the forms labelled dual here.) Like the predicate verb, the relative pronoun permits both syntactic (dual) and semantic (masculine) agreement:

(16) SC: *dva coveka koja* (dual)/*koji* (masc pl) . . .
      two men   who

However, the personal pronoun must take the masculine plural form *oni* (not *ona). We therefore find nil per cent semantic agreement in attributive position, 100 per cent in the personal pronoun. In the two remaining positions there is a choice of agreement forms. This means that the relative requirement of the Agreement Hierarchy comes into play. If our postulated hierarchy is correct, then the frequency of semantic agreement of the relative pronoun will be as high as or higher than that of semantic agreement in the predicate. Figures are available from Sand (1971, 55-6, 63), from a corpus of modern texts, and are given in Table 2.2. These figures lend convincing support to the hierarchy.

Table 2.2: Percentage Distribution of Dual and Plural Forms in Serbo-Croat

	attributive	predicate	relative pronoun	personal pronoun
Percentage showing semantic agreement	0	18 (N = 376)	62 (N = 32)	100

Note: N indicates the total number of examples.

2.1.4 *Serbo-Croat* gazde

The next set of examples also comes from Serbo-Croat; it involves nouns like *gazda* 'master, landlord, boss'. In the singular, nouns of this type are masculine, but when plural (e.g. *gazde*) both masculine and feminine agreements are found.[4] From the meanings of the nouns involved it is clear that the masculine is the semantically agreeing form. Let us first examine the situation in nineteenth-century Serbo-Croat. Maretić (1899, 398–400) gives examples of feminine plural agreements for all positions on the hierarchy. He points out that masculine agreements are possible when the agreeing element is not in the same clause as the controller (in other words, where the target is a relative or personal pronoun). Maretić gives no statistics, but his careful presentation suggests that his examples can be taken as representative. If we examine the examples he gives, we find 24 examples of attributive modifiers, all showing feminine (syntactic) agreement. In the predicate, out of 33 examples there are only two masculine forms.[5] The relative pronoun, however, has a sizeable minority of semantic forms (5 out of 17) while for the personal pronoun the semantic form is predominant (11 out of 14). We therefore have a clear picture of the period Maretić describes – roughly the first half of the nineteenth century: syntactic agreement is obligatory in attributive position, dominant in the predicate and, though less so, with the relative pronoun; but it is the minority for the personal pronoun. This system is totally in accord with the Agreement Hierarchy.

For the modern literary language the most reliable data are provided by Stanojčić (1967), who worked on a corpus taken from the writings of Andrić. Sentences (17) and (18) illustrate the contrast both in attributive position and in predicate position (examples (17)–(20) are from Andrić, quoted by Stanojčić, 1967, 60–2):

(17) SC: *Mlade* (fem) *kalfe*   *su se uozbiljile* (fem) . . .
     The young   journeymen   became serious
(18) SC: *Takvi* (masc sg) *su*   *travnički* (masc) *age* . . .
     Such   are the Travnik   agas

Stanojčić (1967, 59) states that masculine attributes, as in (18) were found in one third of the cases, and that predicate agreements are 'in approximately the same relationship'. This figure is equivalent to that reported by Babić (1973, 207). He gives a combined figure for the two positions: in various literary texts 20 examples out of 30 showed syntactic agreement. Babić adds: 'further agreement [i.e. beyond the clause] is usually semantic' and gives two examples with the relative pronoun. Neither Babić nor Stanojčić gives any figure for the relative pronoun option, as in the following:

(19) SC: . . . *mnoge* (fem) *gazde,*   *koje* (fem) *su se obogatile* . . .
     many   masters who   got rich
(20) SC: . . . *mlade* (fem) *gazde,*   *koji* (masc) *tek počinju*
     the young   masters who   just begin
     da   *izlaze* . . .
     that (they) go out (i.e. who are just beginning to go out)

(In the Eastern variant of Serbo-Croat, as in Bulgarian and Macedonian, *da* plus clause is used in constructions where other Slavic languages use an infinitive.) Given the absence of precise data on the relative pronoun, we can only count up the examples quoted by Stanojčić; this yields five examples of masculine agreement in the seven relative pronouns given. There are no data on the personal pronoun. A corpus of texts taken from Andrić was therefore scanned, so that the results would be comparable with the other three sets quoted. All five examples of personal pronouns showed masculine agreement.[6]

The modern language shows greater acceptance of the semantically agreeing form in this construction than did nineteenth-century Serbo-Croat.[7] The new situation is fully in accord with the Agreement Hierarchy, just as the earlier set of agreements was. The language of the press shows even greater use of semantic agreement, as is suggested by a count of examples quoted by Marković (1954, 95-6) from newspapers of the years 1952-3. It is interesting to note that Modern Standard Serbo-Croat is now approaching the position of the Čakavski dialect of the sixteenth and early seventeenth centuries (the language of Marulić, Hektorović, Lucić, Baraković and Zoronić) as described by Glavan (1927-8, 117-18). He found masculine and feminine forms used equally in attributive and predicate position and exclusive masculine forms in the other two positions. The data are summarised in Table 2.3.

Table 2.3: Semantic Agreement with Plural Nouns like *gazde* in Serbo-Croat

	attributive	predicate	relative pronoun	personal pronoun
	%	%	%	%
Nineteenth century	0 (N = 24)	6 (N = 33)	29 (N = 27)	79 (N = 14)
modern literary language (Andrić)	~33	~33	71 (N = 7)	(100) (N = 5)
press 1952-3	45 (N = 11)	71 (N = 21)	80 (N = 5)	(100) (N = 2)
Čakavski dialect (sixteenth/seventeenth century)	~50	~50	~100	~100

Note: N = total number of examples; ~ = approximation not supported by figures; percentages in parentheses are explained in note 6.

Given the considerable amount previously written on this construction, it is disappointing that more precise figures have not been produced. The best evidence available, though patchy, does present a consistent picture; at each stage of the language's development which has been investigated, we find a monotonic increase in semantic agreement as we move rightwards along the hierarchy — a pattern fully consistent with the hierarchy. This Serbo-Croat construction is particularly interesting because of the considerable change which the language has undergone (constrained by the hierarchy) and also because all four positions on the hierarchy are affected. It was included for these reasons, even though the data in Table 2.3 are less satisfactory than those presented elsewhere in the book.

2.1.5 Serbo-Croat Conjoined Plural Noun Phrases

Serbo-Croat provides further interesting evidence to support the hierarchy, in its rules for agreement with conjoined noun phrases. The rules for resolving gender conflicts, in all the Slavic languages which require them, are discussed in Chapter 10. For the present, we shall consider only examples with two plural nouns (though the rules also apply when more than two are conjoined). When plural nouns of different genders are conjoined in Serbo-Croat, agreement may be with the nearer conjunct only, or with both conjuncts. Agreement with the nearer conjunct can be recognised by the fact that the target takes the gender form appropriate to that conjunct and so agrees fully with it; this is a case of syntactic agreement. If agreement is with both conjuncts, then the masculine plural form is used, which represents semantic agreement. The reason is as follows: in semantic terms, the target clearly relates to both conjuncts. As the masculine plural form signals agreement with both conjuncts, it is in accord with the semantic situation and so can be called semantic agreement. To avoid any possible uncertainty each example includes a feminine and a neuter noun only; masculine agreement must therefore represent agreement with both conjuncts, as it does not show full agreement with either. Note too that all the nouns are inanimate; we are thus keeping the controllers as similar as possible to ensure that any variation found will result from differences in the targets. The examples are from the novel *Travnička Hronika* by Andrić, with the exception of (23) which is from the short story *Anikina Vremena* by the same author. In attributive position agreement is always with the nearer noun:

(21) SC: . . . *najsvirepije* (fem pl) *kazne* (fem pl) *i*
         the cruellest   punishments and
        mučenja (neut pl) . . .
        tortures

Semantic agreement, that is to say the masculine plural **najsvirepiji*, is ungrammatical. However, in the predicate, syntactic and semantic agreement are found:

(22) SC: *Toj*   *službi su bile* (fem pl) *posvećene njene*
        To this job   were   devoted her

> *misli* (fem pl) *i   njena osećanja* (neut pl) . . .
> thoughts   and her   feelings

(23) SC: *Sve njegove molbe* (fem pl) *i   uveravanja* (neut pl)
　　　　All his   prayers   and assurances
　　　　nisu   pomagali (masc pl) *ništa.*
　　　　did not help   at all

Similarly, the relative pronoun shows both types of agreement:

(24) SC: *U svetlosti filozofskih   istina* (fem pl) *i   verskih*
　　　　In the light of philosophical truths   and religious
　　　　nadahnuća (neut pl), *koja* (neut pl) *su se manjala* . . .
　　　　inspirations   which   changed

(25) SC: *Dok   sve one   mučne sumnje* (fem pl) *i*
　　　　While all those painful doubts   and
　　　　kolebanja (neut pl), *koje* (masc pl acc) *je pobeda*
　　　　hesitations   which   victory
　　　　raspršila . . .
　　　　dispersed

In the texts from which these examples are taken, syntactic agreement appears to be more common than semantic agreement in both the predicate and the relative pronoun (examples like (22) outnumber (23), and those like (24) outnumber (25)). There are unfortunately no accurate figures for the relative frequency of semantic agreement in the two positions. The personal pronoun must, however, be masculine plural. Thus the evidence we have is consistent with the Agreement Hierarchy: syntactic agreement is the only possibility in attributive position, both types of agreement are found in the predicate and the relative pronoun, while the personal pronoun permits only semantic agreement.

2.1.6 Russian Dialect Use of Plural with 'Representative' Nouns

We now turn to the Talitsk dialect of Russian as described by Bogdanov (1968). In this dialect, a plural verb is possible with a singular subject, even though the subject is not a collective noun; the noun then refers to a person or persons besides the one indicated directly. The following example is particularly clear (Bogdanov's transcription is retained in transliteration but stresses are omitted):

(26) R: *M'it'ixa dral'is'* (pl)
    Mitixa   had a fight
    (Bogdanov, 1968, 71)

This refers to a fight between neighbours — husband and wife. The verb agreement shows that more than one person was involved; naturally Mitixa was not fighting alone. The plural therefore represents semantic agreement. The same agreement is possible with the personal pronoun:

(27) R: *Pra   Kuz'mu my šypka ab'is'n'it' toža n'e možym,*
    About Kuzma we much explain   also cannot
    paš'imu on'i (pl)   *n'e   p'išut vam.*
    because they (do) not write to you
    (Bogdanov, 1968, 71)

On'i 'they' refers not only to Kuz'ma himself but also to his family. Unfortunately, Bogdanov gives no example of relative pronouns of any sort. However, attributive modifiers must be singular (Bogdanov, 1968, 74) — this special use of semantic agreement does not extend to them:

(28) R: *Moj* (sg) *brat   tam   toža žyl'i* (pl)
    My   brother there also lived
    (Bogdanov, 1968, 69)

In this sentence it is not only the brother who is involved but also people associated with him (most probably his family), as the plural verb shows. However, the attributive modifier remains in the singular. Thus the evidence available — semantic agreement of the personal pronoun and of the predicate but not of attributive modifiers — lends further support to the hierarchy.

2.1.7 Russian Conjoined Noun Phrases

Let us now turn to Standard Russian, and the problem of agreement in number with conjoined noun phrases. This is a question we shall consider in much more detail in Chapters 7 and 9. It is worth establishing the general situation here, however, because it gives particularly strong support to the Agreement Hierarchy. Basically, the singular is normal in attributive position and the plural is more frequent in the other positions. The following example, with a singular attributive modifier and a plural predicate, is typical:

(29) R: *Èta* (sg) *vzyskatel'nost', samokritičnost' tože*
      This   exactingness   self-criticalness   also
      raspolagali (pl) *k   nemu*
      disposed (me) towards him
      (Černov, Introduction to Smol'janinov, *Sredi morennyx xolmov*)

Russian also permits plural attributive modifiers:

(30) R: . . . *Marija zadumalas' ob   ostavlennyx* (pl) *muže*
          Maria thought   about (her) left behind   husband
      i   dočeri: kak   oni (pl) *tam, čto   s*
      and daughter how (are) they   there what (is) with
      nimi (pl)*?*
      them?
      (Maksimov, *Karantin*)

In each case the attributive modifier refers to both conjuncts; the plural agreement form is the one which corresponds to the semantic situation and so represents semantic agreement. Examples like (30), with plural attributive modifiers, are much less common than those with singular modifiers. In literary prose, plural attributives were found in 14 per cent of the examples (N = 44); in the predicate, the plural was found in 71 per cent of the cases (N = 290); details of the corpora are given in §7.1. Thus, while sentences with a plural predicate (as in (29)) are the more common, singular predicates are perfectly acceptable, as in sentence (31):

(31) R: *Byla* (sg) *u   nego   ešče gitara   i*
          Was   at him (i.e. he had) also a guitar and
      samoučitel' k   nej
      a manual   for it
      (Vojnovič, *Putëm vzaimnoj perepiski*)

The relative pronoun normally stands in the plural:

(32) R: *Pečku   mne   počinili* (pl) *brigadir*
          The stove [object] for me mended   the brigade-leader
      i   muž   kladovščicy,   kotorym (pl) *ja*
      and the husband of the storekeeper for whom   I

> *postavil   za   èto   vypit'*.
> provided for this to drink
> (Amal'rik, *Neželannoe putešestvie v Sibir'*)

Occasionally, however a singular relative pronoun is found:

(33) R: *Kazalos',   on skol'zit po   žizni s   toj že*
     (It) seemed he glides   through life with the same
     stremitel'nost'ju i   neprinuždennost'ju, s   kakoju (sg)
     swiftness   and ease   with which
     pero ego skol'zit po   bumage.
     pen his glides over paper
     (Adamovič, Introduction to Nabokov, *Zaščita Lužina*)

With the personal pronoun, the plural (as in the second part of (30)) is overwhelmingly the more common. Exceptions like the use of *on* 'it' in the following sentence are extremely rare:

(34) R: *Um   i   talant gruppy   ne možet* (sg) *prevyšat'*
     The intellect and talent of a group cannot   exceed
     um   členov   gruppy.   On (sg) *niže*
     the intellect of the members of the group. It (is)   lower
     takovyx (pl) *samyx   sil'nyx členov   gruppy.*
     than those   of the most strong members of the group
     (Zinov'ev, *Zijajuščie vysoty*)

These data are particularly significant because alternative agreements are possible at every position on the hierarchy. In attributive position the plural is possible but greatly outweighed by the singular; in the predicate, the plural form is found in the majority of examples, though the singular makes up a sizeable minority; in the relative pronoun the plural is dominant, singular examples being uncommon, while in the personal pronoun, singular pronouns are exceptionally rare. This picture is in perfect accord with the requirement of the Agreement Hierarchy.

2.1.8 Polish łajdaki

Our next set of examples involves an agreement category, the masculine personal, found in West Slavic languages. The examples relevant to the present argument are taken from Polish, though the same category in other West Slavic languages will be discussed in a different context in §10.3. In Polish, masculine personal nouns (masculine nouns referring to male humans) have special nominative plural endings; they also take special agreement forms in the plural. These masculine personal forms may involve consonant alternatives in the noun and in the agreeing elements. Thus, in the following example, *Polacy* is the plural of *Polak* 'a Pole' (data from Rothstein, 1980, 85–6; textual examples in Rothstein, 1976, 248–50):

(35) P: *Ci* (masc pers) *mili* (masc pers) *Polacy mówili* (masc pers)
        These   nice   Poles   said
        . . . *Oni* (masc pers). . .
            They

For comparison, *Polki* 'Polish women' is the plural of *Polka* and takes non-masculine personal agreements:

(36) P: *Te* (non-masc pers) *miłe* (non-masc pers) *Polki*
        Those   nice   Polish women
        mowiły (non-masc pers) . . . *One* (non-masc pers) . . .
        said   They

Some nouns which refer to men may fail to take a masculine personal form in the nominative plural. One such is *łajdak* 'scoundrel' which has the plural form *łajdaki* (the expected *łajdacy* is possible but less common). While *łajdaki* is non-masculine personal in form, agreements with it may be either non-masculine personal (syntactic agreement) or masculine personal (semantic agreement). Attributive modifiers normally take the non-masculine personal form:

(37) P: *Te* (non-masc pers) *łajdaki   były* (non-masc pers)/
        Those   scoundrels were
        byli (masc pers) . . .
        were

As this example also shows, both forms are found in the predicate. Relative and personal pronouns show semantic agreement:

(38) P: *Te* (non-masc pers) *łajdaki,   którzy* (masc pers)
        Those   scoundrels who
        . . . *Oni* (masc pers) . . .
            They

Rothstein (1976, 249) gives an exceptional masculine personal form in attributive position and a case of a relative pronoun in the non-masculine personal form; he points out that pronouns showing non-masculine personal forms are a trifling percentage of the total. Thus in attributive position, these nouns take non-masculine personal forms (with occasional exceptions) and so show syntactic agreement. In the predicate both forms are well attested. Relative and personal pronouns show semantic (masculine personal) agreements, though we have an example of syntactic agreement in the relative pronoun. Once again the data confirm the validity of the Agreement Hierarchy.

2.1.9 Polish Titles

Another point of interest in Polish is the question of titles. They have the appearance of feminine nouns, but they frequently refer to males. Agreements of both genders are found:

> (39) P: *Wasza* (fem) *Królewska Mość,*   *który* (masc)
>   Your   kingly   might (i.e. Majesty) who
>   *wie   więcej od   nas, musiał* (masc) *wiedzieć o   tym.*
>   knows more than us   must have   known   about this.
>   *Niech on* (masc) *nam   wytłómaczy.* (informant)
>   Let   him   to us explain (i.e. Please explain to us)

Here we find syntactic agreement of the attributive modifier *Wasza*, while the predicate (*musiał*), the relative pronoun (*który*) and the personal pronoun (*on*) all show semantic agreement. This pattern clearly conforms to the Agreement Hierarchy.

2.1.10 Russian Titles

In Russian, titles behave similarly to Polish titles, except that most are neuter rather than feminine. (In both languages the majority are no longer in use.) The next example illustrates agreement of the attributive modifier and of the predicate (examples (40)–(42) are from Puškin's *Kapitanskaja dočka*):

> (40) R: . . . *ego vysokoblagorodie prikazal* (masc) *vaše* (neut)
>   his Worship   ordered (me)   your
>   *blagorodie otvesti v   ostrog* . . .
>   Honour   to take to gaol

Note that *ego*, used as a possessive, is indeclinable. However, *vaše*, which modifies the title in object position, shows neuter agreement. The predicate, *prikazal* shows the usual masculine agreement. The following unusual neuter predicate occurs in a letter, in the same novel:

(41) R: . . . *vaše* (neut) *prevosxoditel'stvo ne   zabylo* (neut) . . .
            your   Excellency (did)   not forget

No examples involving a relative pronoun have been found. The personal pronoun is masculine:

(42) R: *On* [*vaxmistr*]   *totčas že   vorotilsja, ob"javiv*
            He [the sergeant major] immediately returned   declaring
            mne   čto ego   vysokoblagorodiju
            to me that to his Worship   (was)
            nekogda   menja prinjat', a   čto
            no time (i.e. he had no time) me   to receive and that
            on (masc) *velel   otvesti menja*
            he   ordered (the sergeant major) to take me
            v   ostrog . . .
            to gaol

The evidence available here is in accord with the hierarchy: we find syntactic agreement in attributive position, semantic agreement in the predicate (with the possibility of syntactic agreement too) and semantic agreement in the personal pronoun.

2.1.11 *Russian Respected Noun*

The agreements just discussed were not the only forms possible. With titles, and also with other nouns denoting persons, plural agreements could be used (even though only one person was involved) in order to show respect. In the following example the subject is a title in the singular, and the intent behind the use of the plural is apparent:

(43) R: *Vaše* (neut sg) *vysokoprevosxoditel'stvo izvolili* (pl)
            Your   Excellency   deigned
            trebovat' ot   menja ob"jasnenija . . .
            to require from me   an explanation
            (Puškin, letter. Quoted in Vinogradov *et al*., 1956, 444)

This usage was not restricted to titles,[8] as the next example shows. A maid is speaking politely of her master and mistress:

(44) R: „*Mamen'ka   plačut* (pl), – *šepnula   ona vsled*
"(Your) mother are crying   whispered she after
uxodivšej Elene, – a   papen'ka gnevajutsja (pl) . . ."
the leaving Elena   and father   are angry"
(Turgenev, *Nakanune*)

The following amusing example has the indeclinable relative *čto*, which
is shown to be plural by the following verb; the speaker is confused
because he is addressing an extraordinary cat:

(45) R: *A   prostite . . . èto   ty . . . èto   vy . . . – on*
But excuse (me) it (was) you   it (was) you   he
sbilsja,   ne znaja,   kak obraščat'sja k
stopped in confusion not knowing how to address
kotu, na „ty‚ ili na „vy‚, – vy –   tot samyi
the cat with "ty" or with "vy"   you (are) that same
kot, čto   sadilis' (pl) *v tramvaj?*
cat which got on   the tram
(Bulgakov, *Master i Margarita*)

Similarly, a plural personal pronoun could be used to refer to a single
person:

(46) R: – *Vy   vojdite k teten'ke, molodye gospoda, . . .*
You go in   to Aunty young   gentlemen
oni (pl)   *ničego, bud'te pokojny.*
they (i.e. she) (are) all right be   calm (i.e. do not worry)
(Pasternak, *Doktor Živago*)

This particular type of semantic agreement, used to denote respect, was
possible in the three positions on the right of the hierarchy, but not in
the leftmost position.

2.1.12 Russian značitel'noe lico *in the Usage of Gogol'*

All the agreements discussed so far have been common to a group of
speakers, sometimes a relatively small group. The final example in this
section concerns the creative use of agreement by a single writer. In his
short story *Šinel'*, Gogol' uses *značitel'noe lico* 'important person' as
the name for a character and, as Peškovskij points out (1956, 190-1),
employs unusual agreements with it. The final version is as follows (for
details of the variants in earlier versions see Corbett, 1981a):

(47) R: *Nužno   znat',   čto* odno (neut) značitel'noe
       (It is) necessary to know that one   important
       lico   *nedavno sdelalsja* (masc) *značitel'nym licom, i*
       person recently became   an important person and
       do   togo vremeni on (masc) *byl neznačitel'nym licom.*
       until that time   he   was an unimportant person
       (emphasis in original)

The attributive modifier *odno* is neuter singular (also in (48)), but the predicate *sdelalsja* is masculine singular, thus showing semantic agreement (as the subject refers to a male). The personal pronoun *on* is masculine singular too. As the hierarchy would predict, the relative pronoun also takes the masculine form:

(48) R: *No my odnakože soveršenno ostavili*   odno (neut)
       But we however   completely have left one
       značitel'noe lico,   kotoryj (masc) *po-nastojaščemu*
       important   person who   really
       edva li ne byl pricinoju fantastičeskogo napravlenija
       almost   was the cause of the fantastic turn   (of this)
       vpročem   soveršenno istinnoj istorii.
       none the less completely true   story

These examples show that even the idiosyncratic usage of a single author, who has a particular literary purpose, is constrained by the Agreement Hierarchy.

2.2 Review of the Evidence for the Agreement Hierarchy

The evidence we have considered is presented in summary form in Table 2.4, which shows the variety of the agreement types we have discussed. *Děvče* permits a choice in one position only, *para* and others separate an end position on the hierarchy from the other three, while conjoined nouns in Russian permit a choice at each position on the hierarchy. Yet all the agreement types we have considered form a coherent pattern; they are all consistent with the requirements of the Agreement Hierarchy. In every case, as we move rightwards along the hierarchy, so the likelihood of semantic agreement increases. This can be seen more clearly in Figure 2.1, where the same data are represented graphically.

Table 2.4: Evidence for the Agreement Hierarchy

	attributive	predicate	relative pronoun	personal pronoun
Cz: *děvče*	neut	neut	neut	neut/FEM
R: *para*	sing	sing	sing	PL
SC: dual noun	dual	dual/(PL)	(dual)/PL	PL
SC: *gazde* (pl, 19th c.)	fem	fem	fem/(MASC)	(fem)/MASC
SC: *gazde* (pl, 20th c.)	fem/(MASC)	fem/(MASC)	(fem)/MASC	MASC
SC: conjoined plural NPs	nearer	nearer/(MASC)	nearer/(MASC)	MASC
R dial: plural for representative	sing	PL	?	PL
R: conjoined NPs	sing/(PL)	(sing)/PL	(sing)/PL	(sing)/PL
P: *tajdaki* (pl)	non-mp/(MP)	non-mp/MP	(non-mp)/MP	MP
P: titles	fem	MASC	MASC	MASC
R: titles	neut	neut/MASC	?	MASC
R: respected noun	sing	PL	PL	PL
R: *vrač*	masc/(FEM)	masc/FEM	(masc)/FEM	FEM
R: *značitel'noe lico* (Gogol')	neut	MASC	MASC	MASC

Notes: a. dial = dialect.

b. non-mp = non-masculine personal; MP = masculine personal.

c. Capitals signify semantic agreement.

d. Parentheses indicate a less frequent variant.

e. Data on Russian *vrač* are included for completeness. A discussion follows in § 2.3.

Figure 2.1: The Varying Possibilities of Semantic Agreement

	← Syntactic		Semantic →	
	Attributive	Predicate	Relative pronoun	Personal pronoun
Cz: *děvče*	□	□	□	◪
R: *para*	□	□	□	■
SC: dual noun	□	◪	◪	■
SC: *gazde,* (pl, 19th c.)	□	□	◪	◪
SC: *gazde,* (pl, 20th c.)	◪	◪	◪	■
SC: conjoined plural NPs	□	◪	◪	■
R dial: representative	□	■	?	■
R: conjoined NPs	◪	◪	■	■
P : *łajdaki* (pl)	□	◪	■	■
P : titles	□	■	■	■
R: titles	□	◪	?	■
R: respected noun	□	■	■	■
R: *vrač*	◪	◪	◪	■
R: *značitel' noe lico*	□	■	■	■

Note: the blacker the square, the greater the likelihood of semantic agreement.

Figure 2.1 makes the pattern absolutely clear and also shows the range of variation in the data discussed. To ensure that any such variation observed related to the target, we restricted the choice of controllers. Let us now check the controllers examined in the previous section, to confirm that they cannot be responsible for the basic pattern we have discovered. The controllers described may be divided into three groups: individual lexical items, sets of lexical items and particular syntactic constructions. We will review each in turn.

The most straightforward cases are the examples of individual lexical items: Czech *děvče* 'girl', Russian *para* 'couple' and the special use by Gogol' of the phrase *značitel'noe lico* 'important person'. In these instances, we may be sure that the differences in agreement are due to the different targets involved, as the controllers are so strictly limited. The evidence in favour of the Agreement Hierarchy is therefore very strong in these cases.

The second group of controllers comprises sets of lexical items. Thus there is a group of nouns in Serbo-Croat like *gazda* 'master', all of which refer to males but belong to a declensional class typical of feminine nouns. When in the plural, nouns like *gazda* permit alternative agreement forms, as we saw above. Similarly, there is a group of nouns like Polish *łajdak* 'scoundrel' which, though referring to male persons, are not necessarily treated morphologically as masculine personal. The Polish and Russian titles also belong to clearly defined sets. However, in the case of plural agreement to show respect, both titles and ordinary nouns referring to humans may be involved. In a similar way, the special use of plural agreements in the Talitsk dialect of Russian was restricted to human nouns. In the latter cases the sets of lexical items are comparatively large. In this second group, therefore, we have treated different controllers together. This is for purely practical reasons: it would take a great deal of time to gather adequate data on agreements with the noun *gazda* alone – it does not occur frequently enough. It is more practical to examine the group of similar nouns as a whole. It may be that the behaviour of these nouns is not exactly identical; for example, *gazda* 'master' may take semantic agreement more, or less, frequently than *kalfa* 'journeyman'. This is a practical rather than a theoretical problem, because we make the strongest possible claim – that the Agreement Hierarchy applies to each controller individually. Whatever the frequency of semantic agreement with any one of these items, the claim is that semantic agreement with each controller taken separately will show a monotonic increase as we move rightwards along the hierarchy. No one has ever claimed that any one of these items shows agreement characteristics which differ from the rest of the group in a way which would run counter to the Agreement Hierarchy (to my knowledge, no one has suggested differences of any type between them). Variation in the behaviour of the group as a whole through time has been documented, as shown above, but at each stage the requirements of the Agreement Hierarchy were met. As we noted, some of the controllers described represent less tightly restricted groups than nouns like *gazda* in Serbo-Croat. However, all the controllers in our first two groups are restricted to reference to humans.

This restriction does not apply to our third group, where the controllers are defined in terms of a particular syntactic construction rather than in terms of a particular group of lexical items. We used three examples of this type. The first consisted of the Serbo-Croat numerals 2–4 combined with a masculine noun. Masculine nouns may be animate or inanimate, so these constructions involve a range of subject types. Similarly, in the case of conjoined noun phrases in Russian, the nouns which may be involved are largely unrestricted. By treating these constructions without regard for the actual nouns involved, we have ignored certain variations which do occur. However, the statistical evidence produced in these two cases is so clear that it is inconceivable that these two constructions hide counter-examples to the Agreement Hierarchy. When discussing conjoined plural noun phrases in Serbo-Croat we could not call on detailed statistical evidence. We did, however, exclude one major potential complicating factor by considering inanimate nouns only. The constructions in this third group all provide evidence to support the Agreement Hierarchy. Nevertheless, we shall analyse all three constructions in more detail below. (Agreement with noun phrases including the numerals 2–4 in Serbo-Croat is discussed in §5.4, and again in §11.3.2, where it is demonstrated that the three numerals have varying degrees of influence on the choice of form. Agreement with conjoined noun phrases is discussed in §6.1.1, §6.2, §7, §8.2 and §10. The details of agreement in gender with conjoined noun phrases in Serbo-Croat are treated in §10.3.3.) As we shall see later, controllers consisting of conjoined noun phrases in particular throw considerable light on the factors which affect agreement variation and which are dependent on the controller. First, however, let us consider in detail a set of controllers of the second type – the type where only lexical items of a defined group are involved. The example, which is remarkable for the amount of data available, shows that lexical items of the same type may have slightly different agreement properties. It gives strong support to the Agreement Hierarchy, and also illustrates variation dependent on factors which we have not met in our investigation so far.

2.3 A remarkable Case of Multi-dimensional Variation

There is a particularly interesting instance of a group of words which allow alternative agreement forms, and for which there is a good deal of data. The words in question are Russian nouns which refer to people belonging to particular professions, such as *vrač* 'doctor'. These nouns have the appearance of masculine nouns, and when referring to males they take masculine agreements. The difficulty arises when they are used of females. This has become a serious problem during the present century, as women have entered many jobs previously occupied exclusively by men. In some instances a separate noun has been derived (by means of a suffix) to denote a woman worker (for an account of the different developments see Janko-Trinickaja, 1966). The agreement problem arises only when the same noun is used for women as for men. Masculine agreement would be in accord with the form of the noun (syntactic agreement), while feminine agreement would be in harmony with its meaning (semantic agreement). When speaking of a man, only (49) can be used:

> (49) R: *vrač*   *prišel* (masc)
>   the doctor   came

But when speaking of a woman, (49) could still be used (syntactic agreement) but so could the form with semantic agreement as in (50):

> (50) R: *vrač*   *prišla* (fem)
>   the doctor   came

In what follows we shall assume that it is always a woman involved, and that there is therefore a potential choice of agreement forms.

The main body of data on this choice of agreement comes from a survey carried out in the early sixties by a team of researchers led by M.V. Panov. They devised a questionnaire, covering variation in Russian phonology, morphology and syntax, and received over 4,000 replies. Four of the questions relate to the problem in hand. The results are available in various publications: first, in the main report from the project (Panov, 1968, 25-40). The relevant section of the report was written by I.P. Mučnik, and he also presents the material on gender in Mučnik (1971, 228-44). The results are discussed in Comrie and Stone (1978, 167-71). However, the account we shall follow is that of Kitaj-gorodskaja (1976), as she provides more of the evidence necessary for our inquiry. The relevant portion of the questionnaire runs as follows (with grammatical notes and glosses added):

What would you say, referring to a woman:

> (B) R: *Vrač*   *prišel* (masc) *ili vrač*   *prišla* (fem)
>   the doctor came   or the doctor came
>
> (A) R: *Upravdom*   *vydal* (masc) *spravku   ili*
>   the house manager issued   a certificate or
>   *upravdom*   *vydala* (fem) *spravku*
>   the house manager issued   a certificate
>
> (C) R: *U nas   xorošij* (masc) *buxgalter   ili u nas*
>   at us (is) a good   accountant or at us (is)
>   *xorošaja* (fem) *buxgalter*
>   a good   accountant (i.e. we have a good accountant)
>
> (D) R: *Ivanova —   xorošij* (masc) *vrač   ili Ivanova —*
>   Ivanova (is) a good   doctor or Ivanova (is)

xorošaja (fem) *vrač*
a good   doctor

For convenience of reference, these sentences have been designated with capital letters, in the order in which they appear in the tables (hence (B) before (A)). Sentences (A) and (B) are fairly straightforward in structure – the past tense verb of the predicate agrees in gender with the subject. Sentence (C) shows the Russian possessive construction: the possessor is marked by the preposition *u* 'at, by'; the verb *byt'* 'to be' shows the null form in the present tense; and the person or thing 'possessed' is the grammatical subject, which is in the nominative. The point of interest is that the subject noun has an attributive modifier which must agree with it in gender. In (D) the verb *byt'* 'to be' is again omitted. The complement noun is in the nominative case and again has an agreeing modifier (we return to the significance of the nominative case in §5.2.2 below). Thus (A) and (B) show predicate agreement, while (C) and (D) show attributive agreement (though in different constructions). Data on the reactions to these sentences are given in Table 2.5 (calculated from Kitajgorodskaja, 1976, 147, 151).

Table 2.5: **Agreement with Nouns like *vrač* in Russian**

sentence	N	informants selecting feminine agreement (%)
(A) Upravdom vydala spravku	3806	60.7
(B) Vrač prišla	3806	51.7
(C) U nas xorošaja buxgalter	3835	25.5
(D) Ivanova – xorošaja vrač	3835	16.9

A few words of explanation are necessary concerning Kitajgorodskaja's data. The total number of informants 'N' varies (differences occur between tables in the same source, and between sources). Though no explanation is given, it can be assumed that some questionnaires were not filled in completely. The percentage figure represents the proportion of the informants opting for the feminine form (semantic agreement); for this reason we have quoted the sentences in that form. Kitajgorodskaja gives only this figure. However, not all the remainder opted for the masculine form; though Kitajgorodskaja does not give the figures, some informants were undecided. From Panov (1968, 27, 28, 30, 39) we can deduce that overall they represent 5–10 per cent of the total. (The figures in Panov, 1968, were not used because there is no data of any kind on sentence (D).)

The most obvious conclusion to be drawn from these data is that there is a marked difference between the responses to sentences (A) and (B) on the one hand, and (C) and (D) on the other. While over half the informants chose the feminine, semantically agreeing form, in the sentences involving predicate agreement ((A) and (B)), only about a quarter chose semantic agreement in attributive position (sentences (C) and (D)). Thus the requirement of the Agreement Hierarchy is met — semantic agreement is more frequent in the predicate than in attributive position. Unfortunately, the other agreement positions were not included in the survey. However, Janko-Trinickaja, who studied women's journals of the twenties, reports more use of semantic agreement with the relative pronoun than in the predicate, with nouns of this type (1966, 193-4). She gives no figures, but of the six examples she cites involving relative pronouns, five show feminine agreement. Finally, the personal pronoun is regularly feminine. This basic information on nouns like *vrač* was included in Table 2.4 and Figure 2.1; again the requirements of the Agreement Hierarchy are satisfied.

While conforming to the hierarchy, the data reveal further patterns of variation. If we return to Table 2.5, we observe that besides the major difference between the two agreement positions, there is also a significant difference between sentences (A) and (B) and between (C) and (D). Though the nouns involved all permit alternative agreements, they differ in their 'preferences'. Three reasons have been offered for the difference between (A) and (B) (Panov, 1968, 30); of these, two can also be applied to (C) and (D). The first is that *upravdom* is a relatively new word (as is *buxgalter*) and so is less associated than is the older word *vrač* with the old norm. As we shall see, the old norm had syntactic agreement with such words. The second, partially overlapping suggestion, is that *upravdom* unlike *vrač*, tends to be restricted to the lower stylistic registers. There is probably some truth in these suggestions — to verify them would require data on several more words of this type. The important thing for our purposes is to have shown that, within the class of nouns which appear to be masculine but which can take feminine agreements when referring to a woman, the agreements used vary in frequency from noun to noun. Nevertheless, all the data available are consistent with the Agreement Hierarchy.

So far we have considered only the total responses to the sentences in the questionnaire. Data are available on the responses of various types of informants. For example, Table 2.6 shows responses according

Table 2.6: Responses According to Education: Number Choosing Semantic Agreement (%)

sentence	education secondary	higher
(A) Upravdom vydala spravku	62.5 (N = 2003)	58.7 (N = 1803)
(B) Vrač prišla	55.0 (N = 2003)	48.1 (N = 1803)
(C) U nas xorošaja buxgalter	30.5 (N = 2020)	20.0 (N = 1815)
(D) Ivanova – xorošaja vrač	20.8 (N = 2020)	12.6 (N = 1815)

Note: N is the total number of informants who responded.

to the education of the informants (i.e. whether they had received secondary or tertiary education).

As mentioned above, the number of replies varies slightly for the different sentences. Table 2.6 shows that those with higher education use the semantically agreeing forms less readily than those with only secondary education; the better educated are more conservative in this respect. However, both groups show the same preferences among the sentences: (A) is the most likely to have semantic agreement and (D) the least likely. We shall see that these preferences are maintained when the informants are divided according to different criteria. For example, in Figure 2.2, which is in the form of a frequency polygon, informants were classified according to the area in which they had spent the greatest portion of their lives (all were native speakers of Russian).

Figure 2.2. shows that Leningrad has the most conservative speakers, followed by Moscow and the Moscow Region, and the North and South of Russia. Areas where Russian is in competition with other languages are less conservative. All the areas show the same ordering of preferences among the four sentences, with the major differences being between sentences (A) and (B), on the one hand, and (C) and (D) on the other. Thus the requirement of the Agreement Hierarchy is met.

In Figure 2.3 the informants' occupation is the criterion according to which they are grouped. As we would expect from the data on education (the better educated are more conservative), graduates and students are less ready to use the semantically agreeing form than are industrial workers. Those whose education involves language study are more conservative than their colleagues, and professional writers are the

Figure 2.2: Area of Longest Stay

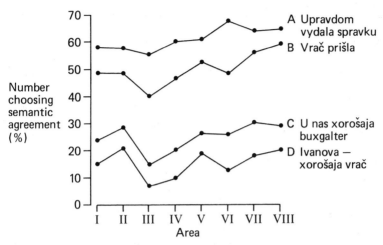

I Moscow (N = 958); II Moscow region (N = 245); III Leningrad (N = 96); IV North (N = 327); V South (N = 689); VI Ukraine (N = 304); VII Belorussia (N = 75); VIII Baltic states (N = 205).

Note: In Figures 2.2-2.4, N is quoted for sentences (A) and (B) (predicate agreement); in almost all cases the figure for sentences (C) and (D) (attributive agreement) is somewhat higher, though in one category in Figure 2.2 it is the same, and in one category in Figure 2.4 it is two lower.

most conservative of all — at least in their pronouncements on the subject. Once again, all groups rank the sentences in the same way, and make the major division between attributive and predicate agreement.

We have referred to 'conservative' usage. This can be justified from a breakdown of informants according to age, as this gives a clear indication of the direction in which the language is moving. As shown in Figure 2.4, the use of semantic agreement is on the increase. Interestingly, agreement in the two different types of sentence has remained roughly in step — as the number of speakers who accept semantic agreement in the predicate increases, so does the number of these who will also accept it in attributive position. However, the youngest group of informants showed slightly less readiness to accept semantic agreement in the predicate (sentences (A) and (B)) than the slightly older group. It has been suggested (Panov, 1968, 31) that this may be a result of schooling. The 1940-9 group comprised the informants nearest to the influence of school, with its emphasis on normative rules.

A more recent survey sheds some light on this suggestion. Wood

Figure 2.3: Professional Grouping

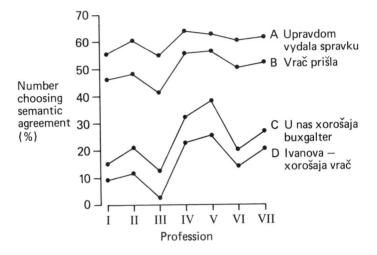

I Modern language graduates (N = 335); II Other graduates (N = 787); III Journalists and writers (N = 62); IV White collar (N = 896); V Workers (N = 419); VI Modern language students (N = 668); VII Other students (N = 167).

Figure 2.4: Year of Birth

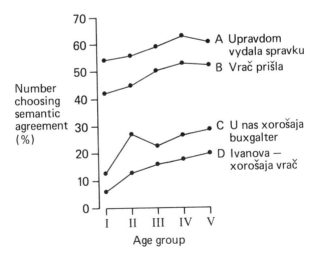

I Up to 1909 (N = 353); II 1910 - 19 (N = 187); III 1920 - 29 (N = 433); IV 1930 - 39 (N = 1280); 1940 - 49 (N = 1647).

(1980, 8-19) gives the results of a questionnaire distributed to fourth and fifth year students at Voronež University (law and philology faculties), and to pupils aged 13 to 14 and 15 to 16, at a school in the Voronež region. Three of the sentences included in her survey are similar to those discussed above (we shall label them (A'), (B'), (C')). They are given below in the variant showing semantic agreement:

(A') R: *Direktor   vošla* (fem) *v   komnatu*
     The director entered   into the room
(B') R: *Nakonec vrač   prišla* (fem)
     Finally   the doctor came
(C') R: *Ona   izvestnaja* (fem) *skul'ptor*
     She (is) a famous   sculptor

Wood does not mention any informants being undecided, but her total number of informants in different categories varies slightly. If we estimate the year of birth of her informants, we can compare her results with those of Panov's team, as in Table 2.7 (again we use Kitajgorodskaja's figures). The figures for the students in Wood's survey, compared with those for the youngest group in Panov's survey, may suggest that the trend towards semantic agreement has not been maintained. The relatively small sample in Wood's survey makes it unwise to make firmer conclusions (as the fluctuations for sentence (C') show).

Table 2.7: Effect of Education: Number Choosing Semantic Agreement (%)

		1930-9	1940-9	Year of birth 1959 and earlier (students)	1963-4	1965-6
sentence						
(A)	Upravdom vydala spravku	63.6 (N = 1280)	61.2 (N = 1647)			
(A')	Direktor vošla v komnatu			58.3 (N = 24)	59.1 (N = 22)	89.5 (N = 19)
(B)	Vrač prišla	53.7 (N = 1280)	53.1 (N = 1647)			
(B')	Nakonec vrač prišla			50.0 (N = 24)	63.6 (N = 22)	70.0 (N = 20)
(C)	U nas xorošaja buxgalter	26.6 (N = 1291)	28.4 (N = 1655)			
(C')	Ona izvestnaja skul'ptor			3.9 (N = 26)	27.3 (N = 22)	10.0 (N = 20)

Similarly the difference between the students and the older school-children is difficult to interpret: it is as likely to represent a difference between town and country (the children were from a village school) as between different age groups. The really interesting comparison is between the two groups of schoolchildren. Here, age is the only variable as far as we can tell. If we look at sentences (A′) and (B′) and compare the figure for those who were 15–16 at the time of the survey (the column headed 1965–6) with the figure for the 13–14 year olds (column headed 1963–4) then we find that those in the slightly older group are much less likely to opt for semantic agreement. This does suggest that schooling has an effect on judgements of these sentences. It will be interesting to see whether the effect is permanent or short-lived.

An obvious question to ask, given the type of sentence we are discussing, is whether the sex of the speaker is important. Panov gives no information on this question, but Wood gives very interesting data from which the figures in Table 2.8 have been calculated. From the

Table 2.8: Sex of Informants: Number Choosing Semantic Agreement (%)

	male	female	total
(A′) Direktor vošla v komnatu	50.0 (N = 36)	85.7 (N = 28)	65.6 (N = 64)
(B′) Nakonec vrač prišla	43.2 (N = 37)	82.1 (N = 28)	60.0 (N = 65)
(C′) Ona izvestnaja skul'ptor	12.8 (N = 39)	14.3 (N = 28)	13.4 (N = 67)

table it is evident that in predicate agreement ((A′) and (B′)) there is a marked difference between the sexes, with females showing a clear preference for the feminine form. It is noticeable that this difference is restricted to predicate agreement; in attributive agreement the difference is slight. A possible explanation for this is that predicate agreement is the most common agreement form − it is also the one which is most discussed and argued about. Perhaps females consciously choose the feminine form for predicate agreement, but do not extend this conscious choice to attributive agreement. Naturally, unsolicited examples are the only means to resolve this question.

Wood's data on the sex of the informants provide a new dimension of variation. Note yet again that the general picture remains the same: the proportion of semantic agreement is markedly different between predicate agreement (sentences (A′) and (B′)) and attributive agreement (as in (C′)) for both groups. In addition, both show a slightly higher proportion for (A') than for (B'). More generally, we have observed that *vrač* and nouns like it provide strong evidence in favour of the Agreement Hierarchy. They nevertheless show considerable variation in agreement, both according to the speaker (age, education, sex, etc.) and according to the particular controller (*vrač*, *buxgalter*, etc.).

2.4 Conclusion

In the previous sections we noted a clear pattern: there is a monotonic increase in semantic agreement as we move from attributive position, to the predicate, to the relative pronoun and finally to the personal pronoun. We observed this pattern in a wide range of data, and so we can safely claim that the Agreement Hierarchy is well founded. The hierarchy places severe constraints on possible agreement systems but still permits a wide range of variation. For example, we observed cases of diachronic change, where the frequency of semantic agreement altered, while the requirements of the Agreement Hierarchy were met at all stages. Thus agreements with *vrač* 'doctor' in Russian (when referring to a woman) have changed in recent times. Similarly, agreements with Serbo-Croat nouns like *gazda* 'master' (when in the plural) have changed since the last century. The latter nouns also furnish a good example of a difference between agreement in the standard language and in a dialect. Another such example was the use of plural agreement in the Talitsk dialect of Russian, in a way which is foreign to Standard Russian. Even within the standard language, we noted that the area in which the speaker lives can influence the agreements he uses — as is the case with *vrač* in Russian. There is also evidence that education, socioeconomic background and the sex of the speaker play their part in determining agreement. Furthermore, register has a role: *vrač* 'doctor' and *buxgalter* 'accountant' in Russian have the same formal properties, but the latter belongs to a lower register than the former, and shows a greater frequency of semantic agreement. An extreme case of variation is Gogol''s completely individual use of agreements with *značitel'noe lico* 'important person'.

The Agreement Hierarchy, therefore, severely constrains the types of variation possible, but within these constraints we still observe considerable divergence in usage. In one position, the predicate, it is possible to distinguish separate agreement positions, and to place further constraints on possible variation. This is the problem to which we turn in Chapter 3.

Notes

1. The abbreviation before each example indicates the language involved. For these abbreviations, and those relating to grammatical information, see p. xii. The transliteration system is given on p. xiii. As stated earlier, glosses are as literal as possible. The glossing of the auxiliary, as in example (10), is explained in the discussion of example (1) in Chapter 3.

2. 'Monotonic' is a term derived from statistics. A monotonic increase describes a series with no decrease in it; the numbers 1, 2, 2, 4, 4, 5, 6, show a monotonic increase, while 1, 2, 5, 4, 7, 6, 8 do not. Formulated in this way, the Agreement Hierarchy also covers the straightforward examples of agreement where all targets take the same form (as in examples (5)–(8)).

3. For further examples of agreement with *para*, Ardov's story *Ošibka Zagsa* is a good source.

4. A reason for the difference between singular and plural is suggested by Belić (1924, 26–7). Originally the feminine was used with these nouns in the singular and the plural. Masculine agreement results from the analogy of male personal names like *Luka* 'Luke', which are masculine despite their apparently feminine form. These are not used in tne plural. Hence masculine agreement with nouns like *gazda* appeared first in the singular.

5. Multiple agreements of the same type with a single controller were counted once only. The figure for the personal pronoun includes examples of *gdjekoji* 'some' used anaphorically.

6. Stanojčić, and other investigators, may have ignored the personal pronoun on the assumption that it must be masculine. If so, they are mistaken, because feminine forms are still found (see Marković, 1954, 94). Or they may have disregarded the personal pronoun because of the scarcity of examples, which is due in part to the fact that all personal pronouns are regularly omitted in Serbo-Croat, unless they are stressed. Thus the natural translation of 'he is good' is *dobar je* literally 'good is'. The form of the subject pronoun can be inferred from the agreements in the clause: *dobar* is masculine singular and *je* is third person singular. Of the five examples quoted of personal pronouns agreeing with nouns like *gazde*, in four the personal pronoun had to be inferred in this way, for example:

(i) . . . *iziđoše   halvadžije   iza   pregratka   gdje*
       went out the halva makers behind the partition where (they)
    su muklo dašćući mijesili (masc pl) *šećer   i   tijesto* . . .
       dully   panting mixed   the sugar and dough
    (Andrić, *Put Alije Đerzeleza*)

Iziđoše is an aorist form, which does not show agreement in gender. In the subordinate clause there is no overt subject; the deleted subject is *oni*, referring to *halvadžije*. It must be the masculine *oni* as the agreeing form *mijesili* proves. The figure which includes such examples and the similar one for the press are parenthesised in Table 2.3.

7. Stevanović (1974, 131–4) states that, while feminine forms are the more common in attributive and predicate position, masculine agreements must now be considered acceptable in the literary language; for the relative pronoun masculine agreement is the more common. His view of the norm is therefore close to what we find in Andrić. Other writers are more conservative than Andrić. Marković (1954, 94) reports that the novels *Daleko je sunce* by D. Ćosić and *Prolom* by Ćopić show no examples of masculine agreement in attributive or predicate position. In contrast, Ječmenica (1966) discusses these agreements in the work of Lalić; she does not consider different agreement positions but it may well be

significant that the only examples she quotes of feminine agreement are in attributive position. For dialect data see Herrity (1977, 266–9) and Marković (1954, 93–4).

8. The use of plural agreement with a singular human referent has also been reported, though it may not still be in use in every case, in the following language areas: Belorussian (Atraxovič *et al.*, 1966, 325), Ukrainian dialects (Shevelov, 1963, 67), Czech (Miklosich, 1868–74, 51), parts of Slovak (Orlovský, 1965, 120), Polish dialects (Makarski, 1973) and Slovene (Toporišič, 1972, 144).

In the previous chapter we compared various agreement targets, one of which was the predicate. If we now concentrate on the predicate, we will discover that within it different agreement positions can be identified. These subdivisions of the predicate were demonstrated by Comrie (1975). As with the Agreement Hierarchy, the Predicate Hierarchy was established on the basis of evidence from a range of languages; however, Slavic languages provide the best evidence found so far in favour of the Predicate Hierarchy. The basic data concern honorific *vy*. *Vy* means 'you', and is the normal form for addressing more than one person. It can also be used politely of a single person (like *vous* in French).[1] We will refer to this pronoun in Slavic as *vy*; it is spelled *vy*, *vi*, *vie* and *wy* in different languages. In all our examples we shall assume that it is appropriate to use polite address (in other words that *vy* or its equivalent is being used of one person) and will concentrate on the agreements found. It is not surprising that there are problems here, because honorific *vy* is plural in form but has a singular referent. Comrie (1975) drew his data on Slavic from Polish dialects, Russian, Czech and Serbo-Croat. As we shall see, the Slavic data support his claims rather better than he may have imagined. Two later studies (Herrity, 1977, Stone, 1977) extended the range of data available; in this account we shall give information on all the modern Slavic languages.

Comrie identifies four main predicate positions. First there is the ordinary verbal predicate. Next we find predicates which include an active participle to form the past tense. This participle agrees with the subject in number and gender. In most of the Slavic languages it is found together with the verb 'to be' as auxiliary; the following example is typical:

(1) SC: *Majka je došla* (fem sg)
    Mother is come

Depending on the context, the compound verb in this sentence could mean 'has come', 'came' or 'did come'; in other examples one of these forms is used when glossing the auxiliary. In East Slavic the verb 'to be', whether an auxiliary or a copula, is not normally used any longer in the present tense; thus the Russian sentence corresponding to (1) has no auxiliary:

(2) R: *Mat'*   *prišla* (fem sg)
     Mother came

Of course, one may wonder whether it is appropriate to use the term 'participle' for a form like *prišla* in (2); we shall return to the status of these forms in §3.3. For present purposes, the important thing is that the ordinary finite verb agrees in person and number with the subject, while the participle agrees in number and gender. The third type of predicate is the adjective; this too is most often accompanied by an auxiliary verb (though, particularly in East Slavic, it may not be). In the following Czech example, the auxiliary is present; it agrees in person and number with the subject, while the adjective agrees in number and gender with the subject:

(3) Cz: *Matka* *je* (3rd pers sg) *zdravá* (fem sg)
     Mother is   well

Finally, we have the predicate noun. The auxiliary may well occur with it, as in the following example:

(4) Sn: *Njen brat*   *je igralec* (nom)
     Her brother is an actor

Providing there is a verb present, some Slavic languages allow the predicate noun to stand in the nominative (as in (4) above) or in the instrumental case:

(5) U: *Vin buv učitel'* (nom)/*učitelem* (inst)
     He was a teacher

The predicative adjective may also stand in the instrumental, though less readily than the noun. The rules governing this choice vary from language to language and the details need not concern us.

The four positions described make up the Predicate Hierarchy, as shown in Table 3.1. These are the four regular positions; as we shall see, there are variations on the basic inventory. Russian, for example, splits the adjective position into two. As we move rightwards along the hierarchy, so the likelihood of semantic agreement will increase monotonically. The controller in question, honorific *vy*, is plural but has a singular referent. This means that plural agreement is syntactic, and singular agreement is semantic. In the case of the finite verb, the plural

Table 3.1: The Predicate Hierarchy

finite verb	–	participle	–	adjective	–	noun

(syntactic) form is found, while in the case of the predicate noun, the singular (semantic) form is normal. Most writers do not even refer to these two positions, considering the forms too obvious to require comment. However, the participle and the adjective show considerable variation. We shall consider each of the Slavic languages in turn: first the West Slavic languages, then those of the Southern group and finally the East Slavic languages.

3.1 The West Slavic Languages

In Standard Czech, only the finite verb takes plural (syntactic) agreement; all other predicates take the singular (semantically agreeing) form, as the following examples illustrate (Comrie, 1975, 408):

(6) Cz: *Vy   jste* (pl) *byla* (sg)   *dobrá* (sg)[2]
      You are   been (i.e. were) good
(7) Cz: *Vy   jste* (pl) *byla* (sg)   *učitelka* (sg)
      You   were   a teacher

Thus in polite address, syntactic agreement is found only in the finite verb, and so we find an increase in semantic agreement as we move from left to right along the hierarchy. While the forms given are Standard Czech, Trávníček (1949, 412) notes that in popular Czech the plural may be found in the participle and adjective, but not in the noun. This variety of Czech also shows an increase of semantic agreement as we move rightwards along the Predicate Hierarchy.

In Slovak, the participle and the predicative adjective take different agreements (Stanislav, 1977, 186):

(8) Sk: *Otec,   čo   ste* (pl)   *robili* (pl)?
      Father what have (you) done
(9) Sk: *Mama, vy   ste* (pl) *taká dobrá* (sg)!
      Mother you are   so   kind

Here we find syntactic agreement in the position to the left on the hierarchy (the participle) and semantic agreement in the position to the right (the adjective). While the forms given above represent the norm (confirmed by Pauliny *et al.*, 1968, 370-1), Orlovský (1965, 120) warns against the use of a singular participle. This suggests that some speakers use singular forms in the participle as well as for the adjective; their agreements are then equivalent to those of Standard Czech, and again they conform to the Predicate Hierarchy. The predicate noun is always singular (Bosák, personal communication).

Sorbian, as we noted above, exists in two variants. In Lower Sorbian, the participle stands in the plural (Stone, 1976, 189):

(10) LS: *Mjejśo   źjek,   až   sćo* (pl) *mje skubłali* (pl)
       Thank you very much that (you) have   me fed

However, the adjective may be either singular or plural (Stone, 1976, 190):

(11) LS: *Bużćo* (pl) *tak dobra*   (sg)/*dobre* (pl)
       Be   so kind

In Upper Sorbian the picture is slightly different. According to Stone, the use of syntactic agreement in the participle used to be almost universal. However, singular (semantic) agreement has spread, largely as a result of the influence of the Czech literary language. This means that both forms can be used in both positions on the hierarchy. The difference is that the singular is preferred (in both positions) in the literary norm, the plural being found in colloquial and non-standard usage. (For sources, examples and discussion see Stone, 1976; 1977, 494; cf. Šewc-Schuster, 1976, 60). In both Upper and Lower Sorbian the noun is found only in the singular (Šewc-Schuster, personal communication).

The remaining West Slavic language, Polish, appears to be the least promising for our purposes. In polite address the forms *pan* 'Mr' and *pani* 'Mrs' are used. These take third person singular agreements and give rise to no conflict between semantic and syntactic agreement. The pronoun *wy* 'you' is also used for polite address, mainly among rural speakers. There is some confusion over the agreement forms required (Stone, 1977, 493-4). Fortunately, usage in certain south-eastern dialects has been described by Makarski (1973). These data are quoted, in standard orthography, by Comrie (1975) and provide some of the best evidence in favour of the Predicate Hierarchy. The finite verb is always plural:

(12) P: *Wy   widzicie* (pl)/**widzisz* (sg)
      You see

And the predicate noun is singular:

(13) P: *Wy   będziecie* (pl) *swatka* (nom sg) /*swatką* (inst sg)
      You will be   a marriage-broker

Note that the predicate noun may stand in the nominative or instrumental case. However, the plural is not found:

(14) P: **Wy   będziecie* (pl) *swatki* (nom pl) /*swatkami* (inst pl)
      You will be   a marriage-broker

(We are, as throughout this section, restricting our attention to polite forms for addressing one person.) In these dialects, the participle used to form the past tense may be singular or plural:

(15) P: *Wyście* (pl) *widzieli* (pl) /*widziała* (sg)
      You   saw

(*-ście* is a clitic form of the present tense of verb *być* 'to be'; orthographically it is attached directly to the pronoun *wy* in these sentences.) Similarly, the predicative adjective may be singular or plural:

(16) P: *Wy   będziecie* (pl) *chorzy* (pl) /*chora* (sg)
      You will be   ill

If we have a sentence with a participle and an adjective in the predicate, there are four logical possibilities for the agreements. Of these, only three are acceptable:

(17) P: *Wyście   byli* (pl) *chorzy* (pl)
(18) P: *Wyście   byli* (pl) *chora* (sg)
(19) P: **Wyście była* (sg) *chorzy* (pl)
(20) P: *Wyście   była* (sg) *chora* (sg)
      You   were   ill

The impossible combination (19) is the one with semantic agreement of the participle and syntactic agreement of the adjective. This is particularly clear evidence in favour of the Predicate Hierarchy.

3.2 The South Slavic Languages

When we turn to Bulgarian, in the South Slavic group, we find convincing evidence of a different kind. In Bulgarian, finite verbs are again plural, and predicate nouns singular:

(21) B: *Vie ste* (pl) *mi răkovoditel* (sg) *i*
You are to me leader and
obrazec (sg). (Vazov)
model
(You are my leader and model)

The active participle, used to form the past tense, is plural:

(22) B: *Vie ste* (pl) *poiskali* (pl) *da bădete* (pl)
You have asked that (you) be
premesten (sg) *văv Varna*
transferred to Varna
(You asked to be transferred to Varna)

Sentence (22) includes a plural active participle (*poiskali*) and a passive participle (*premesten*) which, like a predicative adjective, stands in the singular. (The use of *da* with a finite verb instead of an infinitive is typical of Bulgarian, Macedonian and the eastern part of Serbo-Croat.) The following sentence has straightforward examples of singular predicative adjectives:

(23) B: *Vie ste* (pl) *uctiv* (sg) *i vnimatelen* (sg)
You are polite and attentive

According to Popov (1963, 129, 132–3; 1964, 21–2), from whom these examples are taken, the adjective may be in the plural in official correspondence between government dignitaries (as a result of Russian influence). The evidence given so far suggests that Bulgarian agreements with honorific *vie* (both normal Bulgarian and the variant just mentioned) conform fully with the Predicate Hierarchy. However, the situation is more fluid than most sources suggest, as demonstrated by statistical information on the distribution of the different forms. Dončeva-Mareva (1978) counted all the examples in a corpus of literary texts (400,000 words approximately). The active participle showed singular agreement in four per cent of the cases, while the adjective (including passive participles) was in the singular in 97 per cent of the cases. There appears to be no variation in the finite verb and noun. We can therefore give percentages for each position on the hierarchy (Table 3.2). We can see that there is indeed a monotonic increase in semantic

Table 3.2: Semantic Agreement with Honorific *vie* in Bulgarian (%)

finite verb	active participle	adjective	noun
0	4	97	100
	(N = 167)	(N = 163)	

agreement as we move rightwards along the hierarchy. This is based on a text count, which is to be given greater weight than the descriptive statements we have relied on with the other languages so far. Thus Bulgarian provides strong evidence to support the Predicate Hierarchy.

In Macedonian, which is closely related to Bulgarian, the picture is similar (data from Koneski, 1967, 332). The finite verb is plural, and the predicate noun singular:

(24) M: *Vie ste* (pl) *mi   prijatel* (sg)
        You are   to me friend (i.e. my friend)

The active participle can only be plural:

(25) M: *Vie ste* (pl) *stanale* (pl) /*stanal* (sg)
        You have   got up

However, the predicative adjective can be singular or plural:

(26) M: *Vie ste* (pl) *mnogu dobar* (sg) /*dobri* (pl)
        You are   very   kind

According to Koneski, the singular is preferable. As in Bulgarian, the following combination of forms is quite acceptable:

(27) M: *Vie ste* (pl) *stanale* (pl) *nervozen* (sg)
        You have   become   nervous

In Standard Serbo-Croat, plural agreement is the norm for the finite verb, active participle and predicative adjective (Comrie, 1975, 407–8):

(28) M: *Vi   ste* (pl)*bili* (pl)*dobri* (pl)
       You   were   good

Only the noun stands in the singular:

(29) SC: *Vi   ste* (pl)*bili* (pl)*studentkinja* (sg)
       You   were   a student

However, in colloquial speech the adjective may be singular (Comrie, 1975, 407; Stevanović, 1974, 127):

(30) SC: *Vi   ste* (pl) *pametna* (sg)
       You are   sensible

Herrity (1977, 262) quotes eighteenth- and nineteenth-century writers from Vojvodina and Slavonia and his examples include several singular adjectives, and a singular participle. This usage, while differing from the modern standard, is still in accordance with the Predicate Hierarchy. Singular participles were, it seems, in common use in the speech of intellectuals in the last century (Herrity, 1977, 262-3). It is interesting to note that the trend has been away from the semantic form towards syntactic agreement. There is no evidence for any development in Serbo-Croat to conflict with the Predicate Hierarchy.

In Slovene the situation is fairly similar to that in Serbo-Croat. The standard language requires plural agreement for both participle and adjective:

(31) Sn: *Vi   ste* (pl) *bili* (pl) *dobri* (pl)
       You   were   kind

However, both may occur in the singular in colloquial usage (cf. Jeseno-vec, 1958-9; Legiša, 1958-9):

(32) Sn: *Vi   ste* (pl) *bila* (sg) *dobra* (sg)
       You   were   kind

A singular adjective with a plural participle is unnatural or unacceptable (informants differ):

(33) Sn: ??*Vi   ste* (pl) *bili* (pl) *dobra* (sg)
       You   were   kind

However, a plural adjective with a singular participle is definitely not possible:[3]

> (34) Sn: **Vi   ste* (pl) *bila* (sg) *dobri* (pl)
>   You   were   kind

We shall return to the significance of this last example below (§4.2). Once again the predicate noun is singular. Thus the pattern found in Slovene (syntactic agreement of the finite verb, syntactic or, colloquially, semantic agreement of the participle and adjective and semantic agreement of the noun) is in clear accord with the Predicate Hierarchy.

3.3 The East Slavic Languages

The East Slavic languages, Ukrainian, Belorussian and Russian, differ from the other two groups in an interesting respect: the present tense of the verb 'to be' is not normally expressed. This means that the past tense consists solely of what was historically the past active participle, for example:

> (35) R: *Ja pisal*
>   I wrote

The question arises as to whether in East Slavic past tense forms like *pisal* differ from the normal finite verb form. In one important way they certainly are different: past tense forms show agreement in gender and number, while finite verb forms agree in person and number. However, when we compare them in respect of the agreement category they share – number – then the situation is less clear, as we shall see.

In Ukrainian, finite verb and participle are normally plural:

> (36) U: *Čoho vy   tam   sidite* (pl) *?*
>   Why you there sit
> (37) U: *Može,   vy, djadečku, čoho-nebud' popojili* (pl) *b.*
>   Perhaps you uncle   something   drink   would

Both examples are from Karpenko-Karij, quoted by Petik (1975, 320). With the adjective (and even more so with the noun), the singular is used:

(38) U: *Vy   tam   potribnyj* (sg)
      You there (are) necessary
      (Desnjak, quoted by Shevelov, 1963, 67)

Shevelov points out, however, that a plural adjective may be used to
show greater deference. The use of plural participle but singular adjective seems to be the most common, but as Stone (1977, 495) shows,
there is evidence of variation in both positions. Some writers state that
singular forms occur in the participle; Zahrods'kij (1954, 25) gives
example (39) but warns against the use of such forms.

(39) U: *Vy   skazala* (sg)
      You said

While for some speakers at least the participle can be singular, there is
absolutely no evidence of singular forms being used in other tenses,
and so we must keep the participle as a separate position on the hierarchy. Ukrainian then shows a monotonic increase in semantic agreement as we move rightwards along the hierarchy.

   In Belorussian, there is no evidence for a difference in number
agreement between the (historical) participle and other tenses; this may
be merely because little information is available. (The data given here
were kindly supplied by Father A. Nadson.) The finite verb stands in
the plural:

(40) BR: ... *vy ŭsë   xočace* (pl) *vedac'!*   (Kolas)
            you everything want   to know
(41) BR: ... *vy   tut   sjadzeli* (pl), *čytali* (pl) ...   (Kolas)
            you here sat   read

However, the adjective is singular (as indeed is the noun), according to
Atraxovič *et al.* (1966, 329):

(42) BR: *Vy   –   malady* (sg), *a   paspeli* (pl)   *tak mnoha*
      You (are) young   but have managed so   much
      načytacca.   (Pestrak)
      to read

These data on Belorussian are again fully in accord with the Predicate
Hierarchy.

   When we turn to Russian, the last language to be considered, we find a particularly interesting situation, both as regards the positions on the hierarchy, and in terms of the data available. Let us first consider the past tense form and the finite verb. Both normally take plural agreement with honorific *vy*, though various writers (for example, Bylinskij, 1939, 66; Bulaxovskij, 1958, 30; Rudnev, 1968, 85; Graudina *et al.*, 1976, 254) warn against the use of singular past tense verbs like the following:

(43) R: *Čto   vy   skazala* (sg) *?*
     What you said

However, these writers do not quote actual examples of this usage and it may well be that their warnings are directed towards Ukrainian speakers of Russian.[4] Until genuine examples are produced, we must accept that Russian provides no additional evidence to support the split between finite verb and past tense forms on the hierarchy. (This conclusion is confirmed in §9.2.) However, the fact that Ukrainian provides some evidence for the two positions shows that the loss of the auxiliary does not automatically result in the former participle behaving exactly like other finite verb forms. East Slavic, then, provides only a little evidence to confirm the distinction between the first two positions on the hierarchy. On the other hand, there is strong evidence for the division from other Slavic languages.

When we turn to the other positions on the hierarchy, then we find that Russian provides particularly interesting data. The important additional distinction which must be made is that between the short form (SF) adjective and the long-form (LF).[5] The short-form is the original adjectival form, though the long-form is already present in Old Church Slavic and has been steadily encroaching on the areas of use of the short-form throughout the Slavic family. In most of the Slavic languages, there is now relatively little choice – one or other form is dominant. However, in Modern Russian the short-form survives in the predicate, though the long-form is increasing in frequency. When agreeing with honorific *vy*, the short-form and the long-form behave differently. The short-form, like the finite verb (including the past tense) normally takes the plural:

(44) R: *Vy   vidite* (pl)
     You see
(45) R: *Vy   pisali* (pl)
     You wrote

(46) R: *Vy*   *bol'ny* (SF, pl)
      You (are) ill

The long-form, like the noun, usually stands in the singular:

(47) R: *Vy*   *molčalivaja* (LF, sg)
      You (are) silent
(48) R: *Vy*   *genij* (sg)
      You (are) a genius

When we turn to statistical data, we find that the situation is a little less clear-cut. Table 3.3 incorporates the results of various investigations.

Table 3.3: Agreement with Honorific *vy* in Russian

	past tense pl	sg	SF adjective pl	sg	LF adjective pl	sg	noun pl	sg
Standard language ((44)–(48) above)	✓	*	✓	*	*	✓	*	✓
Dončeva–Mareva (literature)	309	0	105	2	3	11		
Gustavsson (literature)			20	0	1	20		
Vojnovič (*Ivan'kiada*)	41	0	6	0	0	2	0	13
Graudina *et al.* (press)			10	2		0		
Totals expressed as percentages	100	0	97	3	11	89	0	100

The ordinary finite verb is not included, as there are no reports of singular forms and no figures given. A blank indicates that the category was not investigated. The fullest survey is that of Dončeva-Mareva (1978), based on a corpus of approximately 400,000 words of modern fiction. All examples of the past tense verb showed the expected plural agreement (just like the ordinary finite verb). A small number of short-form singulars and long-form plurals was found. Gustavsson (1976, 236-9) also used a corpus of literary texts, but reports only one plural long-form. *Ivan'kiada* is a fruitful source of examples; all conform to the norm of Standard Russian. There is also a study of the press 1968-72, in which Graudina *et al.* (1976, 253) found two singular short-form examples out of twelve. The summary of this evidence, expressed as a percentage figure, shows that there is a small but significant body of deviations from the norm described. The picture of actual usage which emerges, based on a larger body of data than was available for any of the other languages, is absolutely clear. Semantic agreement increases as we move rightwards along the hierarchy.

The system has undergone change in the recent past. In order to establish the position in the first half of the last century, all Puškin's major prose works were scanned (*Povesti pokojnogo Ivana Petroviča Belkina, Istorija sela Gorjuxina, Roslavlev, Dubrovskij, Pikovaja dama, Kirdžali, Egipetskie noči* and *Kapitanskaja dočka*). These were written between 1830 and 1836. There are numerous examples of verbs, many of them past tense forms, agreeing with honorific *vy*; all of them show plural agreement, as in Modern Russian. Similarly, all the examples of short-form adjectives (18, including two past passive participles) show plural agreement. Only one long-form was found. It occurs in *Kapitanskaja dočka*, and is particularly significant because it is supposed to be spoken by the Tsarina, and so represents the educated norm:

(49) R: *Vy, verno   ne ždešnie* (LF, pl) ?
       You probably (are) not local

In this example Puškin uses the plural, while modern usage prefers the singular. In the same conversation the Tsarina uses a predicate noun; this is in the singular:

(50) R: *Vy   sirota* (sg) . . .
       You (are) an orphan

Nine examples with predicate nouns were found; all stand in the singular.

The point at which Puškin's usage differs from the modern norm is the long-form adjective. In Turgenev we find both singular and plural forms here:[6]

(51) R: *Nu, kak   xotite; tol'ko kakoj že vy*
       Well as (you) like   only   how   you (are)
       uprjamyj (LF, sg)*!*
       stubborn (i.e. how stubborn you are!)
       (*Nakanune*, 1860)

(52) R: *Vy   takie dobrye* (LF, pl) . . .
    You (are) so   good
    (*Dvorjanskoe gnezdo*, 1859)

In Turgenev too, the predicate nouns found are in the singular. However, in the last century the less well educated used a plural even for
predicate nouns, as shown by one of Čexov's characters:

(53) R: *Izmenniki* (pl) *vy, čto li?*
    Traitor   you is it
    (Are you a traitor, then?)
    (Čexov, *Xolodnaja krov'*, 1887, quoted in Vinogradov and
    Istrina, 1954, 520)

In this example the predicate noun is plural, even though *vy* refers to
one person. Such examples are particularly important because they
show that predicate noun phrases can obtain their number by agreement
with their subject – they do not always take 'real world' number. Hence
it is necessary to specify whether predicate nouns agree with *vy* or not
in a given language; we cannot, as some investigators do, take it for
granted that they do not. For those speakers who used a plural predicate
with *vy*, the plural occurred in all positions on the Predicate Hierarchy.
They are therefore in accord with the hierarchy, but do not provide
extra evidence to support it. If we ignore for a moment the variation
found within Modern Russian, the three systems we have described may
be presented as in Table 3.4. It is clear that each of these three systems
is in accord with the Predicate Hierarchy.

Table 3.4: Agreement with *vy*: Different Systems in Russian

	verb	SF	LF	noun
19th c. popular	pl	pl	pl	pl
19th c. forms as in Pŭskin	pl	pl	pl	sg
20th c. norm	pl	pl	sg	sg

3.4 Summary of the Evidence for the Predicate Hierarchy

The evidence presented so far is summarised in Table 3.5, which shows
that the evidence in favour of the Predicate Hierarchy is very solid. In
each of the Slavic languages we find a monotonic increase in semantic
agreement as we move rightwards along the hierarchy. Generally we do

Table 3.5: Agreement with Honorific *vy* in the Slavic Languages

	finite verb	participle		adjective		noun
West Slavic:						
Czech	pl	(pl)/sg		(pl)/sg		sg
Slovak	pl	pl/(sg)		sg		sg
Lower Sorbian	pl	pl		pl/sg		sg
Upper Sorbian	pl	(pl)/sg		(pl)/sg		sg
Polish dialects	pl	pl/sg		pl/sg		sg
South Slavic:						
Bulgarian	pl	pl (96%)		sg (97%)		sg
Macedonian	pl	pl		(pl)/sg		sg
Serbo-Croat	pl	pl		pl/(sg)		sg
Slovene	pl	pl/(sg)		pl/(sg)		sg
East Slavic:						
Ukrainian	pl	pl/(sg)		(pl)/sg		sg
Belorussian	pl	pl		sg		sg
			SF		LF	
Russian	pl	pl	pl (97%)		sg (89%)	sg

Note: The sources of the percentage figures have been given above. Other parentheses indicate less frequent or less preferred variants; details were given in the discussion of individual languages. Historical and dialect data, apart from Polish, have been omitted.

not find a single clear break between the two agreement possibilities at one point on the hierarchy. (The clear split in Belorussian may well reflect only the lack of information on this language.) We conclude that the Predicate Hierarchy has been justified. In §9.2 evidence will be presented to show that the Predicate Hierarchy applies with controllers other than honorific *vy*. We shall also have occasion to consider further the place of the Predicate Hierarchy in linguistic theory (§4.2).

3.5 Agreement in Gender with Honorific *vy*

We have concentrated on agreement in number with honorific *vy*. This is certainly the major problem but gender too should be considered. We have seen cases of singular (semantic) agreement with *vy*, and there gender agreement too is semantic. Thus the masculine is used when addressing a man (examples from Bauernöppel *et al.*, 1976, 166):

(54) Cz: *Vy   jste* (pl) *velmi laskav* (masc sg), *pane D!*
        You are   very kind   Mr   D.

And the feminine is used for a woman:

(55) Cz: *Vy   jste* (pl) *velmi laskava* (fem sg), *pani D!*
     You are   very kind   Mrs D.

The more interesting situation arises in those languages where the
participle and adjective stand in the plural (or at least can stand in the
plural) and where gender is distinguished in the plural. Then will a
woman be addressed using a masculine plural or a feminine plural?

Polish has two agreement forms in the plural — the masculine
personal and the non-masculine personal (which would normally be
used for agreement with plural feminine nouns). Recall that the main
forms for polite address are *pan* and *pani*. However, when *wy* is used to
address a woman a problem can arise. In the dialect examples examined
above ((15)–(19)) all the plural forms which distinguish gender are
masculine personal. Thus the effect of polite address is to change both
number (plural for singular) and gender (masculine personal for non-
masculine personal). While this is the recommended form (Doroszewski,
1962, 40–1), some speakers use the non-masculine personal form
(Stone, 1977, 493), for example:

(56) P: *Czy   wyście* (pl)   *to*
        (question) you have   that
        napisały (non-masc pers pl) *?*
        written
        (Did you write that?)

As we saw earlier, the singular can also be used. Thus, for addressing a
woman there are potentially three forms available: masculine personal
plural, non-masculine personal plural and feminine singular.

In Slovene, three genders occur in the plural, matching those of the
singular. The examples given above all have the masculine plural, even
though addressed to a woman, and there is no evidence of the feminine
plural being used. In Serbo-Croat the agreement possibilities are the
same, and the norm is the same as for Slovene (plural forms are masculine). However, Herrity (1977, 262), quoting Bošković, reports examples from the last century like the following:

(57) SC: *Vi   ste*   (pl) *poznavale* (fem pl)
         You have   found out

Given that singular forms were found, as discussed above, as well as the standard masculine plural, this again gives potentially three forms for addressing a woman, as in Polish. This in turn suggests that the simple binary distinction between syntactic and semantic agreement is inadequate. We can tabulate the possibilities (Table 3.6). Feminine plural agreement in these examples is 'more semantic' than masculine plural but 'less semantic' than feminine singular.

Table 3.6: Gender and Number Agreement with Honorific *vy*

	masculine/masculine personal plural	feminine/non-masculine personal plural	feminine singular
number	syntactic	syntactic	semantic
gender	syntactic	semantic	semantic

We shall consider below (§5.2.1) other evidence which forces us to extend the notion of semantic agreement. For our immediate purpose, the justification of the Predicate Hierarchy, these examples are of secondary concern. There is no evidence that any individual speaker ever had three forms available. The little evidence that is available is not in any way contrary to the claims of the Predicate Hierarchy.

3.6 Conclusion

Data have been presented from the different Slavic languages, all fully in accord with the requirements of the Predicate Hierarchy. In some cases more than one set of agreements was described (for example, historical evidence is available for some languages) and all confirmed the hierarchy. The Predicate Hierarchy therefore rests on a sound factual base, as does the Agreement Hierarchy. We must now go on to consider how these two target hierarchies fit into linguistic theory, which we will do in the next chapter.

Notes

1. For information on the use of *vy* rather than *ty* 'you' (familiar) in the Slavic languages see Stone (1977) and references there.
2. In §3.1–§3.3 our main concern is with number agreement. In these sections, forms marked as singular and ending in *-a* are feminine (appropriate for a single female addressee); other singular forms are masculine.

3. I am grateful to Wayles Browne, Rado Lenček and Janez Orešnik for these data.

4. Gerald Stone has made a similar suggestion. Okudžava uses forms such as *Vy ponjala* (sg) *?* 'Have you understood?' in *Dva romana* (Posev, Frankfurt/Main, 1970), 336. But he also uses singular forms in the present tense, e.g. *Vy dumaeš'* (sg)? 'Do you think?'. Russian speakers assure me that this is a humorous use of language for a particular literary effect.

5. A further distinction has been drawn between the past passive participle and the short-form adjective (Dončeva-Mareva, 1978; Corbett, 1981c). The evidence is rather slight, and so we will disregard it here.

6. In Dostoevskij's *Belye noči* (1848) all predicate types already show agreements in accordance with the modern norm.

4.   THE STATUS OF THE HIERARCHIES

We have established that the Agreement and Predicate Hierarchies are supported by and account for a considerable body of data. We must now investigate the status of these hierarchies in linguistic theory. The most interesting question is that of the level at which they operate. They could apply either at *sentence level* or at *corpus level*.[1] Most work in syntax in recent years has been concerned with sentence-level rules, the most familiar type being transformations. Every sentence is subject to these rules, and if they are not applied where appropriate, an ungrammatical sentence results. Less work has been done on corpus-level rules. An example of a rule which can be considered to operate at corpus level is the Keenan-Comrie Accessibility Hierarchy (1977), which specifies that certain NPs are more easily accessible than others to processes such as relativisation. This comparison does not apply to individual sentences but to sets of sentences, or corpora. In fact most of the work on typology in the Greenberg tradition is best seen as applying to corpora rather than to individual sentences. In abstract terms, the distinction between rules which operate at sentence level and those which operate at corpus level is clear. In particular cases it is not always so straightforward. We will therefore consider our two hierarchies in turn to establish the level at which they operate. Once this has been established, the other main aspect of status – the independence of the hierarchies – follows from it. Finally we will examine constraints which complement the Agreement Hierarchy, since this analysis also depends on the distinction between sentence level and corpus level.

4.1 The Status of the Agreement Hierarchy

The Agreement Hierarchy consists of four target types: attributive, predicate, relative pronoun and personal pronoun. As we move rightwards along this hierarchy, the likelihood of semantic agreement increases monotonically. To determine the level at which the hierarchy applies, it is helpful to divide the examples into two: those where the agreement options coincide with divisions on the hierarchy, and those where they do not.

An example where the agreement options and the divisions on the hierarchy coincide is the Russian controller *para* 'couple' (§2.1.2). In the first three positions on the hierarchy, *para* takes feminine singular agreement, while the personal pronoun stands in the plural. Thus we have syntactic agreement in the three positions to the left, and semantic agreement in the remaining position on the right. This situation could be handled by a rule operating at sentence level:

(1) Personal pronouns agreeing with *para* stand in the plural, other targets take the singular.

What then is the role of the Agreement Hierarchy? Given the existence of rules which have the effect of that given above (however they are stated), which require different agreement forms according to the target, there are several theoretically possible agreement systems. For example, we might find semantic agreement in attributive position and syntactic agreement elsewhere. The Agreement Hierarchy stipulates that such a system cannot exist. The theoretically possible systems and the subset permitted by the hierarchy are indicated in Table 4.1. This shows that when agreement options coincide with the positions on the hierarchy, the Agreement Hierarchy excludes eleven of the 16 theoretically possible systems. Implicational universals normally exclude only

Table 4.1: Agreement Systems Permitted by the Agreement Hierarchy

attributive	predicate	relative pronoun	personal pronoun	permitted by Agreement Hierarchy?
SYN	SYN	SYN	SYN	YES
SYN	SYN	SYN	SEM	YES
SYN	SYN	SEM	SYN	NO
SYN	SYN	SEM	SEM	YES
SYN	SEM	SYN	SYN	NO
SYN	SEM	SYN	SEM	NO
SYN	SEM	SEM	SYN	NO
SYN	SEM	SEM	SEM	YES
SEM	SYN	SYN	SYN	NO
SEM	SYN	SYN	SEM	NO
SEM	SYN	SEM	SYN	NO
SEM	SYN	SEM	SEM	NO
SEM	SEM	SYN	SYN	NO
SEM	SEM	SYN	SEM	NO
SEM	SEM	SEM	SYN	NO
SEM	SEM	SEM	SEM	YES

Note: SYN = syntactic agreement. SEM = semantic agreement.

one possibility in four. If we propose that in any language semantic agreement can occur in attributive position only if it occurs also in predicate position, then three possibilities are allowed (semantic agreement in neither, semantic agreement in both and syntactic agreement in attributive position with semantic agreement in the predicate). The only possibility excluded is semantic agreement in attributive position with syntactic agreement in the predicate. Hierarchies are implicational statements linked in chains. This linking gives very considerable predictive power, as Table 4.1 demonstrates. In fact the Agreement Hierarchy makes even stronger predictions, as we shall see below.

First we must conclude our discussion of agreement with controllers like *para*. The particular agreements that this controller requires must be stated in the grammar of Russian. The Agreement Hierarchy tells us that this pattern is one of the relatively small set of permitted patterns; indeed, it is enough to specify that *para* takes semantic agreement in one position only since the Agreement Hierarchy will determine that it is the personal pronoun. Furthermore, if in the course of diachronic change, semantic agreement increases in constructions with *para* as the controller, the hierarchy predicts that this will happen first with the relative pronoun and only then spread to the predicate. As long as the agreement options coincide with the positions on the hierarchy, as is the case with *para*, then a straightforward sentence-level rule such as (1) will specify the required agreements. The role of the Agreement Hierarchy can then be viewed in two ways. It may be seen as a rule which determines the form of sentence-level rules like (1). Or it may be taken to apply to corpora; in this case a corpus which showed examples of semantic agreement with a given controller in one position only would be judged ill-formed if that one position were other than the personal pronoun. Thus rules like (1) would be regulated by their output. In neither case is the Agreement Hierarchy a simple sentence-level rule: it is either a higher level rule specifying the form of sentence-level rules, or it applies to corpora and so is a corpus-level rule.

With cases like *para* there is no compelling evidence for either alternative. If we turn to controllers which permit an agreement option in more than one position on the hierarchy, then we have a much more interesting situation. To take a specific case: suppose a controller takes syntactic agreement in attributive position, syntactic or semantic agreement of the predicate and the relative pronoun, and semantic agreement of the personal pronoun. This must of course be specified in the grammar of the language and the Agreement Hierarchy (operating in one of the two ways just described) tells us that this is a possible agreement system. However, it also tells us that the possibility of semantic agreement in the relative pronoun will be as great as or greater than that found in the predicate. It is therefore insufficient to view the hierarchy as specifying the form of sentence rules. It would have to specify the relative frequency of the outputs of the different agreement rules. It seems logical to opt for the simpler alternative, that of referring directly to the distribution of forms in a corpus; the Agreement Hierarchy requires that a corpus contain a proportion of cases of semantic agreement of the relative pronoun which is as high as or higher than the proportion in the predicate.

The original formulation of the Agreement Hierarchy with its reference to the likelihood of semantic agreement increasing monotonically clearly suggests that it operates at corpus level. However, when controllers which permit agreement choices in two (or more) positions are involved, there is a second type of prediction which the hierarchy can make, which does not arise with controllers like *para*. It could operate as a sentence-level constraint; it would then make different predictions from those which it makes by operating at corpus level. These different predictions deserve investigation.

If the Agreement Hierarchy operates as a sentence-level constraint, then the prediction it makes can be expressed as follows:

(2) If a given language allows a choice of agreement in two positions on the Agreement Hierarchy, and the two positions are filled in a single sentence, then a combination of semantic agreement in the position to the left on the hierarchy and syntactic agreement in the position to the right will produce an ungrammatical sentence.

In the case we have been considering, this excludes any sentence showing semantic agreement of the predicate together with a syntactically agreeing relative pronoun. It operates only when both positions are filled in a single sentence; it does not apply to all those sentences in which only one position is filled. Thus it would be possible for a language to have an agreement controller which almost always took semantic agreement in the predicate and almost always syntactic agreement of the relative pronoun, providing only that when the two were found in a single sentence they did not then both take their usual agreements. If, however, the Agreement Hierarchy applies at the corpus level, then the situation just described is excluded; in a corpus, the proportion of examples of semantic agreement with a given controller will be at least as high in the relative pronoun as it is in the predicate. This is a much stronger claim than that made by the sentence-level constraint, because it relates to all sentences with the given controller and not only to the (probably small) set in which both targets are found.

The Agreement Hierarchy makes different predictions according to whether it applies as a sentence-level constraint or at corpus level. In both instances the class of possible human languages is more narrowly defined: certain language types are excluded which would be permitted if the hierarchy operated at the other level. The stronger claim is that the hierarchy operates at corpus level. This was the original claim made for the Agreement Hierarchy (Corbett, 1979b, 221). All the data presented in Chapter 2 support this claim. It should be noted that as we are considering two agreement forms occurring in any possible proportion and at more than one position on the hierarchy, the number of theoretically possible agreement systems is extremely large. It can readily be established that the Agreement Hierarchy rules out the great majority of these; it is therefore considerably more powerful than Table 4.1 above suggests. While all the data are consistent with the claim that the Agreement Hierarchy applies at corpus level, it is logically possible that it might also apply as a sentence-level constraint. However, we will now examine two constructions where the hierarchy applies at corpus level but definitely does not apply as a sentence-level constraint.

In Serbo-Croat, as we saw earlier (§2.1.3), phrases consisting of *dva* 'two', *tri* 'three' and *četiri* 'four' plus a masculine noun may take two different agreements: a form in -*a* (syntactic agreement: the form is analysed further in §5.4) and a form in -*i* (semantic agreement). The attributive modifier always shows the syntactic form while the personal pronoun always shows the semantic form; the remaining two positions both permit the agreement option. In Sand's sample, in the predicate semantic agreement was found in '18 per cent of the examples (N = 376), while in the relative pronoun it was found in 62 per cent of the cases (N = 32). Thus the Agreement Hierarchy, applying at corpus level, makes the correct prediction. If it were to apply as a sentence-level constraint in the form of (2) above, it would dictate that no sentence could include both the controllers in question, with semantic agreement in the verb and syntactic agreement in the relative pronoun. However, the sample included just such an example:

(3) SC: *Dva tima, koja* (dual) *se   nalaze u donjem*
        Two teams which   themselves find   in the lower

delu tabele,   *Radnički i*   *Olimpija, u*   *Kragujevcu na*
part of the table   Radnički and Olimpija   in   Kragujevac on
teškom   *terenu igrali* (pl) *su prljavo*   *i*   *nesportski.*
a difficult pitch   played   dirtily   and unsportingly
(*Politika*, 9 Dec. 1969)

Sand found only this one example out of 26 containing both an agreeing predicate and an agreeing relative pronoun (1971, 63–5). However,
the fact that there is only one example is not surprising, as it represents
a combination of the less common predicate type (occurring overall in
18 per cent of the examples) with the less common relative pronoun
agreement (found in 38 per cent of the cases). The combination of
these two probabilities is sufficient to account for the infrequency of
sentences like (3). This construction is a clear demonstration of the
Agreement Hierarchy applying at corpus level but not as a sentence-
level constraint.

    Russian provides a similar case. Conjoined noun phrases permit
singular or plural agreement of the predicate and of the relative pronoun
(§2.1.7). As we shall see (§9.1), plural agreement is found more frequently when the target is a relative pronoun than when it is a predicate. Thus the Agreement Hierarchy applies at corpus level. Were it also
to apply as a sentence-level constraint, it would not be possible to have
a semantically agreeing (plural) predicate in the same sentence as a
syntactically agreeing (singular) relative pronoun, but this is precisely
what we find in this next sentence:

(4) R: *Bystrota i*   *uverennost', s*   *kotoroj* (sg) *belye*
      The speed and confidence   with which   white
      „isponili"   *dva poslednix xoda, po-vidimomu,*
      carried out (his) two last   moves evidently
      smutili (pl)   *partnera.*
      confused (his) opponent
      (*Šaxmaty* (Riga, 1978), no. 13, p. 6)

We have established that all the data are consistent with the Agreement
Hierarchy applying at corpus level. There are also instances where it can
be proved that it does not apply as a sentence-level constraint. There
remains the possibility that while it always applies at corpus level, it
may also be invoked as a sentence-level constraint in particular cases.
One possible instance occurs in Russian. *Vrač* 'doctor' can take masculine (syntactic) or feminine (semantic) agreement in both attributive

and predicate positions, providing it refers to a woman. As we saw in §2.3, semantic agreement occurs more frequently when the target is a predicate; this is in accord with the Agreement Hierarchy applying at corpus level. Given the situation just outlined, there are the following four logically possible agreement combinations:

(5) R: *Novyj* (masc)   *vrač*   *skazal* (masc)
(6) R: *Novyj* (masc)   *vrač*   *skazala* (fem)
(7) R: **Novaja* (fem) *vrač*   *skazal* (masc)
(8) R: *Novaja* (fem)   *vrač*   *skazala* (fem)
         The new   (woman) doctor said

According to Švedova (1970, 555), sentence (7) is ungrammatical. Sentence (7) is, of course, the sentence which would be ruled out by constraint (2), that is, by the Agreement Hierarchy operating as a sentence-level constraint.

Another case is found in Czech. Both attributive and predicate agreement with conjoined noun phrases can be singular or plural, but the combination of plural attributive modifier (semantic agreement) with singular predicate (syntactic agreement) is excluded; if the attributive modifier is plural, then the predicate must be plural too (Trávníček, 1949, 419):

(9) Cz: *Moji* (pl) *otec a matka byli* (pl) *chudobní* (pl)
         My   father and mother were   poor

Just the same constraint (semantic agreement in attributive position may not co-occur with syntactic agreement in the predicate) is found with conjoined noun phrases in Russian (see discussion of (28) in §7.4).[2] Two points should be stressed here. The first is that all the evidence for the Agreement Hierarchy applying at sentence level involves the same two positions – attributive position and the predicate. The second point is that in one case at least, the constraint definitely does not apply beyond these two positions. It was stated that with conjoined noun phrases in Russian, plural attributive agreement does not co-occur with singular predicate agreement (as in Czech). However, a plural predicate with a singular relative pronoun is possible, as (4) shows. Thus the evidence for the Agreement Hierarchy applying at sentence level is restricted to the first two positions on the hierarchy, i.e. to agreement within the clause. Thus (2) above must be limited to attributive and predicate targets.

Let us sum up our discussion of the level at which the Agreement Hierarchy operates. All the data found are consistent with the claim that it operates at corpus level. It does not as a matter of course apply as a sentence-level constraint as well (as sentences (3) and (4) prove). There is some evidence to suggest that individual languages may invoke it at sentence level (in the form of constraint (2)). However, we have found such evidence only for the first two positions on the hierarchy. There is no evidence whatever for the Agreement Hierarchy operating as a sentence-level constraint but not at corpus level.

Having settled that the Agreement Hierarchy operates primarily at corpus level, we are in a position to determine whether it has independent status or whether it can be derived from some other measure. The notion that agreement within the clause differs from agreement beyond the clause goes back to Maretić (1899, 399). We have developed that basic distinction. In traditional terms, our four positions represent agreement within the phrase, beyond the phrase but within the clause, beyond the clause but within the sentence and (potentially) beyond the sentence. In the first presentation of the hierarchy, Comrie's measure for the closeness of nodes, Langacker's notion of command and Fauconnier's closeness constraint were considered as possible measures which might make the hierarchy redundant. It was demonstrated that they make the wrong predictions or fail to separate all the positions on the hierarchy (Corbett, 1979b, 216-17). In a sense, it is pointless to consider measures of this type as they involve comparing relative structural distances in a particular syntactic configuration, in other words comparing two targets in a single sentence. This would be appropriate if the Agreement Hierarchy applied at sentence level but, as we have seen, it applies primarily at corpus level. We are therefore justified in claiming that it is a necessary addition to linguistic theory.

4.2 The Status of the Predicate Hierarchy

The Predicate Hierarchy consists of four basic positions in Slavic: finite verb, past active participle, adjective and noun. As we move rightwards along this hierarchy, so the likelihood of semantic agreement increases. As we saw in Chapter 3, the hierarchy is supported by a good deal of evidence. We must now establish the level at which it operates. In the last section we found that the crucial cases are those where there is an agreement option in more than one position on the hierarchy. Consider the case of a language which requires plural (syntactic) agreement of the finite verb with honorific *vy*, singular (semantic) agreement of the predicate noun, but permits either form in both the remaining positions. If the Predicate Hierarchy operates at corpus level, then it requires that semantic agreement must occur in at least as high a proportion of predicative adjectives as it does in the past participle. This is a strong claim which will apply to a large number of sentences in a corpus. The statistical data available for Bulgarian (§3.2) fully support this claim. For Russian (§3.3) different positions on the hierarchy are involved but again statistical evidence indicates that the Predicate Hierarchy operates at corpus level. And, indeed, all the other evidence presented in Chapter 3 is consistent with this analysis.

We must now investigate the possibility that the Predicate Hierarchy also operates as a sentence-level constraint. In Polish dialects we find a situation like that just described: when agreeing with the honorific pronoun, the finite verb is plural, the noun is singular and there is a choice in the remaining two positions. If we have a sentence including both a past participle and a predicative adjective, there are four logically possible combinations:

(10) P: *Wyście byli* (pl) *chorzy* (pl)
(11) P: *Wyście byli* (pl) *chora* (sg)
(12) P: **Wyście była* (sg) *chorzy* (pl)
(13) P: *Wyście była* (sg) *chora* (sg)
        You   were   ill

The sentence which is ungrammatical, (12), is precisely the one which would be ruled out by the Predicate Hierarchy operating as a sentence-level constraint. We may formulate the constraint as follows:

(14) If a given language allows a choice of agreement in two positions on the Predicate Hierarchy, and the two positions are filled in a single sentence, then a combination of semantic agreement in the position to the left on the hierarchy and syntactic agreement in the position to the right will produce an ungrammatical sentence.

This constraint operates in the Polish dialects discussed. It also operates in Slovene, as the data given in (§3.2) demonstrate. In fact, all the data we have examined for all the Slavic languages are consistent with the claim that the Predicate Hierarchy operates as a sentence-level constraint. It is worth emphasising that by operating at two different levels, the hierarchy constrains agreement systems in two separate ways. In the case of the Polish dialect just discussed ((10)–(13)), the hierarchy operating at sentence level requires that semantic agreement must occur at least as frequently with predicative adjectives like *chorzy* as it does with participles like *byli*. This requirement applies to the corpus as a whole — including those sentences with a participle but no adjective and vice versa. Operating as a sentence-level constraint, the hierarchy applies only to sentences with both forms present, and serves to exclude sentences like (12).

We conclude, therefore, that the Predicate Hierarchy, like the Agreement Hierarchy, operates at corpus level. There are clear examples of the Predicate Hierarchy also operating as a sentence-level constraint and no counter-examples have been found so far to the claim that it always applies as a sentence-level constraint. It must also be said that there is no other measure from which it can be derived and so, like the Agreement Hierarchy, it must be recognised as a necessary part of linguistic theory.

4.3 Sentence-level Constraints Complementing the Agreement Hierarchy

In the last two sections we considered, among other things, examples in which two different positions on one of the hierarchies were represented in the same sentence. In this section we examine sentences in which the same position on the Agreement Hierarchy is represented more than once in a single sentence (we have no problematic examples involving the Predicate Hierarchy). For example, a controller which permits alternative agreements may take two attributive modifiers, or it may determine the agreement form of more than one verb. These represent two different possibilities which we shall examine in turn: stacked targets and parallel targets.

4.3.1 Stacked Targets

The notion of stacking is straightforward. Consider the following example:

(15) Cz: *ty   pĕkné žluté   kvĕtiny*
        these pretty yellow flowers

The adjective *žluté* forms a phrase with the noun it modifies, *kvĕtiny*.

This phrase is modified by the adjective *pěkné*, and the larger phrase so formed is modified in turn by the demonstrative *ty*. The relationship involved can be represented clearly with labelled bracketing:

(16) Cz: [$_{NP}$ *ty* [$_{NP}$ *pěkné* [$_{NP}$ *žluté květiny*]]]

In such structures the attributive modifiers are stacked. Suppose that we have a controller which permits alternative agreement forms in a particular position on the Agreement Hierarchy, and that we find stacked modifiers of this type. What does the Agreement Hierarchy predict about this situation? As it stands, it makes predictions only as to the frequency of the two agreement forms relative to their frequency in other positions. It makes no predictions about alternatives within a given position. It must be said that, in the vast majority of instances, stacked modifiers all stand in the same form. However, there are examples where stacked modifiers take different agreements and, as we shall see, these conform to a single pattern.

In §2.1.4 we met a class of nouns in Serbo-Croat which, in the plural, may take masculine or feminine attributive modifiers. Feminine modifiers represent syntactic agreement and masculine represent semantic. In the following example, stacked modifiers show different agreemments:

(17) SC: *Ovi* (masc) *privatne* (fem) *zanatlije* . . .
       These   private   artisans
       (*Oslobođenje* 19 Oct. 1952, quoted by Marković, 1954, 95)

The modifier nearer to the noun shows syntactic agreement while the further shows semantic agreement. A similar situation occurs in the following Russian sentence, recorded from speech by Skoblikova (1971, 183):

(18) R: *U nas byla očen' xorošaja* (fem) *zubnoj* (masc) *vrač*
      At us was a very good   tooth   doctor
      (We had a very good dentist)

The nearer adjective agrees syntactically with the noun, while the further shows the possibility of semantic agreement with nouns of this type (§2.3). The Russian noun *učenyj* is adjectival in form, but functions as a noun, and similarly has alternative agreement possibilities when it refers to a female:

(19) R: *Tak skazala prisutstvovavšaja* (fem) *na operacii*
So said   having been present   at operation
izvestnyj (masc) *amerikanskij* (masc) *učenyj   vrač*
famous   American   scientist   doctor
Èlen Taussing.
Elen Taussing
(So said doctor Elen Taussing, the famous American scientist, who was present at the operation.)
(*Večernjaja Moskva*, 22 May 1958, quoted by Protčenko, 1961, 117)

In this sentence the noun has three stacked modifiers, of which the nearer two show syntactic agreement and the furthest, semantic agreement.

All these examples[3] are in accord with the following constraint:

(20) If stacked targets show different agreement forms, the further target will show semantic agreement.

The Agreement Hierarchy refers to structural differences between possible targets. The smallest structural difference appears to be that between stacked elements; these belong to the same position on the hierarchy, but in a given sentence one stacked target is necessarily structurally closer to or further from the controller than another. This minimal difference is rarely sufficient to allow different agreement forms but, when it does, it will be targets stacked further from the controller which show semantic agreement.

4.3.2 Parallel Targets

Parallelism refers to a situation where two independent elements fill one syntactic slot. Example (21) illustrates the simplest case:

(21) R: *Ivan čital i   pisal*
Ivan read and wrote

In this sentence *čital* and *pisal* are parallel. The question arises as to whether there can be any difference in agreement between parallel elements. They are structurally equivalent, and it might be expected that they would always show the same agreements. However, in natural language absolute parallelism is impossible − one of the elements must be ordered before the other. It can even be argued that this ordering

represents the minimum level of stacking. There are clear cases of parallel constituents showing different agreements; however, the readiness
with which these constructions are permitted varies considerably from
language to language. In Russian they are extremely rare. Our first
example is also unusual because it shows plural agreement with the
noun *dvorjanstvo* 'nobility' which normally takes singular agreement:

(22) R: *Vse dvorjanstvo   voznenavidelo* (sg) *menja vsemi   silami*
         All the nobility has come to hate   me   with all strength
         duši   i   sujut (pl) *mne   palki v   kolesa so   vsex*
         of heart and poke   to me sticks into wheels from all
         storon.
         sides
         (All the nobility has taken a great dislike to me and takes
         every opportunity to trip me up.)
         (Tolstoj, quoted by Rozental', 1974, 219)

In this sentence the nearer verb is neuter singular, showing syntactic
agreement with the subject, while the further verb is plural, showing
semantic agreement. This same situation obtains in the following
sentence, though here the controller is a quantified expression (dealt
with in more detail in §8.4 and Chapter 11 below):

(23) R: *Za četyre goda 43 milliona čelovek pereselilos'* (sg) *v*
         In four   years 43 million people moved   into
         novye doma   i   kvartiry, ulučšili (pl) *svoi   žiliščnye*
         new   houses and   flats   improved   their   living
         uslovija.
         conditions
         (*Sel'skaja žizn'*, 11 May 1966, quoted by Graudina *et al.*,
         1976, 29)

(Note that the parallel targets often occur without a conjunction in
Slavic.) While examples like (23) are extremely rare in Russian, they are
less so in Polish. Consider the following:

(24) P: *Siedm wyszło* (sg) *i   szły* (pl)
         Seven went out   and went (away)

This is actually a sixteenth-century example quoted by Grappin (1950,
90). While constructions of this type were dominant in the sixteenth-

eighteenth centuries, there is now a normative trend towards the use of the singular throughout. Though less common than they were, sentences like (24) still occur in Modern Polish. Once again the further target shows semantic agreement.

In Serbo-Croat, sentences with parallel targets showing different agreements are unusual but not rare. In the following example we see again a noun in *-a* which, when in the plural, may take masculine or feminine agreements (§2.1.4):

(25) SC: *Sarajlije*   *su igrale* (fem) *bolje i   gotovo*
      The Sarajevans   played   better and almost
      potpuno   dominirali (masc) *terenom.*
      completely dominated   the field
      (*Oslobođenje*, 26 Apr. 1953, quoted by Marković, 1954, 95)

In this example the nearer predicate shows syntactic (feminine) agreement and the further shows semantic (masculine) agreement. The same pattern is found in (26), in which the controller is a phrase consisting of *dva* plus a masculine noun (§2.1.3):

(26) SC: *Dva vojnika su stala* (dual) *pred   nas i*
      Two soldiers   stopped   in front of us and
      pomogli (pl) *nam*
      helped   us
      (Kukić, quoted by Stevanović, 1974, 144)

So far all our examples have involved predicates.[4] However, relative clauses may also occur in parallel. As noted above (§2.1.7), conjoined noun phrases in Russian can take a singular or a plural relative pronoun. Both these possibilities are found in the following example:

(27) R: ... *ja čuvstvoval iskrennost',   krovnuju pristrastnost',*
      I felt   the sincerity deep   commitment
      radost' i   bol', s   kakoju (sg) *avtor   issledoval*
      joy   and pain with which   the author investigated
      žizn', bez   kotoryx (pl) *kak   izvestno,*
      life   without which   as (is) well known (there)
      ne možet byt' nastojaščego xudožnika.
      cannot   be   a true   artist

(Černov, Introduction to Smoljaninov, *Sredi morennyx xolmov*)

Both relatives relate to all the conjoined noun phrases; *kakoju* shows singular (syntactic) agreement, and again it is the further target (*kotoryx*) which shows semantic agreement. The constraint which holds for all the examples found is as follows:

(28) If parallel targets show different agreement forms, then the further target will show semantic agreement.

Of course, if one accepts the view that parallel elements are minimally stacked, then this constraint can be subsumed under (20) above.

Constraint (28) must operate at sentence level as it relates specifically to pairs of targets occurring in a single sentence (though, like (20), it also applies when there are more than two targets by applying to each pair). It is possible to envisage a comparable constraint which would apply at corpus level:

(29) The further a target is from its controller, the more frequently semantic agreement will occur.

This constraint refers to 'real' distance; it applies to all sentences where there is an agreement option, not just those with more than one target. If a target is separated from its controller by, say, ten words, it is more likely to show semantic agreement than if it is separated by only five. Various investigators have claimed that such a constraint operates, and it almost certainly does, but unfortunately they do not provide statistical data to prove the point (as Nixon, 1972, does for English). Some evidence in favour of (29) is given in §5.1. While the corpus-level rule requires further demonstration, the case for the sentence-level constraint is quite clear: if, within a single position on the hierarchy, targets are stacked or parallel and show different agreement forms, then the target further from the controller will show semantic agreement.

4.4 Conclusion

We have demonstrated that the Agreement Hierarchy operates at corpus level. The Predicate Hierarchy also operates at corpus level, and places a further restriction on agreement systems in some if not all of the

Slavic languages by further applying as a sentence-level constraint. At sentence level too there are constraints which supplement the Agreement Hierarchy by restricting the options for stacked or parallel targets. The Agreement and Predicate Hierarchies are independent in the sense that they do not duplicate other measures. Nevertheless, as target hierarchies they are clearly related to each other. The nature of this relationship will be investigated in the next chapter.

Notes

1. This distinction stems from that drawn in arc pair grammar by Johnson and Postal (1980, 20-1, 677-87). A corpus is technically the whole collection of sentences of a given language. For practical reasons we normally deal with a representative sample and the term corpus then indicates all the sentences in that sample.

2. The data given by Rothstein (1976, 249) are consistent with the constraint applying in Polish with controllers like *łajdaki* 'scoundrels' (§2.1.8). It is also found with quantified expressions in Russian (see §11.1 example (6) and note 1 of Chapter 11), where a nominative plural modifier of the quantified noun phrase ensures a plural predicate. However, the constraint does not apply to similar Polish quantified expressions as the following example demonstrates:

(i) P: *wszystkie* (pl) *pięć pociągów odjechało* (sg)
    all   five trains   left

(Example from Klemensiewicz, 1930, 122. See Chapter 11, note 2, for references concerning the case of the attributive modifier.)

3. For an Old Russian example see Popova (1955, 92). All the examples given above involve attributive modifiers. We might expect to find similar examples with relative pronouns; however, stacked relative clauses are comparatively rare in Slavic. Zaliznjak and Padučeva (1979, 324) claim that they are unacceptable in Russian. Browne (1980, 161-2) states that stacked relatives are possible in Serbo-Croat, but they are less usual and on average less acceptable than in English.

4. For an example from Old Church Slavic see Xaburgaev (1974, 372). Burzan (1981, 122) gives examples of non-standard agreement with quantifiers in the Serbo-Croat of children whose first language is Hungarian. Even here it is always the further predicate which shows semantic agreement.

5. CLARIFYING AND COMBINING THE HIERARCHIES

Serbo-Croat *deca* 'children' takes a fascinating set of agreements, which seem to violate both the Agreement Hierarchy and the Predicate Hierarchy. *Deca* therefore deserves close attention. An examination of the data makes us clarify and extend our definition of the Agreement Hierarchy and suggests the way in which the two hierarchies are connected. It also leads to an improved analysis of some of the data we have already come across, and confirms the idea put forward in §3.5 that the notion of semantic agreement must be revised. We will first consider the data relevant to the Agreement Hierarchy (§5.1) and refine our analysis where necessary (§5.2), then turn to the Predicate Hierarchy and the way in which the latter connects with the Agreement Hierarchy (§5.3). We will also reconsider certain quantifier constructions as these provide further evidence for the way in which the hierarchies should be combined (§5.4).

5.1 *Deca* : Data Relevant to the Agreement Hierarchy

Serbo-Croat *deca* 'children' declines like a feminine singular noun, but it functions as the plural of *dete* 'child', which is a neuter singular noun. *Deca* shows a remarkable range of agreements; to help the reader to appreciate these possibilities, the typical agreement morphemes of Serbo-Croat (the nominative forms for all positions on the Agreement Hierarchy) are set out in Table 5.1. The masculine singular *i* is an

Table 5.1 : Serbo-Croat Agreement Endings

	masculine	feminine	neuter
singular	ϕ/i	a	o/e
plural	i	e	a

alternative adjectival ending which occurs mainly in attributive position. The *o/e* opposition in the neuter singular is phonologically determined. The important point to note is that the ending *-a* can signal both feminine singular and neuter plural.

Let us consider the agreement forms found in each of the positions on the Agreement Hierarchy. Examples (1)-(5) are from *Na Drini Ćuprija*[1] by Ivo Andrić. In fact, most of the examples in this section are taken from Andrić. The different forms we shall encounter are therefore found in the output of a single writer – they are not limited to varying idiolects. The first example includes an attributive modifier:

(1) SC: *Hrišćanska deca* (nom) . . .
   Christian   children

The ending on *hrišćanska* is a nominative; it might be a feminine singular ending, but it could also be a neuter plural. Forms in oblique cases, however, are unambiguously feminine singular:

(2) SC: . . . *rođenu* (fem sg acc) *decu* (acc) . . .
   born   children
(3) SC: . . . *ove* (fem sg gen) *dece* (gen) . . .
   of these   children

The verbal predicate is always plural, as in:

(4) SC: *Hrišćanska deca* . . . *pređu* (3rd pers pl) . . .
   Christian   children   cross

When the predicate includes an active participle or an adjective, which must agree in gender and number, this form ends in *-a*, for example:

(5) SC: . . . *sva druga deca* . . . *provodila su* (3rd pl) . . .
   all other children spent

The copula *su* is unambiguously plural, but *provodila* could be feminine singular or neuter plural. Maretić assumes that the form is a feminine singular and writes of a 'syntactic mixture' in such sentences (1899, 401). His analysis does indeed involve postulating a mixed predicate; he gives no reason for preferring it to the other analysis (treating the *-a* form as a neuter plural), in which the predicate is consistently plural, and of a type regularly found with ordinary neuter plural nouns. The neuter plural analysis appears the more attractive. There is, furthermore, evidence to show that it is the better analysis, which comes from agreement with subjects consisting of conjoined noun phrases (cf. Megaard, 1976, 100). Normally, conjoined feminine nouns take a feminine plural verb (though there are exceptions, which we discuss in §10.3.3 below). When *deca* is combined with a feminine noun, however, we find masculine agreements:

(6) SC: ... *dok   su je   sa   praga   posmatrali* (masc pl)
           while   her from threshold watched
         gospođa Davil i   začuđena   deca.
         Mrs   Davil and the startled children
         (Andrić, *Travnička Hronika*)

This example shows the agreement which one would expect with a neuter plural and a feminine noun conjoined, and the similar examples found in modern texts show the same agreement (Gudkov, 1974, 60). The predicate agreement form required by *deca* appears, therefore, to be the neuter plural.

The relative pronoun, when in the nominative case, takes the form *koja*:

(7) SC: *Deca   koja su* (3rd pl) *tada bila* ...
         Children who   then were
         (Andrić, *Na Drini Ćuprija*)

This form *koja* could be feminine singular; this interpretation runs into problems since the copula *su* in the relative clause is plural: the relative would be marked as singular yet it requires a plural verb. If we accept the other possibility, that *koja* is neuter plural, then the agreement within the relative clause follows automatically. When the relative stands in the accusative case, we find an unambiguously feminine singular form:

(8) SC: *Tamo su bila u pitanju deca   koju* (fem sg acc)
         There   were in question children whom   (it)
         je trebalo   uzeti   od   propalih roditelja ...
         was necessary to take from ruined   parents
         (Andrić, *Zmija*)

Informants questioned about the following phrase would accept only the feminine singular:

(9) SC: *deca* ⎧ *koju* (fem sg acc) ⎫ *vidite*
　　　　　⎨ **koja* (neut pl acc) ⎬
　　　　　⎩ **koje* (masc/fem pl acc)⎭
　　　children whom 　　(you) 　　see

In other oblique cases a choice exists:

(10) SC: *deca* 　　*koje* (fem sg gen) *se svi boje*
　　　　　　　　　kojih (pl gen)
　　　children whom 　　　　　　all fear

Informants accepted both forms as possible, but had strong and opposing preferences. Both forms are genitive as this is the case governed by the verb. *Koje* is unambiguously feminine singular. In the plural, the oblique cases (apart from the accusative as shown in (9)) have the same agreement forms for all three genders. Thus *kojih* could be masculine, feminine or neuter plural. The same possibilities occur in the next examples in which the relative pronoun is in the dative case (quoted from Pavlović, 1965, 171):

(11) SC: *Zmaj voleo je decu,* 　　*kojoj* (fem sg dat) *je posvetio*
　　　　　Zmaj liked 　children to whom (he) 　　dedicated
　　　　　mnoge svoje veoma lepe 　　*pesme.*
　　　　　many his 　very 　beautiful poems
　　　　　(Jovanović)

In (11) the relative pronoun is singular and is clearly feminine. In (12) it is plural:

(12) SC: *Oko* 　*njih su stajala deca* 　　*kojima* (pl dat)
　　　　　Around them 　stood children to whom
　　　　　oči 　　　　　　　　*gore* 　*kao svitci.*
　　　　　the eyes (i.e. whose eyes) sparkle like glow-worms
　　　　　(Đurović)

Kojima is plural and could be of any gender.

Let us turn to the personal pronoun. In the nominative both *ona* and *oni* occur:

(13) SC: ... *ta* 　　*deca* 　*su* 　*mu* 　*potrebna, jer* 　*ona* 　*jedina*
　　　　　　those children are to him necessary, for 　they 　alone

> *čuju* (3rd pl) *njegovu nemoćnu viku . . .*
> hear   his   weak   shout
> (Andrić, *Travnička Hronika*)

Ona could be feminine singular or neuter plural; the plural verb *čuju* demonstrates that the neuter plural is the correct analysis. In examples like (14) the alternative, *oni*, is unambiguously masculine plural:

(14) SC: *U ovoj istoj kući   spavaju njegova deca.   I*
        In this same house sleep   his   children. And
        oni (masc pl)   *će jednog dana porasti . . .*
        they (i.e. they too) will one   day grow up
        (Andrić, *Travnička Hronika*)

As far as the choice between these two forms is concerned, the limited evidence of a small corpus and casual reading strongly suggests that the further the pronoun is separated from the noun, the more likely is the form *oni* (cf. §4.3.2). In the oblique cases, the personal pronoun is always plural:

(15) SC: *. . . mnogi roditelji sakrivali   decu   u šumu, učili*
           many parents hid (their) children in forest taught
          ih   da   se pretvaraju . . .
          them that (they)   pretend
          (Andrić, *Na Drini Ćuprija*)

The oblique plural forms do not distinguish gender;[2] *ih* could be masculine, feminine or neuter plural.

Before considering the implications of these data, let us review the points established so far, as summarised in Table 5.2. The *-a* ending in the predicate was taken to be neuter plural, since treating it as a feminine singular not only involves postulating an unmotivated mixed predicate but also gives the wrong results when *deca* is conjoined with another noun in the subject. The interpretation of the nominative relative pronoun *koja* and the nominative personal pronoun *ona* as feminine singular was rejected because predicates agreeing with these forms must be plural. If we then reject these three instances of forms being treated as feminine singular, we are left with clear instances of the following types of agreement with *deca*:

1. feminine singular (attributive: oblique cases);

Table 5.2: Agreement Possibilities with *deca*

	attributive	predicate	relative pronoun	personal pronoun
nominative	fem sg *or* neut pl	[fem sg] *or* neut pl	[fem sg] *or* neut pl	[fem sg] *or* neut pl *and* masc pl
accusative	fem sg	–	fem sg	masc pl [*or* fem pl] *or* neut pl
other oblique	fem sg	–	fem sg *and* masc pl [*or* fem pl] *or* neut pl	masc pl [*or* fem pl] *or* neut pl

Note: *or* indicates alternative analyses for a single form. *and* is used when different forms occur. [ ] signifies an alternative to be rejected.

2. masculine plural (personal pronoun: nominative case);
3. neuter plural (predicate; relative and personal pronouns: nominative case).

There are no unambiguous cases of feminine plural agreement with *deca*. We can therefore exclude this possibility from the oblique cases of the relative and personal pronouns. Further analysis will allow us to make an additional slight reduction in the acceptable analyses, as we shall see.

5.2 Clarifying the Agreement Hierarchy

It is evident that the version of the Agreement Hierarchy given in Chapter 2 must be refined if it is to account for the agreements just described. The notions of syntactic and semantic agreement require clarification and the predictions made by the hierarchy must be given greater precision.

5.2.1 Syntactic and Semantic Agreement

Deca controls agreement of three different types: feminine singular, neuter plural and masculine plural. It is, therefore, inadequate to talk merely in terms of syntactic and semantic agreement. The form which would correspond to the semantics of *deca* would be the masculine plural: plural because it refers to more than one person, masculine because this is the form used in Serbo-Croat when humans of either sex or both sexes are involved (as will be shown in §10.4). Neuter plural agreement shows the 'right' number but the 'wrong' gender, while feminine singular is 'wrong' in both respects — it is fully syntactic. Rather than talking of syntactic and semantic agreement we must talk of agreement forms which have greater or lesser semantic justification. The requirement of the Agreement Hierarchy must be restated as follows:

(16)   As we move rightwards along the Agreement Hierarchy, the likelihood of agreement forms with greater semantic justification will increase monotonically.

Deca is unusual in allowing three possible agreements; it is worth comparing it with *vi* when used to a female addressee (§3.5). The form accepted in Standard Serbo-Croat is:

(17)   SC: *Vi   ste   poznavali* (masc pl)
          You have found out

Here the masculine plural form shows the 'wrong' gender and number. Feminine singular predicates are also found:

(18)   SC: *Vi   ste pametna* (fem sg)
          You are sensible

In (18) we have the 'right' gender and number. There is a third possibility, found mainly in the last century:

(19)   SC: *Vi   ste   poznavale* (fem pl)
          You have found out

Poznavale shows the 'right' gender but the 'wrong' number. We may say that the agreement found in (19) has greater semantic justification than that in (17) but that the agreement in (18) has in turn greater semantic justification than that in (19).

Honorific *vi* shows three agreement possibilities, but it differs from *deca* in that the three possibilities all occur in the predicate with different speakers at different times. In the case of *deca*, three forms are found with different targets in the usage of the same speakers: in this respect it is most unusual. However, even in the familiar cases where only two agreement forms are involved, these are best seen in terms of greater or lesser semantic justification. Let us look again at one such case (described in §2.1.4):

(20) SC: *Gazde   su   došle* (fem pl)
          The masters have come

A feminine plural form like *došle* is normally considered to be an example of syntactic agreement. It is indeed less justified in semantic terms than the alternative *došli* (masc pl). However, *došle* shows the semantically justified number (plural); *došli* has greater semantic justification because its gender is also semantically justified. Naturally the restatement of the requirement of the Agreement Hierarchy in (16) covers these cases where there are two alternatives. We conclude that syntactic and semantic agreement is a matter of degree.

5.2.2 *Specifying the Predictions Made by the Agreement Hierarchy*

Given that we must talk in terms of greater or lesser semantic justification, we should ask whether the predictions made by the Agreement Hierarchy adequately account for the agreements described above. The possible agreements with *deca*, in order of increasing semantic justification, are: feminine singular, neuter plural and masculine plural. Let us examine how these agreements are distributed over the positions on the hierarchy.

In attributive position, we found a nominative agreement form which could be feminine singular or neuter plural, while the oblique agreement forms were all feminine singular. It seems logical to assume that the nominative form is feminine singular too. However, we can leave this question open, for it does not affect the adequacy of the Agreement Hierarchy. Whether we analyse the form as feminine singular, ambiguously feminine singular or neuter plural, or solely neuter plural, it will still be in accord with the Agreement Hierarchy. The predicate is neuter plural, and so any of these analyses for attributive agreement would be consistent with a monotonic increase in semantically justified agreement forms.

When we compare the predicate and the relative pronoun, the situation is more difficult. As the predicate shows only neuter plural agreements, we would expect only the neuter plural or masculine plural in positions to the right. The relative pronoun shows exclusively neuter plural agreements in the nominative case, but the feminine singular is found in the accusative and is an alternative in the other oblique cases. This means that the requirement of the Agreement Hierarchy is met or not met, depending on which case of the relative pronoun we consider. The personal pronoun is not so critical, as we find clear masculine plural and clear neuter plural forms in the nominative, while in the oblique cases there are forms which could be of either gender. It is therefore the relative pronoun which forces us to make our claims about the hierarchy more precise: previously it was not necessary to make conditions about case, because case was never crucial. The Serbo-Croat evidence requires us to specify that, when applying the Agreement Hierarchy, nominative case forms are to be considered. This decision is necessary if we are to retain the Agreement Hierarchy; given that the latter accounts for a wide range of data, this approach appears reasonable. It is not, however, an *ad hoc* decision: the special status of the nominative in the case system is well established. If we apply the hierarchy under this stricter definition, then the agreements with *deca* are consistent with it: we have feminine singular (or neuter plural) in attributive position, neuter plural in the predicate and in the relative pronoun, and neuter plural and masculine plural in the personal pronoun.[3] This stricter definition is also consistent with all the data examined in §2.1. We shall therefore take the nominative as the basic case on which the hierarchy rests.

We must next extend the hierarchy to cover variation between the nominative and the oblique cases. On the evidence available at present, we can make the following claim:

(21) Whenever, in a given position on the Agreement Hierarchy, there is a difference between the agreements found in the nominative and in the oblique cases, the form found in the nominative will have the greater degree of semantic justification.

The hierarchy may be represented as in Table 5.3
Let us examine whether this modification is adequate to account for

Table 5.3: The Agreement Hierarchy Including Reference to Case

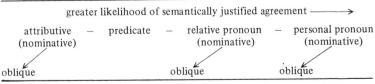

Note: The slanting arrows indicate that any difference in the agreements taken by the oblique cases will be towards forms with lesser semantic justification.

agreements with *deca*. In attributive position, it is simplest to assume the agreements are all feminine singular. However, if we wish to claim that the nominative takes neuter plural agreements, this is acceptable because this form has a greater degree of semantic justification than the feminine singular found in the oblique cases. In the predicate the question of case does not arise, as Serbo-Croat predicates normally stand in the nominative. The relative pronoun is particularly interesting. The accusative (feminine singular) agreement is indeed less justified semantically than the nominative (neuter plural). However, we find a difference even within the oblique cases. As the evidence is restricted, it would be unjustified to draw conclusions from this as yet and so condition (21) does not differentiate between the oblique cases (an alternative approach is mentioned below). The other oblique cases take either feminine singular agreement forms, or forms which could be neuter plural or masculine plural. The Agreement Hierarchy in its revised form requires us to analyse them as neuter plural: if they were masculine plural they would violate condition (21). The same question arises in the personal pronoun – the oblique cases could be taken as masculine or neuter plural; here, however, it is of no consequence as both forms are found in the nominative.

The agreement forms found with *deca* are therefore, we claim, as shown in Table 5.4, from which it is clear that condition (21) does in fact hold: when there is a difference between the nominative and the oblique cases it is the former which have the greater degree of semantic justification. (An alternative approach which should be borne in mind

Table 5.4: Interpretation of Agreements with *deca*

	attributive	predicate	relative pronoun	personal pronoun
nominative	fem sg (*or* neut pl)	neut pl	neut pl	neut pl *and* masc pl
accusative	fem sg	–	fem sg	neut pl *or* masc pl
other oblique	fem sg	–	fem sg *and* neut pl	neut pl *or* masc pl

Note: *or* indicates alternative analyses for a single form. *and* is used when different forms occur. ( ) indicates a possible but less likely alternative.

as further data become available is to apply the hierarchy to each case separately. As can be seen from Table 5.4, the hierarchy holds if applied separately to the nominative, accusative and other oblique cases. On the basis of the evidence available to date, it is preferable to limit ourselves to the more modest claim made by (21).)

It might seem that we have made a major adjustment to the hierarchy merely to account for agreements with *deca*. This is not entirely true: in the original formulation of the Agreement Hierarchy (Corbett, 1979b, 218), it was pointed out that, in diachronic change, the first attributive modifiers to show semantic agreement are those in the nominative case, but no general prediction about case was made. Given that variation in agreement can depend on case, it is essential to make our theory explicit in this area. Furthermore, there are other instances of agreement options which are dependent on case, and these are consistent with the claim that the oblique cases are less likely to show semantic agreement than the nominative. The first of these is already familiar. Russian *vrač* 'doctor' permits masculine or feminine attributive modifiers, when it refers to a woman, as in the following sentence:

(22) R: *ona* $\begin{Bmatrix} xorošij \text{ (masc)} \\ xorošaja \text{ (fem)} \end{Bmatrix}$ *vrač*

she (is) a good   doctor

In all the data on attributive agreement from questionnaires quoted earlier (§2.3), *vrač* appeared in the nominative case. In fact the choice occurs only in this position. In the oblique cases, the masculine is required:

(23) R: *k* $\begin{Bmatrix} xorošemu \text{ (masc dat)} \\ *xorošej \text{ (fem dat)} \end{Bmatrix}$ *vraču*

to a good   doctor

It is the masculine which has the lesser degree of semantic justification, and so these data accord with condition (21) above. For the second confirming case we have to go outside Slavic, a necessary step because data are so scarce. In Finnish, morphologically plural nouns like *Yhdysvallat* 'the United States', which refer to singular entities, normally take a singular predicate. In attributive position both singular and plural adjectives are found; however, the singular (semantically justified form) is more common in the nominative than in the oblique cases (Karlsson, 1968). Other examples will no doubt be found; the problem is that most investigators do not consider that case could have an effect on the distribution of syntactic and semantic agreement, and so present combined figures for agreements of different types.[4]

5.3 The Predicate Hierarchy and its Connection to the Agreement Hierarchy

Examining agreements with *deca* has forced us to clarify the definition of the Agreement Hierarchy. We must now ask whether *deca* can similarly advance our ideas about predicate agreement. The Predicate Hierarchy consists of the following positions: finite verb, participle, adjective and noun. The relevant sentences are those like (24):

(24) = (5) SC: . . . *sva druga deca . . .   provodila su* (3rd pl) . . .
         all other children spent

The finite verb *su* is third person plural, while the participle *provodila* could be feminine singular or neuter plural. If, as is generally believed, the -*a* form represents singular agreement, then the finite verb shows a form with greater semantic justification than the participle and this would be contrary to the Predicate Hierarchy. If both are plural, then the requirement of the hierarchy is met. Thus the Predicate Hierarchy provides a further reason to support our claim that the -*a* form is neuter plural.

There is, however, a problem concerning the predicate. In referring to the predicate as neuter plural in our discussion of the Agreement Hierarchy, we referred simply to the predicate, ignoring the different types of predicate. We have seen that the original formulation of the Agreement Hierarchy was insufficiently precise, as the possibility of agreement varying according to case was not catered for. Similarly, it is insufficient merely to refer to the predicate, for different types of predicate may show different agreements. The question is which type of predicate is involved when, in applying the Agreement Hierarchy, we refer to 'predicate position'. Once again we must specify a basic position. The obvious choice is the finite verb: it enjoys a status similar to that of the nominative case, and is the type of predicate which occurs most frequently. By specifying that the finite verb is the basic predicate which is included in the Agreement Hierarchy, we have again made the formulation of the Agreement Hierarchy more precise. The examples with *deca* are all consistent with the Agreement Hierarchy in this form: *deca* takes plural agreement of the finite verb; the relative and personal pronouns are both plural, while attributive modifiers are singular or possibly plural (in either case the requirement of monotonic increase is met).

However, we have excluded the more interesting part of the data, which concerns gender. We can modify our procedure further to allow us to make a stronger, more interesting claim:

(25) To determine whether a set of agreements is consistent with the Agreement Hierarchy, take the leftmost member of the Predicate Hierarchy which is marked for the category shown by the other positions on the Agreement Hierarchy.

This procedure means that normally the finite verb will be taken. However, when as with *deca* it is not marked for a relevant category (gender in this instance) then the active participle will be substituted, and so on. This formulation adequately covers the agreements shown by *deca*; the predicate will be taken to be neuter plural, and this is consistent with the requirement of the Agreement Hierarchy, given the forms of attributive modifiers and of the relative pronoun.

Let us now return to the earlier point that the finite verb should be taken as the basic predicate for the Agreement Hierarchy. Having previously specified a basic case (the nominative), we then made predictions as to how the other cases could vary in terms of semantically justified agreement forms. We must now make similar predictions for other predicate types, relative to the basic predicate. In this instance, however, the work has already been done: the finite verb is the leftmost position on the Predicate Hierarchy. Other predicates must therefore be increasingly likely to show semantically justifiable agreement forms. This argument suggests that the two target hierarchies should be combined as in Table 5.5. The arrows indicate that semantically justified agreement forms are less likely to occur in oblique cases than in the nominative, but more likely in predicates other than the finite verb. The data on *deca* are fully consistent with this picture.

Table 5.5: The Combined Target Hierarchies

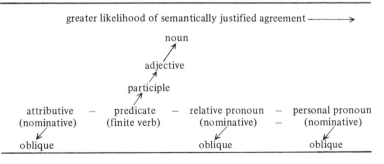

5.4 Evidence to Support Combining the Hierarchies

In the last section a way of combining the hierarchies was proposed, based on the agreements with *deca*. The suggestion is simple, yet it can cope with a complex set of data. This is promising, but before accepting the proposal we must find evidence from other sources. Substantial evidence in favour of combining the hierarchies in the way suggested will be given in Chapter 9. First, however, it is worth reconsidering agreements with controllers consisting of *dva* 'two', *tri* 'three' and *četiri* 'four' plus a masculine noun in Serbo-Croat, because they also provide confirming evidence and because they are best understood in the context of the analysis of *deca*. The unresolved difficulty with this set of controllers was the status of the agreement form in -*a*, as in the following example:

(26) SC: *Dva brata   su* (3rd pl) *došla*
       Two brothers have   come

The form *došla* is normally analysed as a special survival of the dual number (as in §2.1.3). This analysis raises problems. The first is that it involves postulating an irregular predicate type (plural plus dual survival), a step which was avoided in our analysis of *deca*. Second, as the dual is no longer a living member of the semantic category of number in Serbo-Croat, the dual survival form could not be considered semantically justified. However, in this construction the copula found with forms like *došla* is always plural and this use of the plural number is semantically justified. We would then have a violation of the Predicate Hierarchy as the participle (under the dual survival hypothesis) would show a form with lesser semantic justification than the finite verb. The third problem concerns the dual survival form of the relative pronoun:

(27) SC: *dva brata   koja su* (3rd pl) *došla*
       two brothers who have   come

In such cases we would have to give *koja* a special exceptional marker because it too requires an irregular predicate (plural plus dual survival); it cannot be marked in the same way as the antecedent *brata* because *brata* allows alternative agreement forms in -*a* or -*i* while *koja* does not.

By now the parallels with *deca* are becoming evident; we should label the agreement forms in -*a* as neuter plural.[5] This approach does away with the need for a special predicate: forms like *su* and *došla* regularly co-occur as a neuter plural predicate. There is then no question of violating the Predicate Hierarchy as both parts of the compound predicate stand in the plural. And the problem of the relative pronoun is resolved: it is neuter plural and takes neuter plural agreements. We find further strong evidence for treating the agreement forms in *-a* as neuter plural when we consider attributive modifiers:

(28) SC: *ova   dva dobra čoveka*
        these two good men

The traditional account treats *dobra* as genitive singular, which is plausible at first sight since the form of the noun (originally dual) is now equivalent to the genitive singular. There is the further stipulation that the adjective must be in the indefinite form. Serbo-Croat adjectives have both definite and indefinite declensions; however, the indefinite forms are being lost, and are now rarely used in speech except in the nominative. It is somewhat unsatisfactory, therefore, to claim that the common form *dobra* in (28) above is taken from the less usual indefinite declension. This analysis is quite impossible for *ova*, because *ovaj* 'this' has no indefinite forms: the only genitive singular masculine form is *ovog*. It has the neuter plural form *ova*, however. We should therefore analyse both modifiers in (28) above as neuter plural. This analysis avoids the need to postulate two types of morphological irregularity in agreements with quantified expressions. The combination of a neuter plural adjective with a genitive singular noun is indeed surprising; however, the loss of the dual has left equally strange combinations in other Slavic languages (for example, Russian has the noun in the genitive singular but attributive modifiers in nominative or genitive plural; see Corbett, 1978d).

The analysis which treats the forms we have discussed as neuter plural not only solves the morphological problems; it also provides evidence to support the combination of the two hierarchies in the way proposed earlier. The first step towards validating this claim is to establish the relationship between the two possible agreement forms. The neuter plural agreements show the 'right' number but the 'wrong' gender. The other agreement form is the masculine plural:

(29) SC: *Dva brata   su* (3rd pl) *došli* (masc pl)
        Two brothers have   come

The masculine plural is an alternative possibility in the predicate and relative pronoun and is the sole form in the personal pronoun; it shows the 'right' number and the 'right' gender. It therefore has a greater degree of semantic justification than the neuter plural. This claim is evidently true in the case of examples like (26) and (29) where male persons are involved. However, inanimates may also be masculine. In Serbo-Croat, gender has a clear semantic basis for animates only. The inanimates are distributed over the three genders so that no gender has a semantic basis where inanimates are concerned. In such instances the assignment of a form as being semantically justified follows that which applies in the clear cases involving animates. (This point is discussed again in §10.4.) Thus agreement with *dva*, *tri* and *četiri* plus masculine noun may be neuter plural or masculine plural, the latter having the greater degree of semantic justification.

Let us now check that these agreements are distributed in accordance with the hierarchies. Table 5.6 provides the essential data. Attributive

Table 5.6: Agreement with Two, Three and Four plus Masculine Noun in Serbo-Croat

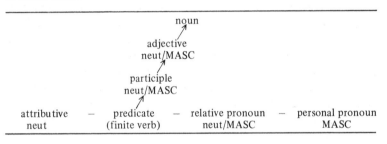

modifiers show the form with the lesser semantic justification – neuter plural (as all agreement forms in our analysis of this construction are plural, this feature is omitted from Table 5.6). The finite verb is plural but does not show gender. Following procedure (25) we therefore substitute the participle, where both agreement forms are found (MASC is in capitals to indicate that this form has the greater semantic justification). The relative pronoun also permits both forms and, as we saw in §2.1.3, the proportion of masculine forms is much higher than it is in the predicate. The personal pronoun always takes the masculine form. We therefore have a monotonic increase in the form with the greater semantic justification, as the Agreement Hierarchy requires. Returning to the predicate, we find that neither the finite verb nor the noun show gender agreement. The two remaining positions both allow either agreement possibility (overall the masculine occurs much less frequently than in the relative pronoun) but there are unfortunately no data on the two predicate forms individually. (Nor is there information on the effect of case: the relative pronoun could provide additional evidence in this regard but only for the nominative and accusative cases.)

Thus our reanalysis of agreements with *dva*, *tri* and *četiri* plus masculine noun avoids the difficulties of the traditional approach; all the data available are consistent with the requirements of the combined hierarchies. Nevertheless we require more substantial evidence before finally accepting that the hierarchies must be combined in the way proposed.

5.5 Conclusion

Analysis of the unusually complex set of agreements with *deca* led us to specify the requirements of the Agreement Hierarchy more precisely (in respect of the effect of case on agreement) and to replace the dichotomy of syntactic and semantic agreement with the notion of varying degrees of semantic justification. We also found a way of linking the Predicate Hierarchy with the Agreement Hierarchy. The evidence so far concerns only a few controllers: *deca* and also phrases with *dva*, *tri* and *četiri*. Naturally, we must find confirming evidence with a less restricted set of controllers. The necessary data can be found in constructions with conjoined noun phrases as the controller. However, by moving to controllers of this type, we introduce a new range of possible variation. It is essential that we should be able to isolate the factors which relate to variation in the controller, in order to confirm our proposed way of combining the target hierarchies. We shall therefore examine agreement controllers in the next three chapters, before returning to our analysis of targets in Chapter 9.

Notes

1. Chapters 1, 2 and 15 are particularly good sources. Given the interest of the data it is difficult to understand why *deca* has received relatively little attention. When it is mentioned, it is generally considered together with *braća* 'brothers', *gospoda* 'gentlemen' and *vlastela* 'landowners'. We will analyse *deca* on its own to avoid confusion (for example, *gospoda* and *vlastela* can refer to a class rather than individuals, and this affects the agreement possibilities).

2. Wayles Browne suggested and undertook informant work on a test to determine the gender of *ih*. The test involved sentences in which *sam* 'alone' (which in

the accusative distinguishes neuter from masculine and feminine) agreed with *ih*. Most informants used the masculine/feminine plural form. However, they did so even when *ih* referred to a neuter noun. The problem here rests with the form *ih*: its accusative matches the genitive, which probably indicates that it carries an irregular animacy marker (see Corbett, 1980b for an account of animacy in other Slavic languages, and Browne, 1980, 71–93 for a related problem in Serbo-Croat). This area deserves further study, but this is likely to tell us more about the personal pronoun and the problem of animacy than about agreement with *deca*.

3. The language of the earlier Čakavian writers differed in that masculine plural agreement was also possible in the nominative case of the relative pronoun (example in Glavan, 1927–8, 121). This system is also in accord with the Agreement Hierarchy.

4. Rozental' (1971, 234) claims that Russian conjoined singular nouns are more likely to take a plural modifier when they stand in the nominative than they are in an oblique case. If this is so, it supports our position. However, Crockett (1976, 170) disputes the claim, and my investigations lend support to Crockett rather than to Rozental'. My examples provide no statistical justification for drawing a distinction between the nominative and the oblique cases in this construction, and so no evidence for or against (21).

Before leaving the question of different agreements in direct and oblique cases, we should consider an apparent counter-example to our claim; it stems from incomplete descriptions of a particular construction. Russian epicenes in *-a* most often take agreements according to the sex of their referents. However, attributive modifiers may show feminine (syntactic) agreement, even when the noun refers to a male. The predicate, too, despite a widespread belief to the contrary, may be feminine (for examples see Kopeliovič (1977, 182). Crockett, following other writers (1976, 70–1, 77, and references there), states that feminine agreement occurs only in predicative phrases (i.e. normally in the nominative). This would be contrary to our claim that the agreement form with the lesser semantic justification is more likely in oblique cases. However, Crockett's statement seems unfounded, as examples in Graudina *et al.* (1976, 76) and Kopeliovič (1977, 184) indicate: feminine agreement is found in oblique cases. Thus the limited evidence relevant to the effect of case on alternative agreement forms is consistent with claim (21). For a survey of epicenes see Herrity, P. (1983) 'Agreement with Epicoena and Masculine Nouns in *-a* in the Slavonic Languages', *Slavonic and East European Review*, 61, 41–54.

5. The interesting data on collective nouns in Old Russian presented by Degtjarev (1966) can also be analysed by treating *-a* endings as neuter plural. His examples show that Old Russian requires the Predicate Hierarchy to be extended to accommodate the present active participle in its predicative use to the right of the predicative adjective.

Our investigation so far has centred on the role of the target in determining agreement. We have established the effect of the Agreement and Predicate Hierarchies and suggested the way in which they are interrelated. Variation in the controller was restricted as far as was practical, so that we could isolate variation which depends on the agreement target. While in some instances we were able to limit the controllers to a small number of lexical items or even to a single item, in other instances we considered controllers of a particular syntactic type.

We must now turn to the controller and to variation within it. When, for example, the controller consists of conjoined noun phrases, the types of nouns involved influence the agreement forms used. To isolate the variation which is due to the controller, we must now limit variation of the target: we must try to keep the target as 'still' as possible. The target we shall use is the predicate. There are four good reasons for this choice. First, this is the type of target which is most sensitive to variation in agreement; in the data presented to support the Agreement Hierarchy, it is the predicate which more often than any other target shows a choice of agreement forms (see Figure 2.1). Second, it is the target type which occurs most frequently. Third, as a consequence of these two factors there is more information available on agreement in the predicate than in other positions. Unfortunately, as we shall see, the studies which have been made to date give only some of the information we would like. And finally, the predicate is the crucial position for linking our two hierarchies; by using the predicate as the target while discussing controllers, we will also be preparing the way for confirming the interrelationship of the two hierarchies.

Our basic strategy is to consider one sort of target only — the predicate — while allowing the controller to vary. Even with this restriction, we are likely to be swamped if we try to take on board too many variables at the same time. We shall therefore review briefly the three main controller types which permit agreement options (§6.1), select the most promising type to investigate further (conjoined noun phrases) and establish the basic possibilities with this type of controller (§6.2).

6.1 Controllers which Permit Agreement Choices

There are three main types of controller which allow variation in the predicate in Slavic: conjoined noun phrases, comitative phrases and quantified expressions. We will consider each in turn with a view to establishing the best type to subject first to more detailed analysis. The agreement choices involved will be illustrated by examples from East Slavic languages.

6.1.1 Conjoined Noun Phrases

When the predicate agrees with conjoined noun phrases, agreement may be with just one of the noun phrases. This possibility is shown in the following example:

(1) R: *Prepodavalas'* (fem sg) *matematika* (fem sg) *i*
     Was taught   mathematics   and
     fizika (fem sg)
     physics

The verb is singular, agreeing with one noun phrase only. However, the plural is also possible (Graudina *et al.*, 1976, 31):

(2) R: *Prepodavalis'* (pl) *matematika* (fem sg) *i*   *fizika* (fem sg)
     Were taught   mathematics   and physics

The verb in (2) agrees with both noun phrases. This form of agreement is clearly the one which has the greater semantic justification – and, as we saw in §2.1.7, the agreements found are in accord with the Agreement Hierarchy. Conjoined noun phrases occur relatively frequently and allow wide variety – nouns of all types occur in conjoined expressions, though within a single conjoined expression the nouns are usually of the same type. While both animate and inanimate nouns occur freely in conjoined expressions, it is rare to find an animate conjoined with an inanimate.

6.1.2 Comitative Phrases

Slavic has an interesting construction consisting of noun phrases linked with *s/z* which means 'with'. They are used in instances where some other languages use a simple conjoined structure. In comitative phrases the first noun may represent the initiator of an action or the dominant participant while the second noun refers to a less important participant, but this is not always so. The second noun, governed by the preposition, appears in the instrumental case. We would expect that agreement would be with the noun in the nominative case, as indeed occurs in the following example:

(3) BR: *Dzed   z   unukam laviŭ* (masc sg) *rybu*
      Grandfather with grandson was catching   fish
      (Grandfather and grandson were fishing)

However, agreement with both nouns is possible, even though only one is in the nominative (both examples from Bukatevič *et al.*, 1958, 292):

(4) BR: *Brat   z   sjastroju pajšli* (pl) *ŭ   tèatr*
      Brother with sister   went   to the theatre

In this construction, too, the plural is the form which has the greater semantic justification, since more than one individual is involved. The information available on the use of the different agreement forms in this construction in the different Slavic languages suggests that the choice is governed by the same factors as for ordinary conjoined noun phrases.[1] There are two reasons for investigating conjoined noun phrases rather than phrases linked with *s/z*. First, phrases linked with *s/z* are less common, which makes collecting data more difficult. To take a Russian example, in Panova's short novel *Sputniki* there were only three examples, compared with 68 examples of predicate agreement with conjoined noun phrases. The second main disadvantage of comitative phrases is that the nouns included are almost always animate. As we will see, one of the major characteristics of controllers which influences agreement is animacy; this can be demonstrated quite clearly with conjoined noun phrases, while finding enough examples of inanimates with *s/z* to form a meaningful comparison with animates would be a very considerable undertaking. We shall therefore postpone further analysis of this construction until §8.3.

6.1.3 Quantified expressions

These are of three types: those headed by numerals; those based on collective nouns, such as Russian *bol'šinstvo* 'majority'; and thirdly, expressions headed by other quantifiers, such as Russian *neskol'ko* 'a few', which are harder to define. There is often a choice between singular and plural agreement, as in the following Ukrainian sentence (Bukatevič *et al.*, 1958, 293):

(5) U: . . . *u lisi   stojit'* (sg) *tri   dubočki*
      in the fence stands   three oaks
(6) U: . . . *u lisi   stojat'* (pl) *tri   dubočki*
      in the fence stand   three oaks

In such instances the plural, as in (6), has greater semantic justification than the singular agreement shown in (5), since reference is made to more than one object. Not all the Slavic languages allow a choice of agreement with all types of quantified expression. The East Slavic languages, which we chose for illustration, allow a greater range of choices than those of West and South. We shall return to the variation between the languages in §11.2. Even if we restrict our attention to a single language we still find many factors at work. There are major differences in the choice of agreement form between the different types of quantifier. Even within a single type the quantifiers are not homogeneous. For example, we have just considered a Ukrainian example with the numeral 3; as we shall see below (Table 11.12), the frequency of semantically justified agreement with the numeral 3 varies from that with 2 or 4, and even more markedly from that with numerals from 5 upwards. It is true that quantified expressions occur relatively frequently, with both animate and inanimate nouns. However, if we have to examine each quantifier separately, in order to isolate the influence on agreement of the particular quantifier, then our task becomes impracticable. It is more sensible to analyse conjoined noun phrases first, in order to isolate the main ways in which the controller influences the choice of agreement; later we shall see how these factors apply to quantified expressions (§8.4).

6.2 Agreement with Conjoined Noun Phrases

We have chosen conjoined noun phrases as the construction to investigate first, in order to establish the main characteristics of the agreement controller which influence agreement. We will consider the normally occurring possibilities and then examine a rare type of agreement.

6.2.1 Normal Possibilities

Let us return to the examples of agreement with conjoined noun phrases which were given above. We saw that plural agreement is possible (as in (2)); this is the form with greater semantic justification. The alternative is for agreement to be with one noun phrase only:

(7) = (1) R: *Prepodavalas'* (fem sg) *matematika* (fem sg) *i*
Was taught   mathematics   and
fizika (fem sg)
physics

Here the verb is singular, agreeing with one noun phrase only; the question is, which one? Both nouns are feminine singular, so agreement could be with either. We must find an example with nouns of different gender:

(8) R: *Byla* (fem sg) *v nej i   skromnost'* (fem sg), *i*
Was   in her and modesty   and
izjaščestvo (neut sg), *i   dostoinstvo* (neut sg)
elegance   and dignity
(*Pravda*, 7.11.1966, quoted by Graudina *et al*., 1976, 31)

(Note that the conjunction may occur before the first item of a list.) In this sentence it is evident that the predicate verb agrees with the noun *skromnost'*; the other nouns are of a different gender. We might assume that the verb agrees with *skromnost'* because it is the nearest noun; but it might also be because it is the first noun in the series. In order to resolve this question we need a sentence in which the conjoined noun phrases are placed before the verb:

(9) R: *Otkaz* (masc sg) *katoržan   ot rabskoj   raboty,*
The rejection   of the convicts of slave-like work
vozmuščenie (neut sg) *rešëtkami i   rasstrelami*
resentment   at the bars and shootings
ogorčilo (neut sg), *udručilo* (neut sg) *i   napugalo* (neut sg)
grieved   depressed   and frightened
pokornyx lagernyx kommunistov.
the meek camp   communists
(Solženicyn, *Arxipelag GULag*)

The gender form of the verbs in (9) makes it clear that they agree with the nearer conjunct. As agreement may be with the nearer (or nearest) conjunct or with all the conjuncts, and the subject may precede or follow the verb, there are four possible configurations, which are illustrated below:

6.2.1.1 Subject-predicate Order, Agreement with all Conjuncts

(10) R: ... *astma i   sil'naja blizorukost'*   *ne*   *pozvolili* (pl)
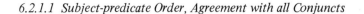
asthma and severe   short-sightedness did not permit
(Vojnovič, *Pretendent na prestol)*

6.2.1.2 Subject-predicate Order, Agreement with the Nearest Conjunct

(11) cf. (9) R: ... *otkaz* ...   *vozmuščenie* ... *ogorčilo* (sg) ...
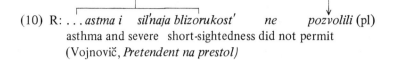
rejection   resentment   grieved

6.2.1.3 Predicate-subject Order, Agreement with All Conjuncts

(12) = (2) R: *Prepodavalis'* (pl) *matematika i   fizika*
Were taught   mathematics and physics

6.2.1.4 Predicate-subject Order, Agreement with the Nearest Conjunct

(13) cf. (8) R: *Byla* (sg) ... *i   skromnost', i   izjaščestvo, i*
Was ...   (and) modesty   and elegance   and
dostoinstvo
dignity

While all four possibilities occur, they do so with markedly different frequency. The factors which govern their distribution are the subject of the next chapter.

6.2.2 Distant Agreement

The four options just described are the ones which normally occur in Slavic. However, there is a fifth possibility, which is found only rarely and about which little is known. It is agreement with the first conjunct, which, when the subject precedes the predicate, is not the nearest conjunct. This type of agreement ('distant agreement') may be represented as follows:

(14)   NP   NP   Pred

In some instances the second conjunct is merely parenthetic:

(15) R: *Celyj   otrjad* (masc sg) *fauny   (i   osobenno ta*
         A whole array   of fauna (and especially that
         dič' (fem sg), *za   kotoroj oxotilis' orly)*
         game   after which   hunted   eagles)
         poglašal (masc sg) *nenormal'no   vysokoe količestvo*
         took in   an abnormally high   quantity
         rtuti.
         of mercury

This example, with several similar ones, is quoted by Crockett (1976, 276). These cases cannot be considered as clear examples of distant agreements, since they do not contain genuine (i.e. non-parenthetical) conjoined subjects. In Modern Russian, genuine conjoined subjects do not normally permit distant agreement.[2] In Old Russian such constructions are attested:

(16) R: *Otec* (masc) *-mat'* (fem) *molodca   u   sebja vo ljubvi*
         Father (and) mother   the youth with them in love
         deržal (masc sg)
         kept
         (Father and mother kept the young man lovingly in their home.)
         (Buslaev, 1959, 456)

It seems that this possibility was restricted to certain common combinations of nouns.

While Russian has largely lost the possibility of distant agreement, this construction is found in Slovene and Serbo-Croat. The following Slovene examples are quoted by Lenček (1972, 59):

(17) Sn: *Groza* (fem sg) *in   strah* (masc sg) *je   prevzela* (fem sg)
         Horror   and fear   has seized
         vso   vas
         the whole village

The fact that the verb is singular indicates that agreement is with one conjunct, and the feminine gender proves that agreement is indeed with the first conjunct only. In the next example both conjuncts are plural:

(18) Sn: *Knjige* (fem pl) *in   peresa* (neut pl) *so*
　　　 Books　　　　　and pens　　　　　 have
　　　 se podražile (fem pl)
　　　 become more expensive

As we shall see below (§10.3.1), the South Slavic languages have a
remarkable rule which requires the masculine gender for agreement
with a mixture of feminine and neuter conjuncts. In this example, the
feminine plural verb cannot therefore indicate agreement with both
conjuncts; it agrees with the first only. Serbo-Croat has the same
construction:

(19) SC: *Ona   stalna,   duboko urezana svijetla* (neut pl) *i*
　　　 Those constant, deeply cut   lights　　　　　　and
　　　 sjene (fem pl) *koje   je   naslikao umjetnikov kist*
　　　 shades　　　　which has painted the artist's brush
　　　 bila (neut pl) *su jača* (neut pl) *od   realne svijetlosti.*
　　　 were　　　　　 stronger　　　 than real   light
　　　 (Desnica, quoted by Megaard, 1976, 80)

For further examples from Serbo-Croat see Maretić (1899, 413), Glavan
(1927–8, 143–5), and especially Megaard (1976, 70, 75, 80–1). Examples like (19) are rare. A corpus of short stories by Andrić produced
no examples of distant agreement. The works included were *Ljubav u
kasabi*, *Smrt u Sinanovoj tekiji*, *Anikina vremena*, *Zmija*, *Mila i Prelac*,
Žena na kamenu, *Mara milosnica*, *Ćorkan i Švabica*, *Put Alije Đerzeleza*,
Jelena, žena koje nema, *Zlostavljanje*, *Mustafa Madžar*, *Priča o kmetu
Simanu* and *Most na Žepi*. (See Table 8.1 for details of the option of
agreement with all conjuncts or the nearest conjunct in this corpus.)
While examples like (19) may be infrequent in texts, Megaard gives too
many examples for us to disregard them. As yet, little is known about
the conditions under which agreement of this type occurs. Certainly,
in the majority of the examples quoted from all three languages, the
noun phrases are inanimate.

　Distant agreement is indeed an unusual phenomenon, but it suggests
certain claims about the way in which agreement operates, which we
shall later verify with more solid data. Consider first the fact that all
the examples of distant agreement have the controller before the target.
No examples have been reported of agreement with a more distant
conjunct following the predicate, as in the following structure:

(20)   *Pred   NP   NP

From this we may deduce that precedence is an important factor in determining agreement: distant agreement is possible in Slavic only when the controller precedes the target. The importance of precedence will be amply demonstrated, with more readily accessible data, in Chapters 7 and 8. Next let us consider the 'rival claims' of a set of conjoined noun phrases, first when preceding the predicate:

(21) NP_1 NP_2 NP_3 Pred
            precedes   precedes   precedes
            first   nearest

All three noun phrases precede the predicate and in this respect have equal claims to the role of controller. However, NP_3 is also the nearest NP, and this advantage is sufficient, in most of the Slavic languages, to ensure that if a single noun phrase is the controller it will be NP_3. However, in a minority of languages, such as Serbo-Croat, the fact that NP_1 is in initial position is occasionally sufficient to make it the sole controller. When we consider noun phrases standing after the predicate the picture is clearer:

(22)   Pred NP_1 NP_2 NP_3
                            first
                            nearest

Here NP_1 has all the advantages; when only one noun phrase is controller in structures like (22) it is always NP_1. When we compare (21) and (22), we observe that in (21) all three noun phrases have some claim to be controller, since all precede the target, whereas there is only one noun phrase in (22) with any claim to be controller. As we shall see in Chapter 7, it is much more common for all the preceding noun phrases to be controllers (for agreement to be with all the noun phrases and therefore for the predicate to be plural) than it is for all the following noun phrases to be controllers.

Distant agreement gives one further clue as to the constraints on agreement. According to Megaard (1976, 80–1), distant agreement is possible only if the noun phrases are either all singular, or all plural. Example (19) quoted above had two plural noun phrases. Megaard gives the following ungrammatical alternatives:

(23) SC: **sjene* (fem pl) *i*   *svijetlo* (neut sg) *bile* (fem pl)
        shades   and light   were
        su jače (fem pl)
        stronger

(24) SC: **svijetlo* (neut sg) *i*   *sjene* (fem pl) *je bilo* (neut sg)
        light   and shades   were
        jače (neut sg)
        stronger

How can Megaard's constraint be explained? I suggest that it follows from our discussion on the different controller positions. As we noted when discussing (21), the prime controller position is that preceding and nearest to the target. In (23) and (24), the noun phrase in prime position is not involved in the agreement and furthermore the number of the predicate is in conflict with it.[3] It is this clash which makes the sentences ungrammatical. However, in sentences showing distant agreement, like (19), the gender of the predicate conflicts with that of the nearer noun phrase (otherwise we could not prove that distant agreement was involved). This implies that agreement in number is in some sense more important than agreement in gender. As we shall see in §10.4, there is good evidence to show that this is the case. However, we are running too far ahead. We must first give a clear demonstration of the claims made concerning precedence.

6.2.3 *The Next Step*

Distant agreement deserves much more study. However, examples are rare. In order to continue our investigation into the main features of controllers which influence agreement, it will be safer to restrict ourselves to the basic choice between conjuncts, as is found in Modern Russian.

So far we have chosen the agreement controller we intend to investigate — conjoined noun phrases, and the target — the predicate. We must now settle the question of which agreement categories are to be included. Conjoined noun phrases may take predicate agreement in gender, person and number. The rules for agreement in gender, for those languages which require them, are quite fascinating, as we shall see below (§10.3). They are not, however, a promising place to begin this part of our investigation. Agreement in person is relatively straightforward (§10.1). Examples occur rarely, and show little variation. Agreement in number occurs much more frequently. Providing we first exclude the complication of the dual number (to which we return in

§10.2) then agreement in number is a suitable starting point. Eliminating gender agreement restricts our choice of language to some extent. Russian has no gender distinctions in the plural, and so fits our requirements. We shall select Russian, rather than one of the other possibilities, because data are available concerning dialect usage; these data will allow us to investigate the extent to which the controller factors we establish vary between dialectal and standard usage.

6.3   Conclusion

Having surveyed the three main types of controller, we have settled on conjoined noun phrases for further study. In Chapter 7 we will undertake a detailed investigation of predicate agreement with controllers of this type, using dialectal and diachronic data in addition to evidence from the modern standard language. The major factors which we find operating in the different language varieties are the animacy of the controller and its order relative to the target. After establishing these two factors in Chapter 7, we can then apply them to other main controller types (comitative phrases and quantified expressions) in Chapter 8.

Notes

1. For Czech data, see Trávníček (1949, 415–16); for Polish, Zdaniukiewicz (1973, 153–4); for Sorbian, Faska (1959, 64–8); and for Ukrainian, Shevelov (1963, 59–61). Russian will be discussed in §8.2.
2. It occurs occasionally with the names of literary and operatic works such as *Vojna i mir*, 'War and Peace' (Rozental', 1974, 219).
3. If sentence (23) showed masculine plural agreement, this would indicate that agreement was with both conjuncts. Then the noun phrase in prime position would be involved in the agreement and there would be no question of ungrammaticality. The constraint under discussion is to be related to the postulated constraint in modern literary Russian by which any preceding plural conjunct makes a plural predicate obligatory (§7.4). Note that while *jače* could be neuter singular or feminine plural in (23) and (24) the verb forms are unambiguous.

In the preceding chapter we considered different controller types and
selected conjoined noun phrases in Russian for further analysis.[1] Here,
we will be concerned with the choice between agreement with all
conjuncts or only with the nearest; the option taken in a given sentence
can be established from the number of the predicate. For data we turn
first to a study by Potapova (1962), which is unusual because she uses
dialectal sources and gives statistical data to back her conclusions.
Surprisingly, there was no similar corpus-based account to give comparative figures for the literary language. So the original aim was to
collect a corpus from the literary language and to compare it with
Potapova's dialect corpus. However, there is interesting variation
within the literary language itself, and so we shall in fact compare five
small corpora: Potapova's, and four from the literary language (§7.1).
Having established the major factors at work (§7.2) we will investigate
their interaction (§7.3) and review other less important influences on
predicate agreement (§7.4). Finally, we consider data from several
further corpora, which confirm the role of the major factors identified
earlier and show the direction of diachronic change (§7.5).

7.1 The Corpora

Potapova's dialect examples were collected from 20 places in the Perm'
region. Her presentation contains several inconsistencies;[2] in order to
have totally reliable figures for comparative purposes, the examples
were transferred to punch-cards, and the numbers belonging to the
different categories were recounted. The corpus analysed below consists
of 94 examples, mostly taken from ordinary conversation; 19 were
taken from folklore sources and two from local written material. We
shall consider Potapova's analysis first, but having the examples on
punch-cards will allow us to calculate figures other than those given in
her account. This may seem a great deal of effort for a comparatively
small corpus. However, examples of predicate agreement with conjoined
subjects occur relatively seldom in spoken language. For example, in
the set of texts of recordings of spoken Russian edited by Zemskaja and

Kapanadze (1978), there are a mere four clear examples in about 50,000 words. Thus the gathering of Potapova's corpus represents a great deal of work and it is, for practical reasons, a corpus of acceptable size. Moreover, given careful interpretation, a small corpus can give reasonably reliable results (see Findreng, 1976, 22-9 for an interesting comparison of results from corpora of different sizes).

For comparative purposes, four corpora were established: they consist of the examples found in Amal'rik's *Neželannoe putešestvie v Sibir'* (hereafter A), in Nabokov's *Zaščita Lužina* (N), in Solženicyn's *Arxipelag GULag* parts V-VII (S) and in two works by Vojnovič: *Pretendent na prestol* (V *Pretendent*) and *Putëm vzaimnoj perepiski* (V *Putëm*).[3] By keeping these corpora separate, we will be able to investigate variation within the literary language. Table 7.1 gives the distribution of our literary examples. We will refer to these corpora simply

Table 7.1: Sources of Examples

Author	examples	words scanned
Amal'rik	84	91,000
Nabokov	66	52,000
Solženicyn	60	171,000
Vojnovič	80	142,000

by the name of the author (by his initial when quoting examples), and to Potapova's data as 'dialects' (D for examples). Examples will be prefixed by LR (Literary Russian) or DR (Dialectal Russian).

Care was taken to ensure that the sets of examples were fully comparable. The criterion adopted for all corpora was that conjoined noun phrases were included providing the noun phrase nearest the predicate had a singular head. The reason for this restriction is as follows. In Modern Russian, agreement with conjoined noun phrases can be of two types: agreement with all the conjuncts (plural), or agreement with the nearest conjunct. (The fact that the possibilities are restricted in this way was established in §6.2 and it is confirmed by the examples in our five corpora.) Suppose we have a sentence in which the conjunct nearest the predicate is plural:

(1) LR: *I   konvoj* (sg), *i   sud'ja* (sg) , *i   zriteli* (pl)
       And the escort   and the judge   and the onlookers

> *prevraščalis'* (pl) *v nečistyx čudovišč*...
> turned into evil monsters
> (V *Pretendent* 310)

In sentence (1), whether agreement is with all the conjuncts or just with the nearest, the plural will result. Since there is no choice of agreement form and so no way of telling which type of agreement is involved, such sentences were excluded. As we shall see, it is possible to have a singular predicate, even though the subject contains a plural form, providing this plural noun does not stand nearest to the predicate. If the nearest conjunct is singular, there is at least a potential choice of agreement form. The other main restriction[4] on the sample was that the noun phrases should be conjoined with the conjunctions *i, da* or *a*, all meaning 'and', or with no conjunction; we are thus dealing with co-ordinated noun phrases.

7.2 Factors Influencing Predicate Agreement with Conjoined Noun Phrases

Having established five fully comparable sets of examples, we can begin our investigation of the role of the agreement controller, and the way in which it varies between literary and dialectal Russian. Potapova discusses three major factors which influence the choice of agreement: word-order, the nature of the subject and the nature of the predicate. We will consider these in turn.

7.2.1 Word-order

Potapova states that when the subject precedes the predicate, the majority of sentences have a plural predicate. Sentences like the following are typical:

(2) DR: *S'em'on-da-žena ne-p'išut* (pl) (D62)
    Simon and wife do not write

(Examples from the dialect corpus are given in a transliteration of Potapova's transcription.) Similar examples are frequent in the literary texts:

(3) LR: *Brigadir i učitel' prišli* (pl)
    The brigade-leader and the teacher came

> *k nemu* . . . .   (A 244)
> to him

(4) LR: . . . *štukaturka i   pobelka   vysoxli* (pl) . . .   (S220)
>   the plaster and the whitewash dried

Examples with a singular predicate are less common, but are found both in dialectal and literary Russian:

(5) DR: *Ran'še ot'ec/   mat'   blagoslovl'ajet* (sg)
>   Earlier father (and) mother blesses
>   *molodyx*
>   the young (couple)
>   (D 63; / denotes an intonational break)

(6) LR: *Otkaz   katoržan   ot rabskoj   raboty,*
>   The rejection of the convicts of slave-like work
>   *vozmuščenie rešëtkami i   rasstrelami ogorčilo* (sg),
>   resentment   at the bars and shootings grieved
>   *udručilo* (sg) *i   napugalo* (sg) *pokornyx lagernyx*
>   depressed   and frightened   the meek camp
>   *kommunistov.*   (S 330)
>   communists

When the predicate precedes the subject, again both plural and singular forms are found in the dialects and in the literary language. Examples (7) and (8) show plural agreement:

(7) DR: *Nap'er'od idut* (pl) *pop   i-djakon*   (D 63)
>   In front   go   the priest and the deacon

(8) LR: *No ne obdeleny* (pl) *byli* (pl) *i   Srednaja Azija, i*
>   But not missed   were   and Central Asia and
>   *Sibir' (množestvo   kalmykov vymerlo na Enisee),*
>   Siberia a great number of Kalmyks died   on the Enisej
>   *Severnyj Ural i   Sever   Evropejskoj*
>   the north Urals and the north of the European
>   *časti.*   (S 408)
>   part

Singular agreement is found in the next two sentences:

(9) DR: *zaplač'et* (sg) *mat'   i-moj   ot'ec*   (D 63)
>   will cry   mother and my father

(10) LR: *Otcu   nravilas'* (sg) *ee samostojatel'nost', tišina,*
         To father was pleasing her independence   quietness
         i   osobaja manera opuskat'   glaza, kogda ona
         and special way   to lower (her) eyes when she
         ulybalas'.   (N 115)
         smiled

Thus both forms of agreement are found when the subject precedes the controller and when it follows. The interesting point is the distribution of these forms,[5] which is given in Table 7.2.

Table 7.2 The Effect of Word-order

	subject-predicate			predicate-subject		
	sg	pl	%pl	sg	pl	%pl
Dialects	16	46	74	14	18	56
Amal'rik	3	27	90	16	38	70
Nabokov	0	23	100	34	9	21
Solženicyn	5	28	85	11	16	59
Vojnovič	0	45	100	15	20	57

In Table 7.2 and subsequent tables, the most useful figure for comparative purposes is the percentage figure – the percentage of plural forms found within a given category. Thus the dialect corpus includes 62 examples with subject–predicate word-order, of which 46, or 74 per cent, show plural agreement. The raw figures are still important: in some categories the number of examples is small, which indicates that those percentages must be viewed with caution. In any event, given the size of the corpora, a difference of several percentage points may not be significant, and for this reason the percentages are rounded to the nearest whole number.

The data in Table 7.2 show that the plural is significantly more likely to occur in sentences with subject-predicate word-order than in those with predicate-subject order. Certainly Potapova is justified in her claim that plural agreement dominates in sentences with subject-predicate order in the dialects. In literary texts too, the plural is favoured in subject-predicate sentences, even more so than in the dialects. Given this similar preference, it would be advantageous to establish whether there is a significant difference between the dialects and the literary language in this respect. If we combine the literary examples, we obtain total figures of eight singular and 123 plural examples. We can compare these with the dialect figures (16 singular and 46 plural), using the chi-square test,[6] which shows that the distribution observed would occur by chance less than once in a thousand instances. We may conclude that plural agreement is favoured in subject-verb sentences both in the dialects and in the literary language, and that there is a significantly greater preference for the plural in the literary language. When we turn to sentences in which the predicate precedes the subject, there is no such clear preference. The plural is favoured marginally both in the dialects and in the literary language, but with a notable exception: Nabokov prefers the singular in these sentences, by a ratio of almost 4:1.

7.2.2 Animate Subjects

We have established that the position of the subject relative to the predicate has an effect on agreement, both in the dialects and in the literary language. We now consider whether animate and inanimate subjects differ in the agreements they take. As far as the dialects are concerned, Potapova (1962, 66–7) claims that when the subject denotes persons, the predicate will normally be plural, and when it denotes objects, then singular. This distinction omits non-human animates. And there are other subject types included in her corpus, for which the classification is not self-evident. All the types of noun phrase which are found in the subject in her corpus are set out in Table 7.3, together with comparable figures for the literary corpora. The table shows that the elements conjoined are normally semantically similar (most

Table 7.3: Agreement with Different Subject Types

corpus subject type	Dialects sg	pl	Amal'rik sg	pl	Nabokov sg	pl	Solženicyn sg	pl	Vojnovič sg	pl
1. all persons	14	54	3	45	2	17	3	18	2	45
2. person + corporate	–	–	–	–	–	–	–	1	–	–
3. all corporate	1	1	–	2	–	–	1	2	–	2
4. person + animal	1	1	–	–	–	–	–	–	–	–
5. all animals	2	6	–	–	–	–	–	–	–	–
6. person + inanimate	1	–	–	2	3	–	–	–	1	1
7. corporate + inanimate	–	–	–	–	–	–	1	–	–	–
8. all inanimate	11	2	16	16	29	15	11	23	12	17

Note: 'Corporate' refers to nouns such as *pravitel'stvo* 'government', *rajkom* 'district committee', *kolxoz* 'collective farm'. In the literary language these normally take singular agreements when standing on their own. In Old Russian the plural was common with comparable nouns and this situation is preserved in the dialects (Potapova, 1960).

commonly two or more nouns denoting persons or two or more nouns referring to inanimates). 'Corporate' nouns, particularly in the literary language, tend to be treated as persons: when conjoined, they usually show plural agreement, as in the following example:

(11) LR: *Oni*   *[kolxozniki]*   *ved'*   *cenjat* (pl)
       They [the collective farm workers] after all value
       svoj sobstvennyj trud stol' že nizko, kak ego cenjat (pl)
       their own   work just as low   as it value
       kolxoz   *i gosudarstvo.*   (A 166)
       the collective farm and the state

It appears too that in the Perm' region animals are treated, for agreement purposes at least, like humans. We can therefore treat subject types 1–5 together: they comprise all personal, corporate and animal subjects and any mixtures of these; we will refer to them as animate subjects.[7] Subjects which include both animates and inanimates show no clear pattern, and there are insufficient examples to permit any conclusions. We will therefore omit them from further discussion in this section. Let us now compare animate subjects (types 1–5) with inanimates (type 8).

Table 7.4 shows that animate subjects (a slightly broader category than that about which Potapova made her claim) generally control plural agreement in the dialects. The correlation between animate

Table 7.4: The Effect of Animacy

	animate subject			inanimate subject		
	sg	pl	%pl	sg	pl	%pl
Dialects	18	62	78	11	2	15
Amal'rik	3	47	94	16	16	50
Nabokov	2	17	89	29	15	34
Solženicyn	4	21	84	11	23	68
Vojnovič	2	47	96	12	17	59

subjects and plural agreement is stronger in the literary corpora. The difference between the combined literary corpora and the dialects is again significant — it would arise by chance less frequently than once in one hundred instances. Moreover, while in the dialects an inanimate subject normally has a singular predicate, this is not the case in the literary language. Here, overall, the two options are almost equally used, with Nabokov favouring the singular and Solženicyn the plural. We conclude that an animate subject has a strong influence on predicate agreement in the dialects and even more so in the literary language. However, while an inanimate subject normally has a singular predicate in the dialects, this is not the case in the literary language. Thus the literary language shows a consistent shift in favour of the plural, as compared with the dialects.

7.2.3 'Active' Predicates

We have seen that both the position of the subject and its type (animate or inanimate) play a role in determining the agreement form of the predicate. These two factors are widely quoted as influencing agreement, in Russian, in other Slavic languages and beyond Slavic. The third factor to be investigated is discussed less often. Potapova (1962, 65–7) claims that if the predicate is a verb of 'activity', then (with conjoined subjects) a plural predicate will normally result. Her 'active' verbs form a more restricted set than those which are merely morphologically active; they contrast with those predicates which denote 'being, state and presence'. While clear in the majority of cases, this distinction is sometimes difficult to draw. Potapova restricts active predicates to sentences with persons as subject; in other words, she considers only sentences which have subjects denoting humans who undertake some activity. Thus (12) has an 'active' predicate:

(12) DR: *Myžik da baba idut* (pl)   (D 65)
Man   and wife are going

The following have 'non-active' predicates:

(13) DR: *Syn da snoxa   bol'nye* (pl)   (D 66)
Son and daughter-in-law (are) ill
(14) DR: *Žyl-byl* (sg) *starik   da staruxa*   (D 66)
Lived was an old man and an old woman

(*Žyl-byl* is a folklore formula equivalent to 'Once upon a time there was/were . . .'; it shows agreement in number and gender.)

The effect of the factor of activity can be seen in Table 7.5; again we consider animate subjects rather than person subjects, and exclude 'mixed' subjects.

At first sight the figures in Table 7.5 appear impressive. However, it must be remembered that 'active' predicates were considered only in

Table 7.5: The Effect of an 'Active' Predicate

| | 'active' predicate | | | 'non-active' predicate | | |
	sg	pl	%pl	sg	pl	%pl
Dialects	6	40	87	23	24	51
Amal'rik	0	31	100	19	32	63
Nabokov	0	10	100	31	22	42
Solženicyn	0	11	100	15	33	69
Vojnovič	2	29	94	12	35	74

the case of animate subjects – a category of examples which already shows a marked preference for plural predicates. Nevertheless, in all corpora except Vojnovič, the percentage of plural agreements in active predicates is greater than the figure for animate subjects given in Table 7.4. This shows that to establish the effect of this factor, we must isolate the other factors at work in the same sentences, rather than merely counting for each factor separately, as Potapova does. We will adopt this approach in §7.3. First, however, let us see what conclusions can be drawn from our analysis so far.

7.2.4 *Comparison of the Factors in the Different Corpora*

We will now reconsider the data, with a view to specifying the differences in the corpora. Table 7.6 gives previous figures, together with some additional measures to be discussed below.

In the table, particularly important figures have been italicised, and will be referred to as each corpus is discussed in turn. In the dialects, the overall total is lower than that for most of the literary corpora. While the same factors favour plural agreement as in the literary texts, in each case they do so to a lesser degree (the lower ratios of plural to singular in subject-predicate sentences and in those with animate subjects were discussed above). In the opposite cases, when the feature which favours plural agreement is absent (predicate-subject order, inanimate subject, non-active predicate), the percentage of plurals found is relatively low, particularly in the case of inanimate subjects. However, the difference between the dialects and the literary corpora is even greater than these figures might suggest. For each factor the proportion of sentences in which it occurs is given: thus, the entry of 66 per cent for 'S-P/total' in the dialects indicates that 66 per cent of the sentences show subject-predicate word-order. It will be observed that, in each case, the dialects have the greatest proportion of sentences in which the factor which favours plural agreement is present. This

Table 7.6: Summary of Data

	Dialects	Amal'rik	Nabokov	Solženicyn	Vojnovič
Total	*68*	77	*48*	73	81
Word-order:					
subject-predicate	*74*	90	100	85	100
predicate-subject	56	70	*21*	59	57
S-P/total	66	*36*	*35*	55	56
Animacy:					
animate subject	78	94	89	84	96
inanimate subject	*15*	50	*34*	64	59
animate/total	85	60	*29*	*40*	61
'Active' predicate:					
'active' predicate	87	100	100	100	94
'non-active' predicate	*51*	63	*42*	69	74
'active'/total	49	38	*15*	*18*	39

Note: All figures are percentages. The three rows which include '/total' indicate the proportion of sentences of that type. The remainder are percentage plural agreement.

shows that the different proportion of sentence-types masks part of the difference in agreement choices.

In the Amal'rik data, the main point of interest is the fact that only 36 per cent of the examples show subject-predicate order. This is largely compensated for by the fact that he shows the highest percentage of plural agreement in predicate-subject sentences. Nabokov's low overall figure of plural agreement results in part from the sentence constructions he uses – in every case he has the lowest proportion of the types which promote plural agreement. When he does use the 'right' sentence types, the proportion of plural agreements is as high as that of the other writers. However, when these factors are absent, his proportion of plural agreements is markedly lower. Solženicyn also uses rather fewer constructions which favour the use of the plural than do Amal'rik and Vojnovič. The latter shows the highest overall proportion of plural agreement mainly because, of all the writers, he shows the greatest preference for sentences of the type which favour plural agreement.

We have established that there is a clear difference in usage between the dialects and the literary texts. This is partially masked by the varying frequency of different sentence types. Moreover, this same variation makes differences between the writers appear sharper than they actually are. The main differences, especially those between the literary corpora, are to be found not in the examples where individual factors which favour plural agreement are found, but rather in the examples where they are absent. In the next section we will investigate the combination of factors in the same sentence, which will give us a clearer picture of the differences between the corpora. It is evident that the total figures, without the data on the contributing factors, would give a poor picture of the true situation. Even bearing this in mind, it is interesting to note that Graudina *et al.* (1976, 31) in their corpus of newspaper texts from the period 1968-72, found 723 examples out of 753 showing plural agreement, equivalent to 96 per cent. It is unlikely that a different distribution of sentence types could explain the difference between the agreements found in literary and newspaper texts – there is surely a real difference in norm, though editing may well be partly responsible for the difference.

7.3 Factor Combinations in Predicate Agreement

Let us now return to our corpora and consider possible combinations of the factors we have discussed so far only in isolation. We have seen that considering each factor separately is insufficient, particularly as there is greater variation in agreement precisely when one or more of the factors favouring plural agreement are absent. We will therefore consider the interaction of the two main factors – word-order and subject type (again omitting the few mixed subjects. We shall then see how 'active' predicates fit into this account.

7.3.1 Word-order and Subject Type

We have observed that subject-predicate word-order and animate subjects both favour plural agreement. As both these factors can be present or absent in a given sentence, there are four possible sentence types to consider. Let us consider first the literary corpora. In Amal'rik the four sentence types show the agreements presented in Table 7.7.

When an animate subject precedes the predicate only plural forms are found:

(15) LR: ... *kogda Katja i   Fedja zapili* (pl) ...   (A 235)
         when Katja and Fedja had a drinking bout

When the subject is animate, but stands after the predicate, the plural is normally found:

(16) LR: *Pečku   mne   počinili* (pl) *brigadir*
The stove [object] for me mended   the brigade-leader
i   muž   kladovščicy . . .   (A 262)
and the husband of the storekeeper

But here the singular is also found:

(17) LR: *V izbuške pri   korovnike   sidel* (sg) *učastkovyj*
In the hut attached to   the cowshed sat   the district
upolnomočennyj i   čelovek v štatskom . . .   (A 230)
representative   and a man · in civilian clothes

When the subject is inanimate, however, singular and plural agreements
are found in roughly equal proportions. For Amal'rik the animacy of
the subject is more important than the word-order.

Table 7.7: Amal'rik

subject type	animate subject			inanimate subject		
word order	sg	pl	%pl	sg	pl	%pl
subject-predicate	0	23	100	3	4	57
predicate-subject	3	24	89	13	12	48

Let us consider Vojnovič next, since he presents a rather different
picture, as Table 7.8 shows. The combination of animate subject with
subject-predicate order again guarantees a plural verb. What is different
is that all predicates which follow the subject show plural agreement.

Table 7.8: Vojnovič

subject type	animate subject			inanimate subject		
word order	sg	pl	%pl	sg	pl	%pl
subject-predicate	0	32	100	0	12	100
predicate-subject	2	15	88	12	5	29

For Vojnovič, unlike Amal'rik, word-order seems of greater weight than
the animacy of the subject. We noted in §7.2.3 that the combination of
animate subject and active predicate is insufficient to guarantee a plural
predicate in the Vojnovič corpus: the two exceptional cases are these:

(18) LR: *Ego rabotoj   rukovodil* (sg) *sekretar'*
His work [object] directed   the secretary

> *rajkoma*   *Borisov,*
> of the district committee Borisov
> *predrajispolkoma*
> the chairman of the district executive committee
> *Samudorov i*   *redaktor*   *Ermolkin.*
> Samudorov and the editor Ermolkin
>   (V *Pretendent* 207)

(19) LR: *Emu zvonil* (sg) *i*   *polkovnik Dobren'kij, i*   *Borisov,*
         Him rang   and colonel   Dobren'kij   and Borisov
         i   *kto-to*   *ešče.*
         and someone else
         (V *Pretendent* 341)

In both of these the predicate precedes the subject. Even so, when the subject is animate, the plural is much more common than the singular. When neither of the factors favouring the plural is present, then the singular predominates:

(20) LR: *Teper' na nej byl* (sg)   *sinij*   *kostjum*
         Now   on her was (i.e. she was wearing) a blue dress
         i   *novaja belaja bluzka* . . .
         and a new white blouse
         (V *Putëm* 132)

Nabokov is similar to Vojnovič in that word-order is more important than the animacy of the subject (Table 7.9). The remarkable feature here is that in the absence of both factors which favour the plural, the singular is greatly preferred.

Table 7.9: Nabokov

subject type word order	animate subject			inanimate subject		
	sg	pl	%pl	sg	pl	%pl
subject-predicate	0	11	100	0	12	100
predicate-subject	2	6	75	29	3	9

Solženicyn strikes an interesting balance, as Table 7.10 shows. The combination of the two factors ensures a plural, either factor by itself favours the plural (roughly to the same degree), and in the absence of both there is no preference. We will now compare and combine the percentage figures, again showing the relative frequency with which each sentence type occurs (Table 7.11).

The column headed '% of corpus' gives the proportion of sentences which fall into the category in question; thus 28 per cent of the examples from Amal'rik have an animate subject standing before the predicate.[8] There is considerable variation between the different authors in their use of the different sentence types. The most notable peculiarity is shown by Nabokov: just over half his examples have inanimate subjects standing after the predicate and the great majority of these show

Table 7.10: Solženicyn

subject type word-order	animate subject			inanimate subject		
	sg	pl	%pl	sg	pl	%pl
subject-predicate	0	11	100	5	17	77
predicate-subject	4	10	71	6	6	50

Table 7.11: Literary Corpora

subject type word-order	animate subject		inanimate subject	
	%pl	% of corpus	%pl	% of corpus
subject-predicate:				
Amal'rik	100	28	57	9
Nabokov	100	17	100	19
Solženicyn	100	19	77	37
Vojnovič	100	41	100	15
Total:	*100*	27	*85*	19
predicate-subject:				
Amal'rik	89	33	48	30
Nabokov	75	13	9	51
Solženicyn	71	24	50	20
Vojnovič	88	22	29	22
Total:	*83*	23	*30*	30

singular agreement. However, the overall picture which emerges is clear and elegant (as shown by the italicised figures). If both factors favouring the plural are present, then the plural results. If either one is present, then the plural is strongly preferred. If neither is present, then the singular is preferred.

Let us compare this with the evidence from the dialects, presented in Table 7.12. The first important difference shown by this table is that in the dialects the combination of subject-predicate word-order and an

Table 7.12: Dialects

word-order	subject type	animate subject			inanimate subject		
		sg	pl	%pl	sg	pl	%pl
subject-predicate		8	45	85	7	1	13
predicate-subject		10	17	63	4	1	20

animate subject does not guarantee a plural predicate, as the following examples illustrate:[9]

(21) DR: *Ot'ec/   mat'   prišla* (fem sg)   (D 64)
         Father (and) mother came

(Recall that / denotes an intonational break.)

(22) DR: *Dva syna-da-doc'   byla* (fem sg)...   (D63)
         Two sons and daughter was

In these sentences agreement is with the nearer conjunct only. Table 7.12 also shows that the nature of the subject is more important in determining agreement than the word-order. Predicate-subject word-order is unusual and the plural is rare in such sentences, but there are too few examples to draw any conclusion about the effect of word-order when the noun phrases refer to inanimates.

In this section we have cross-classified the examples according to two factors – the animacy of the subject and its position relative to the predicate. When the subject is animate and precedes the predicate, plural agreement is found in all instances in our literary corpora, and in the majority of cases in the dialects. If only one factor favouring plural agreement is found then this will give a higher frequency of plural agreement than when neither factor is present (the only instance where this does not hold, in the dialects, is not significant as there are insufficient examples). It is important to observe that neither factor has absolute priority over the other. If it were the case that the word-order mattered only for inanimate subjects, then we would conclude that the animacy of the subject was of a different order of significance to the word-order. But this is not the case. We did observe that for Nabokov and Vojnovič all the examples with subject-predicate word-order show plural agreement irrespective of animacy. Unless this situation persists with larger samples it would be safer not to claim that they differ radically from the other writers (and those presented later in Table

7.17); rather we should restrict ourselves to the more modest claim that for Nabokov and Vojnovič word-order is more important than animacy. While the literary and dialect corpora differ in the relative importance of the two factors, and indeed the authors differ among themselves, the likelihood of plural agreement depends on the presence or absence of both factors. We shall return to the nature of these two factors in §8.1. For our present purposes, the important thing is to have established that both factors affect agreement, that their relative importance varies, but that neither is completely subordinate to the other.

7.3.2 The 'Active' Factor

Since cross-classifying for the two main factors has produced such encouraging results, we should now ask whether the 'activity' of the predicate can be incorporated into this scheme. Recall that an 'active' predicate is not just one that is morphologically active, but one that refers to an activity rather than a state. Potapova restricted consideration to subjects referring to persons, but this seems unjustified. It is reasonable to label the following predicate as 'active':

(23) LR: ... *grob,   muzyka,   toržestvennaja pečal'*
          the coffin the music the solemn   sadness
          obstanovki   dejstvovali (pl) *na   nee tak,*
          of the surroundings acted   upon her in such a way
          čto ona zaplakala ...
          that she started to cry
          (V *Pretendent* 237)

In fact it is preferable to view the question from the point of view of the controller: subjects may be animate or inanimate, and in addition they may operate as animates (moving, doing, etc.) or as inanimates (being, remaining, etc.). Thus some subjects are more animate than others. We have a scale of four possibilities; as shown in Table 7.13.

Let us examine the agreements found when subjects are classified in these terms. In order to ensure a reasonable number of examples of the different types, we combine the literary corpora in Table 7.14 (again the few 'mixed' subjects are omitted). The regularity displayed in the table is quite remarkable: in each of the main sentence types where there is a choice of agreement, the subjects which are 'active' show a higher proportion of plural predicate agreement. In the dialects, the number of inanimate subjects is too small for meaningful figures

Table 7.13: Degrees of Animacy

animate		inanimate	
operating as animate ('active')	not operating as animate ('non-active')	operating as animate ('active')	not operating as animate ('non-active')
(1)	(2)	(3)	(4)

←——most animate   least animate ——→

to be calculated, but in the animate subjects an interesting picture emerges (Table 7.15).

We can see from Table 7.15 that the animate subjects are clearly differentiated according to 'activity';[10] this is relevant in subject-predicate sentences, whereas in the literary corpora the distinction is irrelevant in such sentences, as there the plural is obligatory. It is evident, particularly from Table 7.14, that the 'activity' of the subject is a subsidiary classification, at a lower level than animacy. If the first classification were according to 'activity', then the regularity of Tables 7.14 and 7.15 would be lost. This indicates that the factors of animacy and 'activity' are hierarchically related, with animacy being the more significant factor. This hierarchical relationship confirms the view that 'activity' should be viewed as a factor relating to the subject, being a subdivision of animacy rather than an unrelated factor.

In this section we have observed the way in which the major factors influencing agreement interrelate. We will return to word-order and animacy in §7.5, where we investigate their position in diachronic change. First, however, we must consider less important factors which also affect predicate agreement.

7.4 Other Factors which Influence Predicate Agreement

The factors we have isolated so far have a major influence on predicate agreement. They operate both in the literary language and in the dialects, though their relative importance varies between the two. There are two other, less significant factors, relating to the nature of the subject, which influence predicate agreement and so require attention.

As explained earlier, subjects with one or more plural conjuncts were included, providing there was a singular conjunct next to the predicate. The number of such examples in the sample is relatively small (e.g. 6/84 in Amal'rik, 7/80 in Vojnovič). When the subject occurs after the

Table 7.14: The 'Active' Factor in the Literary Corpora

subject type	animate						inanimate					
	active			inactive			active			inactive		
word-order	sg	pl	%pl	sg	pl	%pl	sg	pl	%pl	sg	pl	%pl
subject-predicate	0	52	100	0	25	100	3	22	88	5	23	82
predicate-subject	2	29	94	9	26	74	7	8	53	53	18	25

Table 7.15: The 'Active' Factor in the Dialects

subject type	animate						inanimate					
	active			inactive			active			inactive		
word-order	sg	pl	%pl	sg	pl	%pl	sg	pl	%pl	sg	pl	%pl
subject-predicate	4	32	89	4	13	76	5	0	(0)	2	1	(33)
predicate-subject	2	8	80	8	9	53	1	1	(50)	3	0	(0)

predicate, both singular and plural agreement forms are found. In (24), the verb agrees with the nearer (singular) conjunct:

(24) LR: *Na sosednem stule ležala* (sg) *furažka* (sg) *s   vysokoj*
On a nearby   chair lay   a cap   with high
tul'ej   i   brošennye poverx nee belye perčatki (pl).
crown and thrown   over   it   white gloves
(V *Pretendent* 178)

In (25), however, a plural is found:

(25) LR: *V magazine prodajutsja* (pl) *vodka* (sg), *vino* (sg),
In the shop are sold   vodka   wine
saxar (sg), *krupi* (pl), *pečen'e* (sg), *konfety* (pl), *rastitel'noe*
sugar   groats   biscuit(s)   sweets   vegetable
maslo (sg), *konservy* (pl), *mužskaja i   ženskaja*
oil   tinned foods men's   and women's
odežda (sg) *v nebol'šom vybore,*
clothing   in restricted choice
posuda (sg) . . .   (A 175)
crockery

Of course, in such examples a plural predicate is possible even without a plural conjunct. While we find singular and plural predicates when a subject containing a plural conjunct stands after the predicate, the picture is different with subject-predicate word-order. In the literary corpora, plural agreement is found in all the examples in which a plural occurs before the predicate:

(26) LR: *Ego ruki* (pl), *život* (sg), *koleni* (pl), *i   daže odna*
His hands   stomach knees   and even one
ščeka (sg) *byli* (pl) *v grjazi*
cheek   were   muddy
(V *Pretendent* 49)

Given that the number of examples is small, we must be cautious. Nevertheless, it is a reasonable hypothesis that a plural conjunct standing before the predicate requires plural agreement (unless, of course, it is parenthetic). We will call this hypothesis the Preceding Plural Constraint. This constraint does not hold for the dialects, as the following example shows:

(27) DR: *Kartoški* (pl) / *morkoška* (sg) / *r'it'ka* (sg) / *luk* (sg)
       Potatoes   carrot   radish   onion
       rost'ot (sg) / *br'ukva*   (D 65)
       grows (and) swede

Thus the Preceding Plural Constraint may be valid, but only for the literary language, not for the dialects. (Nor does it hold for Serbo-Croat. Though there were no counter-examples in the corpus described in §6.2.2, Megaard (1976, 109) notes the existence of rare examples.) The fact that the constraint is not generally valid indicates that it is a minor factor.

Our second point concerns conjoined noun phrases which have a plural attributive modifier referring to them all. In such instances the predicate is plural, for example:

(28) LR: ... *v toj že   komnate na Nikitstkom, vposledstvii*
          in that same room   on Nikitskij   subsequently
          Suvorovskom bul'vare, gde   prošli (pl) *moi* (pl)
          Suvorovskij   boulevard where passed   my
          detstvo   i   junost' ...   (A 204)
          childhood and youth

As we saw in §2.1.7, the presence of a plural attributive modifier like *moi* is itself rare — the singular is more common. All the examples with plural attributive modifiers in the literary corpora, and all the others found elsewhere, show plural predicate agreement (there were no examples in the dialect corpus). This is a case of the Agreement Hierarchy applying as a sentence-level constraint (§4.1). Note that a singular modifier does not demand a singular predicate; both predicate types are found:

(29) LR: ... *no kakovo* (neut sg) *že bylo* (neut sg) *moe* (neut sg)
          but what   was   my
          udivlenie (neut sg) *i   ogorčenie* (neut sg), *kogda*
          surprise   and dismay   when
          ja uvidel ...   (A 261)
          I saw

(30) LR: *No kakovy* (pl) *že byli* (pl) *moe* (neut sg)
          But what   were   my
          udivlenie (neut sg) *i   užas* (masc sg), *kogda Novikov*
          surprise   and horror   when Novikov

> *otkryl sejf...* (A 211)
> opened the safe

These two sentences are similar in structure and are from the same author, but they show different agreements. It may be that the fact that the nouns in (30) are of different genders favours the plural, but in the corpora as a whole the evidence does not justify such a claim. It seems, rather, that this is a sentence type where there is a genuine choice (and where the attributive modifier is irrelevant). As we saw in §7.2.1, when inanimate conjoined noun phrases follow the predicate, both agreement forms are found, and there is considerable variation between the corpora. Thus, although we have established factors which clearly favour a particular agreement form, these factors still permit considerable variation.

7.5 Diachronic Change

It is worth considering the development of the two systems we have discussed. Borkovskij (1978, 35-8) outlines the position in Old Russian (his monograph covers the eleventh to seventeenth centuries). In Old Russian, animate subjects preceding the predicate took plural agreement (or dual agreement, up to the fourteenth century, if there were two singular conjuncts); singular agreement was rare. In all other sentence types, however, singular agreement was normal. Unfortunately he gives no statistics. This situation is represented in Figure 7.1. The shaded area represents plural agreement, which was dominant – though not obligatory – if animate noun phrases preceded the verb, and in the minority elsewhere. Figure 7.2 represents the dialect data in the same fashion, and shows that in the dialects the animacy factor has become sufficient to produce plural agreement in many cases, irrespective of the word-order; the overall use of plural agreement has increased. Modern Literary Russian shows a further increase in plural agreement, as shown in Figure 7.3. Here the presence of either factor makes plural agreement very likely; furthermore, the likelihood is about the same for the two factors.

It must be borne in mind when comparing the dialects and literary Russian that we are comparing across two dimensions – dialect versus standard, and spoken versus written (the dialect examples are largely from the spoken language). Spoken Standard Russian may be nearer to the dialects than to the written standard: the single shred of evidence

Figure 7.1: Old Russian

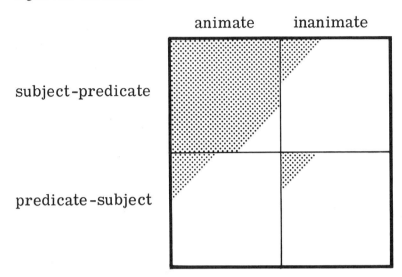

Figure 7.2: Dialects

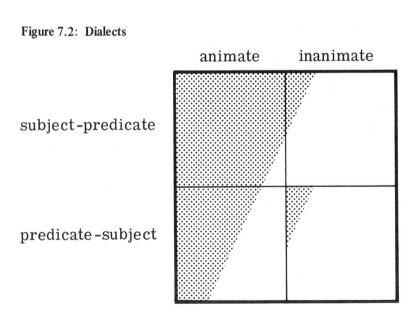

Figure 7.3: Modern Literary Russian

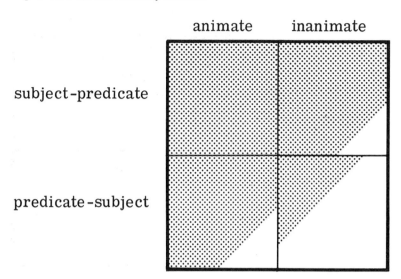

concerns the transcripts of spoken Russian published by Zemskaja and Kapanadze (1978). These include four clear examples of predicate agreement with conjoined noun phrases, of which three show singular agreement. While our understanding is not complete of the way in which agreement of this type varies through time and between language varieties, cross-classifying examples for the two main determining factors gives a much clearer picture than was previously available. From a situation where plural agreement was found only when everything was in its favour (i.e. animate subject and subject-predicate order) we have reached the position when the plural is most likely unless everything is against it (inanimate subject and predicate-subject order).

We have now established the basic trend of development. Earlier we noted that in Modern Literary Russian there is considerable variation between writers. Let us now compare these two sources of variation — diachronic and stylistic — by examining the usage of writers over the last two centuries. As representatives of the nineteenth century, the following works were scanned: all Puškin's major prose works (*Povesti pokojnogo Ivana Petroviča Belkina, Istorija sela Gorjuxina, Roslavlev, Dubrovskij, Pikovaja dama, Kirdžali, Egipetskie noči* and *Kapitanskaja dočka*), which were written between 1830 and 1836; *Mertvye duši* by Gogol' (published 1842); four novels by Turgenev (*Rudin, Dvorjanskoe gnezdo*, *Nakanune*, *Otcy i deti*), published between 1856 and 1862; and Čexov's short stories of the period 1898 to 1903, which we have counted as belonging to the nineteenth century (*U znakomyx*, *Junič*, *Čelovek v futljare*, *Kryžovnik*, *O ljubvi*, *Slučaj iz praktiki*, *Po delam služby*, *Dušečka*, *Novaja dača*, *Dama s sobačkoj*, *V ovrage*, *Na svjatkax*, *Arxierej*, *Nevesta*).

The results are given in Table 7.16. In each sample, when conjoined noun phrases referring to animates precede the predicate, a plural predicate results. Inanimates standing before the verb very often take a plural predicate, while animates after the predicate do so less frequently. When the noun phrases are inanimate and follow the verb, the plural is found only in a minority of cases. The effect of precedence is more marked than that of animacy (the total figure for inanimates before the predicate, 91 per cent, is much higher than the 61 per cent found for animates after the predicate). The sentence types where we find the greatest differences between writers are the two with predicate-subject word-order. While there is indeed considerable variation, it is interesting to note that two profiles are very similar – those of Puškin and Čexov. Thus the two writers furthest separated in time are the closest in terms of the agreements shown, while writers closer in time show greater variation in their patterns of agreement. This indicates that for the period covered in Table 7.16, individual stylistic differences outweigh chronological differences.

Let us turn to the twentieth century for comparison. The data presented in Table 7.17 are from the corpora examined earlier in the chapter, with the addition of Panova's *Sputniki* (1946)[11] and *General'-naja repeticija* (1974) by Galič.

Table 7.17 reveals the now familiar pattern – plural when animacy and word-order both favour it, a majority of examples in the plural when only one factor favours it, and a generally substantial minority of plural forms even when inanimate noun phrases stand after the predicate. Compared with the nineteenth century, there is a smaller difference between agreement with inanimates before the subject and with animates after it; the totals in fact are very close (85 per cent as opposed to 84 per cent). In this respect Amal'rik stands out as the only writer in our selection whose figure for post-predicate animates (89 per cent) is significantly higher than that for pre-predicate inanimates (57 per cent); Panova shows a marginally higher figure for post-predicate animates (91 per cent). When we compare the total figures with those from the nineteenth century, we see that the effect of animacy has increased considerably. In those sentences where the animacy of the

Table 7.16: Nineteenth-century Russian

		animate			inanimate		
		sg	pl	%pl	sg	pl	%pl
Puškin (1830–6)	subject-predicate	0	30	100	2	31	94
	predicate-subject	3	2	40	9	4	31
Gogol' (1842)	subject-predicate	0	19	100	1	7	88
	predicate-subject	3	5	63	14	8	36
Turgenev (1856–62)	subject-predicate	0	31	100	3	17	85
	predicate-subject	2	10	83	19	1	5
Čexov (1898–1903)	subject-predicate	0	63	100	1	15	94
	predicate-subject	6	5	45	19	11	37
Total	subject-predicate	0	143	100	7	70	91
	predicate-subject	14	22	61	61	24	28

Table 7.17: Twentieth-century Russian

		animate			inanimate		
		sg	pl	%pl	sg	pl	%pl
Nabokov (1930)	subject-predicate	0	11	100	0	12	100
	predicate-subject	2	6	75	29	3	9
Panova (1946)	subject-predicate	0	28	100	1	7	88
	predicate-subject	1	10	91	17	3	15
Amal'rik (1970)	subject-predicate	0	23	100	3	4	57
	predicate-subject	3	24	89	13	12	48
Galič (1974)	subject-predicate	0	10	100	1	5	83
	predicate-subject	2	10	83	5	3	38
Solženicyn (1975)	subject-predicate	0	11	100	5	17	77
	predicate-subject	4	10	71	6	6	50
Vojnovič (1979)	subject-predicate	0	32	100	0	12	100
	predicate-subject	2	15	88	12	5	29
Total	subject-predicate	0	115	100	10	57	85
	predicate-subject	14	75	84	82	32	28

subject but not the word-order favours plural agreement, the latter type of agreement is found in 84 per cent of the cases as opposed to 61 per cent in the last century. The two factors are now of about equal weight (84 per cent and 85 per cent) while there was a marked discrepancy in the last century (61 per cent and 91 per cent).

The data are presented graphically in Figure 7.4, which shows particularly clearly how the presence of both factors favouring plural agreement guarantees a plural predicate, while in the absence of both factors the percentage for plural agreement is always the lowest. When one factor is present but not the other, then there is considerable variety, though the gap between the two factors (animate subject but after the predicate, as opposed to inanimate subject before the predicate) has narrowed over the course of the last two centuries. Nevertheless, the differences between the writers are more striking than this trend. We have a fine illustration of the theme of pattern and variation. On the one hand, there are two factors which favour plural predicate agreement. With both present, we find plural agreement; if either one is present, then the percentage of plural agreements is higher than if neither is present. This pattern holds absolutely. On the other hand, within these constraints we find considerable variation, both diachronic and stylistic.

7.6 Conclusion

In order to determine the factors relating to the controller which influence agreement, we investigated predicate agreement with conjoined noun phrases. We have demonstrated that there are two major factors at work: animacy and word-order. The influence of these two factors is quite clear, in all the various corpora we have investigated. While animate subjects and subject-predicate word-order always favour plural agreement, they may do so with different intensity both taken together and relative to each other. While in Old Russian the plural was normally found only when both factors were present, in Modern Russian the plural predominates if either of the factors is present. In the modern literary language the two factors are of approximately equal weight, while in the dialects, animacy has the stronger influence; in the literary language of the last century it was word-order which was the stronger. Thus the overall pattern of agreement is clear, but within this pattern there is still room for considerable variation through time, between dialectal and literary usage, and resulting from differences in individual styles.

Figure 7.4: Diachronic and Stylistic Variation

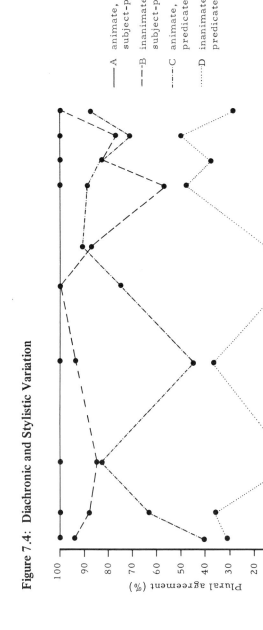

Notes

1. For previous research in this area see Potapova (1962, 59–60), Crockett (1976, 209–313) and the references given in both. Sobinnikova (1969, 11–18) gives dialect examples, but no statistical data.

2. For instance, the total number of examples varies without explanation between pages 62 and 64, 66 and 67. In fact a careful study of pages 66–7 will convince the reader that it would be unwise to use Potapova's figures without a careful recounting.

3. Page references are to the following editions: A. Amal'rik (1970) *Neželannoe putešestvie v Sibir'*, New York, Harcourt Brace Jovanovich; V. Nabokov (1930) *Zaščita Lužina*, Paris, Éditions de la Seine; A. Solženicyn (1975) *Arxipelag GULag*, V–VI–VII, Paris, YMCA; V. N. Vojnovič (1979a) *Pretendent na prestol: novye priključenija soldata Ivana Čonkina*, Paris, YMCA and (1979b) *Putëm vzaimnoj perepiski*, Paris, YMCA.

(The Solženicyn text was scanned for a different project, and it is possible that a small number of relevant examples has been omitted; if so, this is most unlikely to affect the percentage figures to any significant degree.)

4. Examples in which the nearest conjunct was a quantified noun phrase were eliminated. As we saw in §6.1.3, quantified expressions may take singular or plural agreement. If the nearest conjunct is a quantified expression, plural agreement could result either from agreement with the quantified expression or from agreement with all conjuncts.

Two other examples were eliminated from our sample. In one, the subject consists of so-called 'unspecified noun phrases':

(i) LR: *I   to,   i   drugoe,   i   tret'e,*   *razumeetsja, bylo* (sg)
     And that and the other and the third (thing) of course   was
     vypolneno (sg) *nemedlenno.*
     carried out   immediately
     (V *Pretendent* 326)

As has been pointed out elsewhere (Corbett, 1979a, 2–31), a special 'neutral' form is normally used in such sentences. The last sentence excluded from the sample was the following:

(ii) LR: *I   ètot čvanlivyj   samodur   i   groza vsej roty . . .*
      And this swaggering petty tyrant and terror of the whole company
      bežal (sg) *po   vsemu   koridoru . . .*
      ran   along the whole corridor
      (V *Putëm* 224–5)

In such sentences, where the conjoined noun phrases have the same singular referent, the predicate always stands in the singular.

5. Two examples have compound predicates consisting of a plural verb and a singular noun and are recorded in this chapter as having a plural predicate. They are presented and discussed in §9.2 (examples (15) and 16)); see also note 3 in that chapter.

6. Chi-square is the appropriate statistical test for situations in which examples are classified into different categories. If, in the case in question, we believed there was no difference in agreement between the literary language and the Perm' dialects, then any difference in the distribution of singular and plural forms between the corpora would be random. Chi-square gives us the likelihood of a particular distribution arising by chance. (Any statistics textbook will describe

how chi-square is calculated. For a clear account, which includes the reasoning behind the calculation, see Chase, 1967, 174–84.) Though we are given the likelihood of the distribution arising by chance, we must still make the judgement as to whether our result is significant or not. Herdan (1964, 101), writing on statistics for linguistic purposes, suggests that a distribution which would occur by chance on one occasion in 20 should be regarded as significant. We will adopt a stricter position, accepting only distributions which would occur by chance once in 100. On every occasion the result of the chi-square test will be spelt out in terms of the likelihood of the distribution resulting by chance, so that readers with no statistical background can evaluate the data for themselves. In the case in question, we obtain a value for chi-square of 15.00, which is well above the value required for significance at the .001 level, given one degree of freedom. In other words, the distribution observed would occur by chance less than once in a thousand tries. It is therefore reasonable to believe that this difference between the literary language and the dialects is a significant one.

7. An alternative is to divide the subjects into three groups: persons (type 1), any other animates, including mixed subjects (2–7) and inanimates (8). We then combine the literary corpora, in order to obtain a reasonable figure for the 'other animate' category.

Table 7.i: Alternative Division of Subject Types

corpus	dialects			literary texts		
subject type	sg	pl	%pl	sg	pl	%pl
person	14	54	79	10	125	93
other animate	5	8	62	6	10	63
inanimate	11	2	15	68	71	51

The percentage figures reveal an attractively clear picture; we should view this picture with considerable caution, however, in view of the small number of examples in the middle category. Since we wish to be able to compare the literary corpora with each other in what follows, we will retain the simpler division into animates and inanimates, excluding mixed subjects.

8. The percentage figures for the total corpus add up to 99, due to rounding to whole numbers. Apparent discrepancies between Table 7.11 and Table 7.6 result from the exclusion of mixed subjects.

9. Similar sentences are quoted by Xitrova (1964, 125) from the Novo-Usmanskij district (Voronež region):

(iii) DR: *Timoxa i   tovarišč jago ušel* (sg)
      Timoxa and friend   his   left
(iv) DR: *Dva   Van'ki dy Njus'kja dy Andrjuxz pajexzl* (sg)
      The two Van'kas and Njus'kja and Andrjuxa set off
      kudy   nja pomnju
      whither (I do) not remember
      (z indicates a reduced central vowel)

10. To continue the investigation of the subject, it appears sensible to subdivide the inanimate subjects into concrete and abstract. If we omit all mixed subjects, along with any subjects whose status is open to any doubt, the distribution is as in Table 7.ii. The results here are spectacularly unimpressive. It may be that a larger corpus would reveal a distinction.

Table 7.ii: Concrete and Abstract Subjects

subject type corpus	concrete subject			abstract subject		
	sg	pl	%pl	sg	pl	%pl
Dialects	10	1	9	1	1	(50)
Amal'rik	8	8	50	8	8	50
Nabokov	14	8	36	10	6	38
Solženicyn	2	7	78	8	10	56
Vojnovič	9	11	55	3	6	67
Total (literary corpora)	33	34	51	29	30	51

11. One example with two animates and an inanimate conjoined (and a plural verb) was necessarily omitted.

12. For the sake of clarity, the spacing between authors is only approximately proportional to the chronological difference.

In the previous chapter we established the effect of animacy and word-order on predicate agreement with conjoined noun phrases in Russian. Animate subjects are more likely to take plural (semantically justified) agreement than are inanimates. Similarly, subjects preceding the predicate give rise to plural agreement more frequently than do those which follow. It was claimed that these two factors are the main controller factors. In this chapter we will first make this claim more explicit, by reviewing the two factors in question and discussing why they are treated as controller factors (§8.1). We will then extend our claim in two ways: first, by showing that animacy and word-order affect agreement with conjoined noun phrases in Slavic languages other than Russian (§8.2); and second, by demonstrating their role in agreement with other types of subject – with comitative phrases (§8.3) and with quantified expressions (§8.4). (We move on to positions beyond the predicate in Chapter 9.) We will see that although the impact of the two factors varies from language to language and from construction to construction, their basic effect remains unchanged: animate controllers and controllers preceding their targets favour semantically justified agreement forms.

8.1 Animacy and Precedence as Controller Factors

The influence of these two factors in Russian has already been demonstrated, and we will confirm their importance in later sections. Let us now review their status as controller factors.

Animacy, beyond any doubt, relates to the controller: the noun or nouns which are included in the controller may refer to animates, in which case the controller is considered animate. This is not to say that animacy is completely straightforward. As we observed in §7.2.2, there is a small proportion of subjects which it is difficult to classify as animate or inanimate. Given a very large corpus, it might be possible to justify setting up subdivisions of animacy, for example by separating humans from non-humans (as suggested in Chapter 7, note 7), although evidence to be presented in §8.3.1 indicates that this is by no means certain. However, we did establish in §7.3.2 that both animate and inanimate subjects can be subdivided according to whether the subject is operating as an animate or not. This suggests that some controllers are more animate than others (cf. Ransom, 1977, 421-4; Comrie, 1981, 178-93).

While there is no doubt that animacy is a controller factor, the position is not so clear in the case of word-order.[1] We saw in §7.2.1 that when the controller (subject) precedes the target (predicate), this favours semantically justified agreement. But we must still consider why this should be treated as a factor relating to the controller, rather than to the target or both.

There is one general argument why we should consider the positioning of the controller before the target to be a controller factor, which runs as follows. There are various ordering phenomena reported in the linguistic literature. In these, word-order is normally treated in terms of the preceding element. A clear case is Langacker's account of pronominalisation, where he refers explicitly to 'precedence' (1969).

Our second argument rests on the well-documented fact that definite noun phrases in Slavic tend to occur earlier in the sentence than do indefinites. The following, oft-quoted minimal pair gives a clear illustration:

(1) R: *Prišel poezd*
        came train
        (A train came)
(2) R: *Poezd prišel*
        train came
        (the train came)

When the noun phrase is definite, as in (2), it precedes the verb. The motivation for placing it there — definiteness — is clearly a factor which relates to the noun phrase. It is therefore reasonable to treat position before the target as a factor relating to the controller. This argument is not vitiated by the fact that the subject-verb order is normal in Slavic, because it is also the case that subjects are more often definite than not.

More specifically still, the data presented in Chapter 7 showed a close interplay between the factors of animacy and word-order. While they are independent, they have tended in Russian to 'balance' each other during the present century. This suggests — no more than that — that they are factors of the same type.

Animacy and word-order are related through a number of other properties, notably that of topic. One factor which makes a noun phrase more likely to be treated as the topic is definiteness: thus the noun phrase in (2) is definite and is the topic. A second such factor is animacy – animate noun phrases are more likely to be topics than are inanimates. Given that topic noun phrases typically stand in initial or near-initial position, animacy and word-order are linked. Further proposals for 'topic-worthiness' include individuation and the closely related notion of salience, both of which include reference to animacy (cf. Givón, 1976, 152; Ransom, 1977, 424-7; Comrie, 1981, 191-2). The interrelationship of all these concepts confirms the link between animacy and word-order – in particular, the positioning of the noun phrase early in the sentence, certainly before the verb. In view of these links and of the earlier arguments, we will treat word-order as a controller factor, and so refer to 'precedence' for the case where the controller precedes the target. It is not, however, essential that this view be adopted. The data to be presented below demonstrate the effect of word-order and readers can if they wish interpret this in a different way. We will continue our analysis in terms of animacy and precedence, rather than adopting the notion of topic. Topic is a particularly difficult term, which has a wide variety of interpretations (but see note 1 for a discussion of an unusual but unambiguous definition). While there are occasional difficult cases involving animacy or precedence, in the vast majority of examples the animacy of a noun phrase and its position relative to the predicate are beyond doubt. It is therefore methodologically more sound to establish patterns based on the clear criteria of animacy and precedence. The way is then left open for interpretation in terms of topic, while the presentation of the data is not weakened by the use of unclear criteria.

While we will in the main treat animacy and precedence as binary properties in this chapter, it is worth repeating that further division may be possible, as has already been discussed for animacy. In the case of precedence, if we treat certain controllers as preceding their targets 'more' or 'less' than others, then we can accommodate the notion of 'real distance', which was discussed in §4.3.2 and §5.1. As noted there, several researchers have claimed that when the subject and predicate are widely separated, the likelihood of semantically justifiable agreement increases (e.g. Faska, 1959, 51; Mullen, 1967, 55). The sentences quoted involve subject-predicate word-order. This means that the further the controller is to the left of the target, the more likely is semantically justifiable agreement. Thus the subject may precede the predicate to a greater or lesser extent.

Refinement of the criteria of animacy and precedence deserves further attention. It is, however, normally quite clear whether a controller precedes its target or not, and the basic distinction of animacy is usually unproblematic. As we will confirm below, these two controller factors exert a major influence on agreement choices.

8.2 Conjoined Noun Phrases in Serbo-Croat and Other Slavic Languages

Having established animacy and precedence as major controller factors, we can now extend the claims based upon them to languages other than Russian. Various investigators who have analysed predicate agreement with conjoined noun phrases have reported the effect of animacy and precedence: in every case animate subjects and subjects standing before the predicate favour the semantically justifiable form. Thus Megaard (1976, 108–39) states that both factors operate in Serbo-Croat, and Faska (1959, 58–60) makes similar claims for Sorbian. Kallas (1974, 67–8) shows the effect of word-order in Polish, but does not consider animacy, while Zdaniukiewicz (1973, 152–3), ignoring word-order, suggests that animacy has an effect. Comments on the role of word-order are made by Popov (1963, 135) in Bulgarian, Trávníček (1949, 414–15) in Czech, Pauliny *et al.* (1968, 370) and Orlovský (1965, 118–19) in Slovak, Krivickij *et al.* (1973, 173) in Belorussian and Shevelov (1963, 62) in Ukrainian. Unfortunately, even those who mention both animacy and word-order do not cross-classify for the two factors, as was done in §7.3. In order to establish comparable data, a Serbo-Croat corpus was scanned; it consisted of fourteen short stories by Andrić (listed in §6.2.2). Noun phrases conjoined with *i* 'and', *pa* 'and' and with no conjunction were included. Serbo-Croat has gender agreement in the plural and in Table 8.1 this complicating factor is disregarded (it is discussed in §10.3.3); only agreement in number is considered. The sentences are divided into the familiar four types.

When both the animacy and the word-order favour plural agreement, then this is found in all the examples (just as in literary Russian). When neither factor favours plurality, then the singular predominates. When one factor, but not both, is present, then the plural is preferred. Thus the picture which emerges is very similar to that found for Russian (in particular, Russian of the last century, as indicated in Table 7.16). All the evidence available — that provided by other investigators and

Table 8.1: **Predicate Agreement with Conjoined Noun Phrases in Serbo-Croat**

subject type	animate			inanimate		
word order	sg	pl	%pl	sg	pl	%pl
subject-predicate	0	21	100	3	32	91
predicate-subject	7	16	70	46	16	26

the data on Serbo-Croat in Table 8.1 — indicate that both animate subjects and subject-predicate word-order favour the semantically justifiable agreement form in other Slavic languages, just as they do in Russian. Naturally the degree of preference, and the influence of the two factors relative to each other, can vary.

8.3 Comitative Phrases and Precedence

We now turn to consideration of the role of animacy and precedence in other constructions. In our discussion of controller types which permit agreement options (§6.1), we considered comitative phrases and quantified expressions, before selecting conjoined noun phrases as the first controller type to investigate. An important reason for rejecting comitative phrases, besides their relative infrequency, was the fact that the nouns involved are almost always inanimate. This gives little scope for investigating the influence of animacy, but we can still consider the role of word-order. Nichols *et al.* (1980, 375) asked native speakers for their judgements on the following textual example:

> (3) R: *Avdeev so   svoim   vedomym čut'   bylo ne otpravili* (pl)
>   Avdeev with his own co-pilot   almost   sent
>   *na tot   svet   fon Manštejna.*
>   to the other world von Mannstein
>   (N. I. Krylov)

Their informants favoured the plural verb, as in the example. The singular form *otpravil*, which shows agreement with the head noun *Avdeev* only, was considered marginally acceptable. However, when the sentence was rearranged with the comitative phrase after the predicate, both forms were found equally acceptable:

(4) R: *Fon Manštejna   čut' bylo ne*
    Von Mannstein [object] almost
    otpravil (sg) /*otpravili* (pl) *na tot   svet   Avdeev so*
    sent   to the other world Avdeev with
    svoim   vedomym.
    his own co-pilot

These informant responses indicate that semantically justified agreement with comitative constructions is more likely when the subject precedes the predicate than when it follows. Our examples are from Russian, but a similar claim has been made for Ukrainian (Shevelov, 1963, 60).

While the general effect of precedence matches that found with conjoined noun phrases, it is worth noting that the result is not exactly the same. With conjoined noun phrases in literary Russian, the combination of animacy and precedence (animate subjects before the predicate) was sufficient to guarantee a plural predicate. With animates in a comitative phrase standing before the predicate, as in (3) above, the singular was not excluded by the informants. Furthermore, such examples with a singular predicate can be found in texts:

(5) R: . . . *padčerica   s   detjami priexala* (sg) *gostit'* . . .
    stepdaughter with children came   to visit
    (Panova, *Sputniki*)

The fact that we find a singular verb, even though it is preceded by animates, shows that in comitative constructions the plural is less favoured than with comparable conjoined expressions. The reason is clear – in comitative expressions one of the noun phrases is in the instrumental, and instrumentals do not usually control verb agreement.[2] Note that in (5) the instrumental phrase is plural, which shows that comitative phrases are not subject to the Preceding Plural Constraint, providing that the plural noun phrase stands in the instrumental. In §7.4 we saw that in the literary language agreement with conjoined noun phrases complies with this constraint; here again, therefore, comitative constructions favour the plural less strongly than do conjoined noun phrases. However, the main conclusion to draw from sentences (3) and (4) is that precedence influences comitative constructions in a similar manner to that in which it influences agreement with conjoined noun phrases. Nichols *et al.* also give examples to show that it has a similar effect on agreement with quantified expressions. Here, as mentioned earlier, the picture is complicated by conflicting factors. It is never-theless possible to demonstrate the effect of animacy and of precedence. as we shall see in the next section.

8.4 Quantified Expressions, Animacy and Precedence

Quantified expressions are the main controller type which we have yet to investigate. We have already noted (§6.1.3) that quantified expressions in Slavic may frequently take either singular or plural predicate agreement. These alternatives are illustrated in the following sentences from Rozental' and Telenkova (1972, 285):

(6) R: *V   komnatu vošlo* (sg) *pjat' čelovek*
        Into the room entered   five people
(7) R: *V   komnatu vošli* (pl) *pjat' čelovek*
        Into the room entered   five people

Both these sentences are fully acceptable. It has been claimed that in such cases animacy and precedence both play their part. It is clearly plural agreement which has the greater semantic justification (since more than one individual is involved) and this form is more likely if there is an animate controller or if the controller stands before the target. We must look for unambiguous evidence to back these common but rarely justified claims. This task is complicated by the fact that the quantifiers themselves differ markedly in their influence on the agree-ment form to be used. For example, taken as a group the numerals 5-10 in Russian take singular and plural agreement with equal fre-quency; in fact Suprun (1969, 185) found 220 examples, of which exactly half showed singular agreement, and half plural agreement. For the quantifier *mnogo* 'many', on the other hand, he found a total of 168 examples, of which only two showed plural agreement. (Further data are given in Table 11.13.) If we were to classify examples only according to animacy and word-order, our results could be dis-torted by the distribution of the actual quantifiers within the different categories. There are two ways to avoid this problem. The first is to use a very large corpus; it is then most unlikely that individual quanti-fiers will influence the totals to an unacceptable degree. The second method is to investigate a single quantifier only; this ensures that any variation observed must have its source elsewhere. (An alternative to the second approach is to use a small and clearly defined group of quantifiers.) Using these techniques, we will first consider evidence showing the effect of animacy on agreement with quantified expressions (§8.4.1) and then move on to precedence (§8.4.2). Having established that both factors do indeed have an effect we then consider their interaction. We will compare this relationship in agreement with quantified expressions with the role of these factors in agreement with conjoined noun phrases (§8.4.3).

8.4.1 Animacy

There are clear statistical data to demonstrate the effect of animacy on agreement with quantified expressions in Russian, in a doctoral dissertation by Patton (1969), based on a substantial corpus. Patton took examples from literary works of the last and present century, and from the newspaper *Pravda*. She divided the quantified expressions into those referring to persons, those referring to animals and those referring to inanimates. The figures in Table 8.2 have been calculated from different sections of her account (Patton, 1969, 35, 63, 148, 160). (The effect of these calculations is to combine her main and secondary corpus, and to eliminate examples with a plural determiner such as *èti* 'these', where a plural predicate is obligatory.)

Let us first look at the examples where the quantified noun refers to animals. Even in this large corpus, the number of such instances is small and the differences between the three types of text are too large to allow us to draw any firm conclusions about these examples. Given that the overall percentage of plural agreement with expressions referring to animals (62 per cent) matches the percentage for those referring to persons, the two groups can be treated together as animates (which was the approach adopted in §7.2.2). In fact, since the number of examples referring to animals is so small, we may take the figure for persons as representative of the animate category. Let us now compare the animates (persons) with the inanimates. In each section of the corpus — nineteenth-century literature, twentieth-century literature and *Pravda* — the figure for animates is markedly higher than that for inanimates. It is important to note that there is considerable difference between the usage in literature and that of the press, but that the influence of animacy is evident in both areas.

The development of the literary language is particularly interesting. The total percentage of plural agreement has risen from 63 per cent in the nineteenth century to 71 per cent in the twentieth.[3] However, this is not the major change which has occurred. Agreement with quantified expressions referring to animates has remained almost static, but inanimates have become more likely to take plural agreement. (This mirrors the development with conjoined noun phrases seen in Tables 7.16 and 7.17.) In the literary language, therefore, the difference between sentences with an animate quantified subject and those with an inanimate has been considerably reduced; in the language of the press, however, animacy has a major influence. While the extent of the effect of animacy varies between the three sets of texts, the direction of its influence remains constant: animates are always more likely to take plural agreement than are inanimates.

We have demonstrated the effect of animacy using data from a large corpus. Fortunately Patton singles out the quantifier *neskol'ko* 'some, a few' for special attention, and there is comparable evidence available from alternative sources, as we shall see. We can therefore confirm our findings by reference to an individual quantifier, as Table 8.3 shows.

If we consider the columns headed 'animate' and 'inanimate' it is immediately obvious that animacy has a considerable effect. In each part of the corpus, animate nouns quantified by *neskol'ko* are much more likely to show plural agreement than are inanimates. This is the major conclusion to be drawn from the data. It is clear too, however, that there has been a slump in plural agreement from the last to the present century. The overall drop results from a major decline in plural agreement with animates (78 per cent to 39 per cent) balanced against an insignificant rise with inanimates (28 per cent to 29 per cent). Thus agreements with *neskol'ko* have developed in a way diametrically opposed to the overall trend seen in Table 8.2. There we saw inanimates 'catching up' with animates in terms of plural agreement; with *neskol'ko* the animates are 'falling back' to a position nearer the inanimates.

The figures for *neskol'ko* discussed so far (the animate, inanimate and total columns in Table 8.3) are calculated from data in Patton (1969, 51, 154). The number of examples is impressive, given that a single quantifier is involved. However, in view of the dramatic change suggested, we might still wonder whether the result could be a freak. Evidence from other sources suggests strongly that it is not. The data for the nineteenth and twentieth centuries in the 'alternative source' column are taken from Suprun (1969, 185, 188). The difference in agreements between the two centuries which he found would occur by chance less than once in 100 instances (chi-square = 6.84, significant at the 0.01 level, given one degree of freedom). While Suprun does not specify the type of material scanned, the remarkably close correspondence with Patton's figures suggests that he too used literary sources.

Table 8.2: Agreement with Quantified Subjects in Russian

	persons			animals			inanimates			total		
	sg	pl	% pl	sg	pl	% pl	sg	pl	% pl	sg	pl	% pl
nineteenth-century literature	67	180	73	5	20	80	97	94	49	169	294	63
twentieth-century literature	73	192	72	1	8	89	46	98	68	120	298	71
press (*Pravda* 1967–8)	631	890	59	13	3	19	904	548	38	1548	1441	48
total	771	1262	62	19	31	62	1047	740	41	1837	2033	53

Table 8.3: Agreement with *neskol'ko* in Russian

	animate[4]			inanimate			total			alternative source		
	sg	pl	% pl	sg	pl	% pl	sg	pl	% pl	sg	pl	% pl
nineteenth-century literature	7	25	78	29	11	28	36	36	50	151	139	48
twentieth-century literature	20	13	39	10	4	29	30	17	36	137	78	36
press (*Pravda* 1967–8)	13	16	55	57	10	15	70	26	27	174	60	26
total	40	54	57	96	25	21	136	79	37	462	277	37

He does not, unfortunately, give any information on animacy. Nevertheless, the fact that the results match those of Patton so closely suggests that her results can be viewed with confidence. This view is reinforced by the figures given for the press. Here the 'alternative source' is Graudina *et al.* (1976, 28), who investigated newspapers of the period 1968–72. Their larger corpus confirms Patton's figure; we can therefore be confident that plural agreement with *neskol'ko* is used less in the language of the press than in literature. To sum up the discussion of *neskol'ko*, we may say that animacy favours plural agreement in texts of all the types investigated; there has been a decline in plural agreement since the last century in literary texts, while journalistic usage shows least examples of plural agreement.

The data from Patton provide convincing evidence for the effect of animacy on agreement with quantified expressions. First we considered all the quantifiers, assuming that the extremely large number of examples would avoid distortion caused by individual quirks. Then we examined the quantifier *neskol'ko*, which turned out to be particularly interesting, and which confirmed the role of animacy. Patton discussed the effect of word-order on agreement, but does not give figures in the way she does for animacy. However, data are available which demonstrate the role of precedence just as convincingly as Patton's data prove the effect of animacy.

8.4.2 Precedence

In a doctoral dissertation rather like Patton's and based on a similarly impressive number of examples, Sand (1971) investigated agreement with quantified expressions in Serbo-Croat. She drew her examples from literature (works published during the 1960s), non-fiction (mainly history and social sciences, 1951–68) and the press (*Politika* 1969–70). Most of her sources represent the Eastern variant of Serbo-Croat. Sand gives data on various quantifiers and the effect of precedence is apparent.[5] We will first consider a large set of data and then turn to an individual quantifier. The largest category discussed is the cardinal numerals from 5 upwards, including compounds (but excluding compounds with 2, 3 and 4). The data presented in Table 8.4 are derived from Sand (1971, 73–5). It is clear that in each type of text the word-order has a definite effect on the agreement form used. In each case the plural is more frequent when the subject precedes the predicate than when it follows. As in Russian, the semantically justifiable (plural) form is more common in literature than in the press. It is noteworthy that, unlike the Russian examples, these Serbo-Croat quantifiers greatly

Table 8.4: **Agreement with the Numerals Five and Above in Serbo-Croat**

	subject-predicate			predicate-subject			total		
	sg	pl	%pl	sg	pl	%pl	sg	pl	%pl
literature	34	15	31	43	2	4	77	17	18
non-fiction	50	12	19	251	12	5	301	24	7
press	165	34	17	536	7	1	701	41	6
total	249	61	20	830	21	2	1079	82	7

favour singular agreement overall: plural agreement is found in only seven per cent of the cases. Nevertheless, within this strong bias to the singular, the role of precedence has been fully established.[6]

Let us now turn to an individual quantifier to check that the effect of precedence can also be detected here. We will consider the numeral *tri* 'three'. (There are more examples with *dva* 'two' but Sand includes with these the figures for *oba* 'both'. Since we wish to investigate one quantifier only, we will therefore use *tri*.) As we saw in §2.1.3, *tri* — when quantifying a masculine noun — may take agreements in *-a* or *-i*:

(8) SC: *tri   brata   su došla* (neut pl)
        three brothers   came
(9) SC: *tri   brata   su došli* (masc pl)
        three brothers   came

The form *došli* in (9) is unambiguously masculine plural and we concluded in §5.4 that the *-a* form in (8) should be analysed as a neuter plural. It is the masculine plural as in (9) which has the greater semantic justification and which, therefore, we should expect to be favoured by subject-predicate word-order. The data in Table 8.5 are derived from Sand (1971, 57–60); we combine her three corpora, as there are relatively few examples. Precedence obviously has a major effect on the agreement form used. While the neuter plural is the more common, the semantically justified masculine form is used in 22 per cent of the

Table 8.5: **Agreement with *tri* Plus Masculine Noun in Serbo-Croat**

	subject-predicate			predicate-subject			total		
	neut	masc	%masc	neut	masc	%masc	neut	masc	%masc
all texts	35	10	22	41	0	0	76	10	12

cases when the subject precedes the predicate. There were no examples of its use in predicate-subject order in Sand's corpus, though it is not completely excluded there.

Serbo-Croat has an interesting set of quantifiers in which a similar agreement problem occurs and which provides further evidence of the role of word-order. The quantifiers in question are those ending in *-ica*, which refer to groups of males, for example *dvojica* 'two (males)'. These take plural agreement: targets which show gender may take the ending *-i* or *-a*:

(10) SC: *Dvojica od njih   otišli* (masc pl) *su* . . .
                two   of them went away . . .
                (Andrić, *Anikina vremena*)
(11) SC: . . . *ostala   su samo njih   petorica-šestorica* . . .
                remained   only of them five (or) six . . .
                (Andrić, *Mila i prelac*)

The form *otišili* in (10) is masculine plural. Forms like *ostala* in (11) are normally labelled feminine singular but, following our analysis of the similar situation with *deca* and the numerals 2–4 in §5.4, we will consider such forms to be neuter plural. The masculine plural form, as in (10), is the one with greater semantic justification. Data on the use of the competing forms are given in Table 8.6 (derived from figures in

Table 8.6: **Agreement with Quantifiers like** *dvojica*

| | subject-predicate | | | predicate-subject | | | total | | |
	neut	masc	%masc	neut	masc	%masc	neut	masc	%masc
all texts	40	110	73	31	7	18	71	117	62

Sand, 1971, 123), which provides another clear illustration of the effect of precedence: subject-predicate order favours the semantically justified form. The use of masculine plural agreement is much more frequent with quantifiers like *dvojica* than with *tri*, but the effect of precedence is equally evident.

While the evidence in Table 8.6 is of the same type as that presented before, quantifiers such as *dvojica* confirm the role of precedence in a second, more striking way. There are examples in which both word-orders and both agreement forms occur in a single sentence:

(12) SC: ... *pojavila* (neut pl) *su se dvojica   u zelenkastim*
       appeared   two (men) in greenish
       uniformama, zagledali (masc pl) *leš   ne dodirujući*
       uniforms   looked at   the corpse not touching
       ga, i   vratili (masc pl) *se . . .*
       it and went back
       (Vučo, *Mrtve javke*)

This example is quoted by Sand (1971, 123), and she reports another five similar cases. In every instance the predicate showing neuter plural agreement stands before the subject, and that showing masculine plural agreement follows. A comparable example has been found in Russian, involving the numeral *dva*:

(13) R: *Vot prišlo* (sg) *dva nadziratelja v   barak,   posle*
      Then came   two warders   into the barracks after
      raboty, budnično, i   skazali (pl) *:,,Sobirajsja, pošli".*
      work   in civvies and said   get ready let's go
      (Solženicyn, *Arxipelag GULag*)

Here again we find syntactic agreement before the controller, and agreement with greater semantic justification after the controller. (Rozental', 1971, 218, gives similar examples but does not identify the regularity involved.) Our next illustration of the effect of precedence is particularly clear. In two successive sentences the lexical items involved in the controller and the target remain the same, but different word-orders are used, and there are different agreements:

(14) R: *Prinjato   govorit', čto čeloveku   nužno* (sg) *tol'ko*
      (It is) usual to say   that to a man (is) necessary only
      tri   aršina   zemli.   No ved'   tri
      three arshins (seven feet) of ground But you know three
      aršina   nužny (pl) *trupu,   a ne čeloveku.*
      arshins (are) necessary to a corpse and not to a man
      (Čexov, *Čelovek v futljare*)

Here the main difference between the two sentences is the word-order (though the presence of *tol'ko* 'only' in the first may also play a role) and the plural is found in the case where the controller precedes the target.

The regularity that we have observed in examples taken from texts has been matched by informant work. Nichols *et al.* (1980, 375–6) asked native speakers for their judgements on the following sentence:

(15) R: *Množestvo   žonglerov kidajut* (pl) *desjatki*
A large number of jugglers throw   tens
tysjač   šarov.
of thousands of balls
(Sent-Èkzjuperi)

This example has subject-predicate word-order; the original has plural agreement, but informants found the singular (*kidaet*) equally acceptable. In a sentence with the same subject but with predicate-subject word-order, the Russian translator used a singular verb:

(16) R: *V   pljasku   vstupilo* (sg) *množestvo   žonglerov.*
Into the dance entered   a large number of jugglers
(Sent-Èkzjuperi)

In this example the plural (*vstupili*) was considered only marginally acceptable. Thus for informants, just as in all the data discussed earlier, subject-predicate word-order makes the semantically justifiable agreement form more likely than in predicate-subject order.

8.4.3 The Relationship of Animacy and Precedence

In the last two sections we examined data which demonstrate quite clearly the effect both of animacy and of precedence on agreement with quantified expressions. The evidence is considerable and the corpora involved are of an impressive size. But the two factors were discussed in isolation: the published sources do not consider their interrelationship. In order to take the analysis a stage further, four Russian corpora were scanned for examples[7] – those labelled 'Gogol'', 'Turgenev', 'Čexov' and 'Solženicyn' in §7.1 and §7.5. In order to avoid the distortions which can be caused by certain individual quantifiers while including enough types of quantifier to make it possible to find a satisfactory number of examples, a restricted number of the more common quantifiers was selected for inclusion.[8] So that we will not be confronted by an unmanageable amount of data, we will first take the evidence concerning animacy and precedence separately, and only then cross-classify for the two factors.

The evidence for the role of animacy shown in Table 8.7 is strikingly consistent. In each corpus there is a considerable margin between plural

Table 8.7: **Agreement with Quantified Expressions: Animacy**

subject type corpus	animate sg	pl	%pl	inanimate sg	pl	%pl	total sg	pl	%pl
Gogol' (1842)	2	14	88	18	10	36	20	24	55
Turgenev (1856–62)	4	11	73	33	12	27	37	23	38
Čexov (1898–1903)	11	12	52	22	6	21	33	18	35
Solženicyn (1975)	18	34	65	18	10	36	36	44	55
Total	35	71	67	91	38	29	126	109	46

Table 8.8: **Agreement with Quantified Expressions: Precedence**

word-order corpus	subject-predicate sg	pl	%pl	predicate-subject sg	pl	%pl	total sg	pl	%pl
Gogol' (1842)	3	16	84	17	8	32	20	24	55
Turgenev (1856–62)	11	11	50	26	12	32	37	23	38
Čexov (1898–1903)	6	10	63	27	8	23	33	18	35
Solženicyn (1975)	12	31	72	24	13	35	36	44	55
Total	32	68	68	94	41	30	126	109	46

agreement with animate subjects and with inanimates. (Note that the actual percentages are not directly comparable with those of Patton, as not all quantifiers were included.) When we turn to precedence (Table 8.8), the evidence is equally conclusive. While there is considerable variation between the writers (resulting in part no doubt from the size of the sample), the overall pattern is absolutely clear. Subject-predicate word-order is more likely to result in the semantically justified agreement form than is predicate-subject word-order. It is interesting to note that the effect of precedence in the corpora as a whole almost exactly balances that of animacy: with animate subjects, plural agreement was found in 67 per cent of the instances compared to 68 per cent in subject-predicate sentences. In sentences of the opposite types a similar situation obtained: 29 per cent plural agreement in sentences with inanimate subjects, compared with 30 per cent in sentences with predicate-subject word-order. Given these similarities, it will be especially interesting to cross-classify for the two factors, as in Table 8.9.

This table shows a strikingly regular pattern. In each corpus, the

Table 8.9: **Quantified Expressions: Animacy and Precedence**

		animate			inanimate		
		sg	pl	%pl	sg	pl	%pl
Gogol'	subject-predicate	1	8	89	2	8	80
	predicate-subject	1	6	86	16	2	11
Turgenev	subject-predicate	1	5	83	10	6	38
	predicate-subject	3	6	37	23	6	21
Čexov	subject-predicate	3	8	73	3	2	40
	predicate-subject	8	4	33	19	4	17
Solženicyn	subject-predicate	6	27	82	6	4	40
	predicate-subject	12	7	37	12	6	33
Total	subject-predicate	11	48	81	21	20	49
	predicate-subject	24	23	49	70	18	20

highest percentage figure is recorded when both factors which favour semantic agreement (animate subject, subject-predicate word-order) are present. Conversely, when neither factor occurs (inanimate subject, predicate-subject word-order), then we find the lowest percentage. The main area of variation is in the types of sentence where one only of the two factors is present. In all corpora the percentages for inanimates standing before the predicate and for animates occurring after are fairly close. However, these stand in differing relationships to the other two figures. For Gogol', the main distinction is between having both factors or either one factor on the one hand (89 per cent, 86 per cent and 80 per cent plural agreement), and neither factor on the other (11 per cent). Solženicyn is the reverse of Gogol'; here the major contrast is between having both factors present on the one hand (80 per cent), as opposed to just one or neither on the other (40 per cent, 37 per cent, 33 per cent). When we combine the four corpora under 'Total' we find an elegant symmetry. Given an animate subject preceding the predicate, the plural agreement is found in the majority of cases (81 per cent); when one of the two factors is present, then singular and plural are equally balanced (49 per cent plural); if neither factor is present then the plural is found only in a minority of examples (20 per cent).

Table 8.9 is similar to those constructed for agreement with conjoined noun phrases. We can now compare the relationship of animacy and precedence in the two different constructions. Table 8.10 combines the data of Table 8.9, with data from Table 7.10 and 7.16. As the

Table 8.10: Conjoined Noun Phrases and Quantified Expressions (Percentages)

		conjoined noun phrases		quantified expressions	
		animate	inanimate	animate	inanimate
Gogol'	subject-predicate	100	88	89	80
	predicate-subject	63	36	86	11
Turgenev	subject-predicate	100	85	83	38
	predicate-subject	83	5	67	21
Čexov	subject-predicate	100	94	73	40
	predicate-subject	45	37	33	17
Solženicyn	subject-predicate	100	77	82	40
	predicate-subject	71	50	37	33
Total	subject-predicate	100	85	81	49
	predicate-subject	67	31	49	20

actual number of examples are available there, Table 8.10 contains only the percentages, and the two main sections of the table reflect the familiar pattern established for conjoined noun phrases in §7.3 and for quantified expressions in this section. When we compare the two controller types, the most striking difference concerns controllers which are animate and which precede the predicate; in this situation, conjoined noun phrases always take plural agreement in our corpora while with quantified expressions, the plural is much the more common form, but there is a sizeable minority of singulars. Similarly, under other conditions the percentage of plural forms is normally higher for conjoined noun phrases than for quantified expressions. This is true overall (see the totals), and for most cases in the individual corpora. The two exceptions are Gogol' — animate subjects standing after the predicate, and Turgenev — inanimate subjects standing after the predicate. In both instances the number of examples involved was relatively small so it may be that larger corpora would reveal complete regularity even here. The basic pattern is as follows: when both factors favouring semantic agreement are present, the plural is greatly preferred, less so when only one is present, and least of all when neither is present. In general the proportion for plural agreement is higher with conjoined noun phrases than with quantified subjects.

8.5 Conclusion

We had already established the major influence of animacy and precedence on agreement with conjoined noun phrases in Russian. In this chapter we reviewed the two factors and considered reasons for judging them to be controller factors. Next it was shown that their effect is not limited to Russian, but that they operate in other Slavic languages. Similarly, they extend to other constructions; this was demonstrated first, for precedence only, in agreement with comitative phrases. Then we examined a considerable amount of evidence which confirms the effect of both these factors individually on agreement with quantified expressions. Finally, we investigated their interaction, and obtained results similar to those found previously in the case of conjoined noun phrases.

Notes

1. I am very grateful to Alan Timberlake for suggesting to me that word-order should be viewed in terms of the controller. This view is incorporated in a fascinating paper of which he is a joint author (Nichols *et al.*, 1980). In that paper the notion of 'topic' is defined operationally as any constituent which occurs pre-verbally. It is claimed that topics are stronger controllers than non-topics. Suppose we have a sentence with possible alternative predicate agreement forms, and in which the subject precedes the verb. Nichols *et al.* claim that the greater likelihood of the semantically justified agreement form cannot be explained simply by the fact that the controller precedes the target. They suggest that since the subject precedes the verb it is the topic, and for that reason it is more likely to control semantic agreement (or 'maximal scope of agreement' in their terms). For subject-verb agreement this appears to be only a change of label, as the target is the verb and the topic is determined relative to the verb. However, Nichols *et al.* give examples, such as reflexivisation, where the target is an element other than the verb but where nevertheless the topic (which if it is also the controller will be a stronger controller) is determined by its position relative to the verb, and not to the target. If this analysis can be maintained it will be a useful advance, as it links agreement to other syntactic phenomena. Unfortunately there is an apparent flaw. In the next chapter (note 2) we meet a type of agreement where the topic analysis and the simple precedence analysis make different predictions. The evidence available supports the latter analysis. For this reason we will not adopt the approach based on their notion of topic. Nevertheless, it is worth stressing that Nichols *et al.* convincingly demonstrate the need to distinguish rigorously between grammatical relations and the topic relation; grammatical relations are not simply derivatives of discourse relations. In their separate writings too, all three authors have contributed to our understanding of controllers and targets.

2. An idea of the difference in agreement preferences between conjoined and comitative constructions can be gained from Table 8.i. The literary corpus consists of Panova's *Sputniki* (1946) and Nekrasov's *Kira Georgievna* (1961). Data on the usage in the press come from Graudina *et al.* (1976, 31, 346). In both

Table 8.i: Conjoined Noun Phrases and Comitative Constructions

	conjoined noun phrases			comitative phrases		
	sg	pl	%pl	sg	pl	%pl
literature	5	4	44	28	57	67
press	15	15	50	30	723	96

types of text the plural occurs less frequently with comitative than with conjoined constructions. It is worth pointing out that in texts from the very end of the seventeenth century, Popova (1955, 93) found the plural used with comitative constructions in 90 per cent of the cases (N = 29). There has, therefore, been a marked decrease in the use of the semantically justified agreement form (as is also the case with corporate or collective nouns – see note to Table 7.3). Unfortunately, the literary corpus is too small to allow division according to word-order and Graudina *et al.* do not give the relevant data.

3. There is, however, evidence against an increase in plural agreement since the last century, for which see Table 11.13 and the discussion there. For further data on animacy from a smaller corpus see Mathiassen (1965, 77–90); he also gives information on word-order (1965, 66–75). Note that an arithmetical error in Patton (1969, 148) has been corrected in Table 8.2.

4. Two examples referring to animals are included here, both found in nineteenth-century literature. One showed singular agreement, and the other plural.

5. The figures had to be reorganised and recalculated as Sand divided her examples first according to the agreement form, and then gave the proportions of the different word-orders. To demonstrate the effect of word-order, we will classify the sentences according to that factor, and within it give the agreement forms found.

6. In Ukrainian, as we shall see in §11.2, there is greater freedom of choice with numerals 5 and above. Buttke (1972, 632–3) gives data on all the cardinal numerals taken together. Like Sand he gives the figures for word-order as a percentage of those with singular and plural agreement. However, unlike Sand, he does not give the actual number of examples involved, so it is impossible to calculate the figures we would like. We must therefore be content with the figures given, which relate to materials published between 1967 and 1970.

Table 8.ii: Agreement with Cardinal Numerals in Ukrainian

	%sg	% of these which are subject-predicate	%pl	% of these which are subject-predicate
scientific	37	4	63	47
social science	79	3	21	56
journalistic	44	12	56	51

The figures in the first column give the singular agreements found as a percentage of the total in that corpus. The second column gives the percentage of those with singular agreement which also show subject-predicate word-order. It is evident that there are comparatively few sentences which have singular agreement together with subject-predicate order. On the other hand, of the sentences with plural agreement approximately half have subject-predicate order. This indicates that overall subject-predicate order is more likely to combine with plural agreement than is predicate-subject order. (The high figure for singular agreement in the social science corpus results, according to Buttke, from the particular type of text – presentation of historical data.)

7. Not all the texts scanned for agreement with conjoined noun phrases in Chapter 7 are included here. This does not mean – no more do similar instances elsewhere – that information is being withheld. It simply indicates that the texts were read at different times and that not every text was scanned for each construction.

8. These are: the cardinal numerals 2–10; collective numerals like *dvoe* 'two', *desjatok* 'ten'; the quantifiers *mnogo* 'many', *nemnogo* 'a few', *nemalo* 'many', *neskol'ko* 'some' and *stol'ko* 'so many'; and the collective nouns *bol'šinstvo* 'majority' and *množestvo* 'multitude', providing they are followed by a noun in the genitive plural. Phrases modified by a plural determiner such as *èti* 'these' are excluded since these invariably take plural agreement (cf. Chapter 11, note 2). Phrases including a numeral 2–4 and a nominative plural adjective, for example *dve krasivye rozy* 'two beautiful roses' were excluded for the same reason.

9 INTERACTION OF TARGET HIERARCHIES AND CONTROLLER FACTORS

In Chapters 2 and 3, we investigated the effect that the target has on agreement and established the validity of two hierarchies, the Agreement Hierarchy and the Predicate Hierarchy. We suggested the way in which these two hierarchies should be combined (Chapter 5), though we were not able fully to justify our proposal, since we considered a restricted set of controllers. In Chapter 6 we turned our attention to the controller factors which influence agreement. Agreement with conjoined noun phrases was analysed first (Chapter 7) and we found that the major factors are the animacy of the controller and its order relative to the target. These factors are also major factors in agreement with quantified expressions (Chapter 8). It is now time to consider target and controller factors together, in order to discover how they interact. We will see that this analysis will provide the justification for our earlier combining of the two Target Hierarchies.

In our account of the Agreement Hierarchy (Chapter 2), among other evidence we cited we quoted data on agreement with conjoined noun phrases, in Serbo-Croat and in Russian. When we moved on to consider controller factors, we also investigated conjoined noun phrases (Chapter 7), this time restricting our attention to predicate agreement. Having done the groundwork on conjoined noun phrases, we will now take the analysis a stage further, considering both target and controller factors. Though conjoined noun phrases provide the best starting point, other controller types could be used: the effect of the Agreement Hierarchy on quantified expressions is shown in §11.1, while the role of the Predicate Hierarchy in agreement with comitative phrases and quantified expressions is described in Corbett (1979a, 83-95). In this chapter we will avoid unnecessary complications by dealing with conjoined noun phrases in Russian, considering both the positions on the Agreement Hierarchy (§9.1) and those on the Predicate Hierarchy (§9.2), in each case investigating interaction with controller factors. We can then confirm the way in which the two Target Hierarchies should be combined (§9.3).

9.1 The Agreement Hierarchy

The Agreement Hierarchy consists of the following agreement positions: attributive, predicate, relative pronoun and personal pronoun. According to the formulation reached in §5.2.1, as we move rightwards along the hierarchy, the likelihood of agreement forms with greater semantic justification will increase monotonically. The considerable amount of evidence presented in Chapter 2 was consistent with this claim. Agreement with conjoined noun phrases in Russian provides particularly strong confirming evidence. Examples found in the four literary corpora described in §7.1 show the distribution of agreement forms given in Table 9.1 (we retain the corpus labels and abbreviations used in Chapter 7).

Table 9.1: Agreement with Conjoined Noun Phrases: the Agreement Hierarchy

	attributive			predicate			relative pronoun			personal pronoun		
	sg	pl	%pl	sg	pl	%pl	sg	pl	%pl	sg	pl	%pl
Amal'rik	16	2	11	19	65	77	0	5	100	0	14	100
Nabokov	7	1	13	34	32	48	0	4	100	0	1	100
Solženicyn	8	2	20	16	44	73	data		not		available	
Vojnovič	7	1	13	15	65	81	0	1	100	0	11	100
Total	38	6	14	84	206	71	0	10	100	0	26	100

The percentage of plural agreement forms in the different categories is given for each corpus. These percentage figures show that in every corpus the condition of monotonic increase of the semantically justified (plural) form is fulfilled, even though the corpora show considerable differences between themselves (particularly in predicate agreement, as discussed in §7.2.4). Comparable data are rare: Drejzin (1966, reported in Crockett, 1976, 162) investigated attributive agreement in a non-fiction text, and found eight plural forms to 66 singulars (11 per cent); in newspaper texts, Graudina *et al.* (1976, 31) found 723 examples of plural predicate agreement out of 753 (96 per cent plural agreement). While the variation between registers deserves further investigation, the difference in agreement between attributive and predicate positions is clearly established. Our corpora suggest that while there is a difference between the predicate and the relative pronoun, there is no difference to be observed between the relative and the personal pronoun. Even so, the condition of monotonic increase is fulfilled. However, examples of singular relative pronouns do occur. One such example (ironically from Adamovič's introduction to *Zaščita Lužina* and therefore not included in the corpus) was given as example (33) in §2.1.7. Such examples are rare but not exceptional:

(1) R:... *rabotnik   prosto ne   otvečaet na zaprosy,*
     the worker simply does not answer   to inquiries
     otnošenija, ankety, vedomosti, smety   i   pročij material,
     memoranda forms   records   estimates and other material
     kotoryj (sg) *emu   dostavljajut počta   i   posetiteli.*
     which   to him bring   the post and callers
     (Ardov, *Tak ono i byvaet*)

In (1) the relative pronoun agrees with the nearest noun only. In §4.3.2, example (27), both agreements are found (in such examples, the pronoun showing the semantically justified form must be further from the conjoined noun phrases). We conclude that singular relative pronouns in this construction are unusual, but certainly not excluded. In the personal pronoun, the singular is quite exceptional (see §2.1.7, example (34)). Thus the agreements with conjoined noun phrases in Russian provide particularly strong evidence in favour of the Agreement Hierarchy. Alternative agreements are possible at each position on the hierarchy: in attributive position the singular is strongly preferred; in the predicate there is a marked preference for the plural; the relative is normally plural but occasional singulars are found, while the personal pronoun is plural in the overwhelming majority of cases.

So far we have considered only target factors (the Agreement Hierarchy) and have ignored controller factors. The clear pattern shown by Table 9.1, which fits into the broader picture of evidence for the hierarchy (Table 2.4), indicates that the Agreement Hierarchy is the major constraint on variation in agreement. On the other hand, we have seen that the controller factors of animacy and precedence also play a role in the choice of agreement. This influence was demonstrated using predicate agreement; we must now investigate their influence in other syntactic positions.

We will consider first the role of animacy, starting with instances where the target is a relative or personal pronoun. Both types of pronoun strongly favour plural agreement; no singulars were found in our corpora, but pronouns showing singular agreement do occur, as we have just seen. It is significant that in all the examples referred to the controller is inanimate. No examples of animate controllers with a singular relative or personal pronoun have been found. This suggests that the controller factor of animacy does have an effect here: the singular occurs only with inanimate controllers. When we turn to agreement in attributive position we find a greater degree of choice than with the pronouns, and so it is easier to establish the role of the controller factors. There are 44 examples of attributive agreement with conjoined noun phrases in our four corpora. One example includes both animate and inanimate nouns:

(2) R:... *so   svoej* (sg) *ženoj, domom i   fabrikoj*...   (A 200)
with his own   wife,   house   and factory

In all the other examples, the noun phrases are consistently animate or inanimate; the distribution of agreement forms in these instances is given in Table 9.2. Given the small number of animate controllers, we

Table 9.2: Attributive Agreement According to Animacy

	sg	pl	%pl
animate controller	1	3	75
inanimate controller	36	3	8

can draw no definite conclusion. The figures give the impression that the animacy of the controller is an important factor. For our corpora, the following examples are typical. In (3) with animate conjuncts we find a plural modifier:

(3) R:... *nesuščix* (pl) *ego Serafima i   Samodurova*...
the carrying him Serafim and Samodurov
(V *Pretendent* 242)

With the inanimates in (4) we find a singular attributive form:

(4) R:... *nazovite vaše* (sg) *imja,   otčestvo   i   familiju*...
give   your   first name, patronymic and surname
(V *Pretendent* 294)

Other examples found outside the corpora support the claim that animacy is significant, and Crockett (1976, 163-97) subscribes to that view. Thus the evidence available suggests that the animacy of the controller has an effect on agreement in all positions on the Agreement Hierarchy.

Let us now consider precedence. Its effects on predicate agreement has been fully established (§7.2.1). When we consider relative and personal pronouns, we find that in practically all cases the controller precedes the target and so there is no possibility of demonstrating any effect caused by precedence. It may nevertheless be significant that in the sole example Crockett gives of a singular personal pronoun agreeing with conjoined noun phrases the controller does not precede the target (1976, 178):

(5) R: *Vot ona* (fem sg)*, glubina* (fem) *i   vjazkost'* (fem)
Here it (is)   depth   and viscosity
perežitogo
of the experienced
(Here it is, the depth and viscosity of what has been experienced.)

When we turn to attributive agreement, we face the opposite problem. In almost all instances Russian attributive modifiers precede their controllers:[1] this is true of all the examples recorded in Table 9.2. However, postpositive attributives do occur, as in the following example from Durnovo, quoted by Rezvin (1970, 238; cf. Crockett, 1976, 206):

(6) R: *Na nem   šapka i   šuba mexovye* (pl)
On him (are) cap   and coat fur
(He is wearing a fur cap and coat.)

Rezvin states that the plural in (6) is felt to be fully natural precisely because the adjective is postposed. If it were preposed, then he would find the singular *mexovaja* preferable.

We have seen that the Agreement Hierarchy applies irrespective of the type of controller. Within the positions of the hierarchy, controller factors have an influence. This was clearly demonstrated for animacy and precedence in predicate position. For the other positions on the hierarchy there is less evidence; however, in all instances where it is theoretically possible for animacy and precedence[2] to have an effect, there is evidence to support the view that they both favour agreement forms with greater semantic justification.

Before leaving the Agreement Hierarchy it is worth considering a plausible but false hypothesis, namely that the hierarchy is an artefact whose apparent effect is due to word-order. In the evidence just discussed, we noted that attributive modifiers normally precede the noun in Russian; predicates may precede or follow the subject; relative pronouns follow the antecedent; and personal pronouns almost always follow the noun to which they refer, though occasionally they precede. Could this be sufficient explanation for the differences in agreement we have noted? There are two sets of evidence readily available to show that this claim is untenable. First, it predicts that the relative pronoun, which always follows its controller, should show semantically justified agreement no less frequently than the personal pronoun (which occasionally precedes its controller). In fact, precisely the opposite is the case, as we have seen both with conjoined noun phrases, and more generally in §2.2. Second, we can compare attributive modifiers with preposed predicates — if the Agreement Hierarchy were explicable in terms of word-order alone, these two sets of examples should show no difference in agreement. The relevant data from our corpora are given in Table 9.3.

Table 9.3: Attributive Modifiers and Preposed Predicates

	attributive modifiers			preposed predicates		
	sg	pl	%pl	sg	pl	%pl
animate controllers	1	3	75	11	55	83
inanimate controllers	36	3	8	60	26	30
total	37	6	14	71	81	53

If we consider inanimate controllers, where there is an adequate number of examples, then the data in Table 9.3 show that the two positions on the hierarchy have markedly different frequencies of plural agreement, even when word-order is held constant. This demonstrates that the Agreement Hierarchy cannot be explained in terms of word-order. Therefore our previous conclusion stands: the Agreement Hierarchy is the major factor determining the distribution of agreement options but, within the divisions it sets, the controller factors of animacy and precedence both have an effect.

9.2 The Predicate Hierarchy

In Chapter 3 we considered agreement with honorific pronouns in the different Slavic languages, and found that the Predicate Hierarchy has a great deal of evidence to support it. The hierarchy consists of four main positions: finite verb, participle (in *-l*), adjective and noun. In Russian, the predicative adjective may take two forms, giving five possible positions: verb, participle (in *-l*), short-form adjective, long-form adjective and noun. The .claim is that as we move rightwards along the hierarchy, so the likelihood of agreement forms with greater semantic justification will increase monotonically. Let us consider the evidence from agreement with conjoined noun phrases in our four corpora, as presented in Table 9.4.

Table 9.4: Agreement with Conjoined Noun Phrases: the Predicate Hierarchy

verb			participle (in *-l*)			short-form adjective			long-form adjective			noun		
sg	pl	%pl	sg	pl	%pl	sg	pl	%pl	sg	pl	%pl	sg	pl	%pl
9	21	70	62	143	70	11	27	71	0	8	100	4	5	56

Note: Compound predicates are included once only, the element to the right on the hierarchy being counted.[3]

At first sight, these figures might suggest that the Predicate Hierarchy is misconceived. However, they will repay further investigation. Let us begin with the first two elements on the hierarchy, the verb and the participle in *-l*. In Russian the form in *-l* (originally the past active participle) serves as the past tense in its own right, without any auxiliary. However, it agrees in gender and number, rather than in number and person as do present and future tense verbs, and so it is conceivable that its number agreement forms might differ, at least in their frequency relative to each other, from those of other finite verbs. Table 9.4 suggests strongly that they do not, confirming our conclusion in §3.3.

To dispel any doubt that different subject types may be hiding a difference in agreement, let us consider for a moment agreement with a different controller. When relative *kto* 'who' has a plural antecedent, it may take singular or plural agreement. In (7) we find singular agreement:

(7) R:... *tex, kto ešče ne vstal* (sg)... (S 63)
those who yet not got up
(those who had not yet got up)

While this is the more usual form in the written language, the plural is
also possible:

(8) R: *Poètomu te,   kto napravljali* (pl)
Therefore those who directed
zabastovku...   (A 274)
the strike

Table 9.5 gives figures for agreement with relative *kto* (with a plural
antecedent) from two of our corpora, Amal'rik and Solženicyn, and
from Vojnovič's *Žizn' i neobyčajnye priključenija soldata Ivana Čonkina*
(abbreviated as *Čonkin*). There is no significant difference between the

Table 9.5: Agreement with Relative *kto*

	finite verb			participle in *-l*		
	sg	pl	%pl	sg	pl	%pl
Amal'rik	7	0	0	18	0	0
Solženicyn	18	4	18	43	6	12
Vojnovič (*Čonkin*)	3	0	0	3	0	0
Total	28	4	13	64	6	9

agreements found in the ordinary finite verb (present and future) and
the past tense. In the absence of firm evidence to the contrary it is
reasonable to treat them together.

It might appear that relative *kto* would be an ideal controller to use
for investigating the Predicate Hierarchy: it occurs first in the clause,
so that its order relative to the predicate does not vary, and it is always
animate. There are however two problems: first, examples with non-
verbal predicates are rare; and second, the singular predominates, in
the written language, to such an extent that a very large number of
examples would be needed to detect any variation. These problems
are evident in Table 9.6, where the verb forms are combined, as discussed above, and compared with other predicate types. The first three
corpora are the same as in Table 9.5. The Zinov'ev examples are taken
from *Zijajuščie vysoty*, a book of approximately 210,000 words.[4] This
illustrates particularly clearly the problem with *kto*: Zinov'ev uses only

Table 9.6: Agreement with Relative *kto*: the Predicate Hierarchy

	verb			short-form adjective			long-form adjective			noun		
	sg	pl	%pl	sg	pl	%pl	sg	pl	%pl	sg	pl	%pl
Amal'rik	25	0	0	1	0	0	0	0	–	0	(1)	(100)
Solženicyn	60	10	14	6	2	25	0	0	–	0	0	–
Vojnovič (*Čonkin*)	6	0	0	0	0	–	0	0	–	0	0	–
Zinov'ev	36	0	0	3	0	0	0	0	–	0	0	–
Total	127	10	7	10	2	17	0	0	–	0	(1)	(100)

two of our predicate types and all his agreements are singular. The entry for the noun example found in Amal'rik is in parentheses because it is a secondary predicate:

(9) R: *Te,   kto uže   rabotal* (sg) *na ferme   teljatnicami* (pl)
    Those who already worked   on the farm as calf-herds
    i   dojarkami (pl)...   (A 251)
    and milk-maids

This example is particularly interesting as the verb is singular and the predicate nouns are plural (they are counted as one example). This is an example of the phenomenon discussed in §4.2; the element to the right on the hierarchy is the one which takes the agreement form with greater semantic justification. Note too that *rabotal* is masculine singular, agreeing syntactically with *kto*, while the predicate nouns are both feminine. While predicate nouns and long-form adjectives are rare, as Table 9.6 amply demonstrates, examples of both types, with singular and plural agreements, are given in Corbett (1979a, 50–6). These examples are taken from casual reading and secondary sources, rather than from a defined corpus.[5] The figures in Table 9.6 suggest a difference between agreement of the verb and the short-form adjective but this difference is not statistically significant. However, while *kto* ensures that animacy and word-order remain constant, activity – the subdivision of animacy – can vary. The examples counted under verb include active and non-active subjects, while those under short-form adjective are all non-active. This implies a greater difference between verbs and short-form adjectives than that shown by the figures in Table 9.6. Unfortunately there are just not enough examples to demonstrate a significant difference with *kto*. We should therefore return to our main line of analysis — agreement with conjoined noun phrases — where examples are more plentiful. The basic conclusion to retain from this excursus into agreement with *kto* is that there is no adequate evidence for separating past tense forms from ordinary finite verbs.

Let us reconsider the agreements with conjoined noun phrases found for the different positions on the Predicate Hierarchy, when the past tense is included with the other finite verb forms, as in Table 9.7. While we see a clear distinction between the agreements with

Table 9.7: Agreement with Conjoined Noun Phrases: the Predicate Hierarchy (Modified Version)

verb			short-form adjective[6]			long-form adjective			noun		
sg	pl	%pl	sg	pl	%pl	sg	pl	%pl	sg	pl	%pl
71	164	70	11	27	71	0	8	100	4	5	56

long-form and short-form adjectives, there is no significant distinction between verbs and short-form adjectives. This is surprising, because in Chapter 3 we found a great deal of evidence from different Slavic languages for separating the predicative adjective from the verb; indeed, Russian was one of the languages which provided evidence for this distinction (§3.3). On the one hand, therefore, the data from agreement with honorific *vy* indicate that verbs and short-form adjectives differ in their agreement choices; on the other hand the data from agreement with conjoined noun phrases (Table 9.7) suggest no such distinction. It may be that there are other factors which are hiding a genuine difference. The obvious possibilities are the controller factors of animacy and precedence.

In Chapter 7 we established that animate subjects and subject-predicate word-order both favour plural agreement. If both factors are present, then in the literary language a plural predicate is required. If either one of the factors is present, a plural predicate will probably result, while if neither is present, the singular is the most frequent form. If the short-form adjective and verb are not equally distributed among these four sentence types, this will blur the picture of the agreements they take. We will therefore divide the examples from our corpora into the four sentence types, and within each type, give separate figures for the different sorts of predicate.

As can be seen from Table 9.8, the combination of an animate

Table 9.8: Agreement According to Predicate Type and Controller Factors

		animate subject			inanimate subject[7]		
		sg	pl	%pl	sg	pl	%pl
subject-predicate	verb	0	68	100	5	31	86
	SF	0	2	(100)	2	10	83
	LF	0	4	100	0	2	(100)
	noun	0	3	(100)	3	0	(0)
predicate-subject	verb	11	46	81	51	17	25
	SF	0	6	100	8	8	50
	LF	0	2	(100)	0	0	–
	noun	0	1	(100)	1	1	(50)

Note: SF = short-form adjective; LF = long-form adjective.

subject and subject-predicate word-order ensures a plural predicate. Such sentences therefore tell us nothing about a possible difference between the verb and the short-form adjective. When only the word-order favours a plural subject (subject-predicate order, inanimate subject), we find slightly more plural verbs than short-forms, and when only the animacy of the subject favours a plural we find a rather higher percentage of plural short-forms. However, when neither factor is present, the percentage of plural agreements for short-forms is markedly higher than for verbs.

Let us now examine the distribution of the two predicate types in question among the different sentence types, as presented in Table 9.9. In each section of this table, the first figure gives the number of

Table 9.9: Distribution of Predicates According to Sentence Type

		animate subject		inanimate subject	
		examples	% of total	examples	% of total
subject-predicate	verb	68	30	36	16
	SF	2	6	12	33
predicate-subject	verb	57	25	68	30
	SF	6	17	16	44

examples (e.g. our corpora contain 68 verbs in sentences with an animate subject standing before the predicate), and the second figure gives the proportion represented by the first (thus 30 per cent of the verbal predicates occur in sentences of this type)[8] It is immediately obvious that short-form adjectives occur most often precisely in the sentence type which has no factors favouring plural agreement, and least often in sentences where plural agreement is required. It appears that the odds are stacked against the short-form; the fact that, overall, the figure for plural agreement of the short-form adjective is as high as that for the verb in Table 9.7, is in itself highly significant.

There is a further factor which is loaded against the short-form. As we saw in §7.3.2, if the subject (whether animate or not) is presented as behaving like an animate, i.e. engaged in an activity rather than being in a position or a state, then this will make a plural predicate more likely. In such sentences, of course, only verbs are found. We should exclude these sentences, and allow the short-form to 'compete on equal terms', by considering only sentences with 'inactive' subjects. Then a clearer picture emerges, as shown in Table 9.10.

Table 9.10: Agreement with 'Inactive' Subjects Only

		animate subject			inanimate subject		
		sg	pl	%pl	sg	pl	%pl
subject-predicate	verb	0	16	100	2	9	82
	SF	0	2	(100)	2	10	83
predicate-subject	verb	9	17	65	44	9	17
	SF	0	6	100	8	8	50

When short-form adjectives are compared with verbs with 'inactive' subjects, we find they have an equal or higher proportion of plural predicates, in each sentence type. If we apply the chi-square test (described in Chapter 7, note 6) to the total number of singular and plural forms in verbs with 'inactive' subjects and in short-form adjectives (verbs 55 sg to 51 pl, SF 10 sg to 26 pl), we find that the difference in agreement between the two would arise by chance less than once in 50 tries (chi-square = 6.29, significant at the .02 level given one degree of freedom). But if we exclude the 18 examples which occur in sentences with an animate subject standing before the predicate, where there is no choice of form, then the chi-square test applied to the remaining totals indicates that this distribution would result by chance less than once in 100 tries (chi-square = 9.94, significant at the .01 level). We are therefore fully justified in concluding that there is a difference in agreement between the verb and the short-form

adjective. In order to demonstrate the difference with subjects consisting of conjoined noun phrases, it is first necessary to exclude the
factors of precedence, animacy, and even the 'activity' subdivision of
animacy, since their effect is directly opposed to that of the short-
form adjective. Once the short-form adjective and verb are isolated in
fully comparable sentences, then the difference becomes evident.
Why then did agreement with honorific *vy* provide evidence for the
difference, without the necessity for such careful analysis? *Vy* is an
ideal controller as it is always animate and, being a personal pronoun,
is less likely to follow the verb than is a subject consisting of noun
phrases. Even under these almost ideal conditions, the short-form
agreeing with honorific *vy* showed only three per cent singular forms,
as opposed to none in the verb (§3.3).

We have observed a particularly interesting example of the interaction of target and controller factors. The short-form adjective is a
target which, all things being equal, is more likely to show semantically
justified agreement forms than is the verb. However, it tends to
occur in sentence types where the controller factors of precedence
and animacy (including activity) do not favour semantically justified
agreement. In our corpora, these conflicting factors are perfectly
balanced, making it appear at first sight that there is no difference
between the verb and the short-form adjective.

Let us now return to the other positions on the Predicate Hierarchy,
as in Table 9.7, which is repeated for convenience as Table 9.11. We

**Table 9.11: Agreement with Conjoined Noun Phrases: the Predicate
Hierarchy (Modified Version)**

verb			short-form adjective			long-form adjective			noun		
sg	pl	%pl	sg	pl	%pl	sg	pl	%pl	sg	pl	%pl
71	164	70	11	27	71	0	8	100	4	5	56

have seen that the apparently insignificant difference between verb and
short-form adjective hides a significant difference when other factors
are removed. However, the difference between the short-form and long-
form adjective is clear-cut. Though no singular long-form adjectives
were found in the corpus, these do occasionally occur, for example:

(10) R: *Dostoinstvo i   masterstvo upotreblenija ètix*
       The quality and the mastery of the use   of these

> *snarjadov bylo ravnoe* (LF sg) *zdes' i   tam.*
> shells   was equal   here and there
> (The quality of the shells and the ability to use them were
> equal on both sides.)
> (Annenkov, quoted by Prokopović, 1974, 134)

When we turn to the noun we find an apparent break in the pattern.
It could be argued that predicate nouns should not have been considered because they cannot possibly agree. Such an objection is unjustified, for there are cases of predicate nouns agreeing with their
subject; as we saw in §3.3, in nineteenth-century Russian honorific *vy*
could take an agreeing plural nominative predicate (referring to one
person):

(11) R: *Izmenniki* (pl) *vy, čto li?*
         Traitor   you perhaps
         (Are you a traitor, perhaps?)
         (Čexov, quoted by Vinogradov and Istrina, 1954, 520)

Another construction where agreeing nominal predicates can occur
involves relative *kto* with a plural antecedent, as discussed above;
the semantically justified form here would be the plural:

(12) R: *Iz geroev,   kotoryx mne prišlos' voploščat' v*
         Of the heroes which (it) to me fell   to embody in
         teatre   i   v kino,   naibolee mne blizkimi
         the theatre and in the cinema the most to me close
         byli te,   kto dobyval čelovečestvu sčast'e,   kto
         were those who gained   for mankind happiness who
         byl neutomimym stroitelem (sg) *buduščego,   borcom* (sg),
         was a tireless   builder   of the future a fighter
         preobrazovatelem (sg), *revoljucionerom* (sg).
         a reformer   a revolutionary
         (Čerkasov, quoted by Gvozdev, 1973, 241)

These examples show that it is possible for predicate nouns to take
forms which are not justified in semantic terms. In general, this form
of agreement is rare; the Predicate Hierarchy predicts that it can occur
only when the same type of agreement is possible in all other positions
on the hierarchy. However, though agreement of predicate nouns
cannot be simply ruled out, it does not occur in the case of conjoined

noun phrases in Russian – the form of the nominal predicate is determined purely by semantic criteria. The following typical examples
support this analysis:

(13) R: . . . *zavedujuščaja   klubom   vremja   ot vremeni*
    the woman in charge of the club from time to time
    čitala na ferme   kosnejuščim jazykom kakuju-nibud'
    read at the farm getting tongue-tied   some
    malo   ponjatnuju   ej   samoj stat'ju v
    scarcely comprehensible to her herself article in
    gazete   i   zatem raz"jasnjala ee slušateljam:
    the newspaper and then   explained   it to the listeners
    vrode togo, čto Sinjavskij i   Daniel' byli amerikanskimi
    such as   that Sinjavskij and Daniel' were American
    špionami (pl).   (A 267)
    spies

In (13) the predicate noun is semantically plural, and so stands in the
plural. In (14), the preposed predicate noun is semantically singular
(*cel'ju* must be the predicate as it is in the instrumental case):

(14) R: . . . *osnovnoj cel'ju* (sg) *zagovora   javljalos'*
    the basic aim   of the conspiracy was
    širokoe   vosstanie   mestnogo   naselenija   protiv
    widespread insurrection of the local population against
    Sovetov . . . , zaxvat   dannoj   territorii i
    the Soviets   the seizure of a given territory and
    uderžanie   ee   do   podxoda   germanskix   vojsk.
    the holding of it until the approach of the German troops
    (V *Pretendent* 290)

These examples are covered by our formulation of the Predicate Hierarchy, in that as we move rightwards along the hierarchy, so the likelihood of semantically justified forms increases monotonically. For the
verb, short-form and long-form adjective, the semantically justified
form, when the subject consists of conjoined noun phrases, is the
plural, and indeed the likelihood of plural agreement does increase.
The predicate noun, in this construction, takes its number independently of the subject – it is therefore always semantically justified. This
means in turn that a compound predicate may show different numbers.
Two such examples exist in our corpora:

(15) R: ... *pospešnaja kollektivizacija i   forsirovannoe*
             hurried   collectivisation and the forced
     razvitie   promišlennosti za sčet   razorenija
     development of industry   at the expense of the ruining
     sel'skogo   xozjajstva   byli (pl) *bol'šoj*
     of the rural economy (i.e. agriculture) were   a big
     ošibkoj (sg) , *kotoraja dorogo obošlas' strane* ...   (A 247)
     mistake   which   dearly cost   the country
(16) R: *To   obožestvlenie Stalina   i   ta   vera   vo vsë,*
     That idolisation   of Stalin and that belief in everything
     bez   somnenija i   bez   kraja, sovsem   ne
     without doubt   and without limit absolutely not
     byli (pl)   *sostojaniem* (sg)
     were (i.e. were not at all) a state
     obščenarodnym ...   (S25)
     general (i.e. a general state)

In these examples, all the predicate forms are semantically justified —
the verbs are plural to agree with more than one subject noun phrase,
while the predicative noun phrases are singular because their referents
are singular. Given that the predicate noun in these constructions
always takes the semantically justified number, then there is indeed a
monotonic increase in the use of semantically justified forms as we
move rightwards along the Predicate Hierarchy.

We have now established that data on conjoined noun phrases from
our corpora confirm the validity of the Predicate Hierarchy. Our
investigation was complicated by the interaction of controller factors
with the hierarchy in the first two positions (verb and short-form
adjective). We cannot find any effect of controller factors in the other
two positions on the hierarchy (long-form adjective and noun) simply
because all the examples in the corpora show semantically justified
agreement, which makes it impossible to separate out conflicting
factors.

9.3 The Relationship of the Predicate Hierarchy to the Agreement Hierarchy

We have seen that both the Agreement Hierarchy and the Predicate
Hierarchy have a role in determining agreement with conjoined noun
phrases in Russian. The raw figures on agreement forms are quite

adequate to demonstrate the effect of the Agreement Hierarchy. Within its divisions, animacy and precedence also have an effect, but these controller factors are overshadowed by the Agreement Hierarchy. When we consider the Predicate Hierarchy, the picture is rather differen. The effect of the Predicate Hierarchy is counterbalanced by controller factors, so that the difference between verbs and short-form adjectives is masked. It is only when the effect of the controller factors is removed that the difference resulting from the Predicate Hierarchy is clear. The original evidence produced in favour of the Predicate Hierarchy — agreement with honorific pronouns — largely avoided these problems; the restriction of the subject to a single type of animate pronoun provided almost laboratory conditions, in which controller factors varied only minimally, so that the effect of the Predicate Hierarchy was obvious. In other cases such as the one we have analysed, the Predicate Hierarchy has to compete with other factors and, unlike the Agreement Hierarchy, it does not dominate them.

Now that we have demonstrated the validity of the Predicate Hierarchy, using a broader range of subject types than the single type considered in Chapter 3, we are justified in combining the two Target Hierarchies, as suggested in §5.4. We may represent their relationship as in Table 9.12. The data examined in the previous two sections

Table 9.12: Combined Target Hierarchies

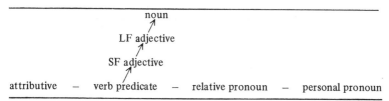

demonstrate that as we move rightwards in this diagram, so the likelihood of semantically justified forms increases monotonically. The predicate forms are indicated by oblique arrows because the difference between the positions on the Predicate Hierarchy are not so great as between those on the Agreement Hierarchy. The two hierarchies meet at the verbal predicate. To be strictly accurate, therefore, the figures we quote for the predicate position on the Agreement Hierarchy should be those for the verbal predicate only (cf. §5.3). Normally this will be unimportant for practical purposes, as non-verbal predicates form a small proportion of the total and do not greatly distort the picture (the figure for all predicates given in Table 9.1 is 71 per cent plural agreement and for verbal predicates alone, in Table 9.7, it is 70 per cent).

Having established how the Agreement and Predicate Hierarchies relate to each other and to controller factors we should ask what other hierarchies may be involved. The Relational Hierarchy (Johnson, 1977, 156) and the Accessibility Hierarchy (Keenan and Comrie, 1977, 66) share the following positions: subject, direct object, indirect object, other object (this last position is further divided in the Accessibility Hierarchy but not in the Relational Hierarchy). Moravcsik (1978, 364) has claimed that if a language shows verb agreement then there will be cases of agreement with the intransitive subject. Agreement with direct objects will be found only if there is also agreement with intransitive subjects, and agreement with indirect objects is possible only if agreement with direct objects occurs. This is in accord with the Relational and Accessibility Hierarchies, which were originally proposed to account for other syntactic phenomena. The Slavic languages provide supporting evidence for this claim in that they all have verb agreement with the subject, which is normally the only constituent which controls verb agreement. Bulgarian and Macedonian have constructions in which an accusative clitic pronoun is obligatory (Sussex, forthcoming). This may prove to be the first stage in the development of object agreement, which would further support Moravcsik's claim.

9.4 Conclusion

Conjoined noun phrases provide controllers of a wide range of different types but agreements with them meet the requirements of the Agreement Hierarchy, without regard to variation in the controller. Nevertheless, the controller factors influence agreement, but only within the limits of the Agreement Hierarchy. The Predicate Hierarchy, which draws finer distinctions of target types than does the Agreement Hierarchy, is also confirmed by the data from conjoined noun phrases. However, controller factors counteract the effect of the Predicate Hierarchy, so that the different factors must first be isolated to demonstrate their individual effect. Once this is done, we obtain evidence which confirms that the two Target Hierarchies can be combined.

Notes

1. Modifiers which stand after conjoined nouns are usually heads of adjectival phrases. Participles make up a large proportion of the examples, as in:

(i) R:... *sideli francuženka   i   èkonomka,   nenavidevšie* (pl)
   sat   the Frenchwoman and the housekeeper hating (i.e. who hated)
   drug družku.   (N 27)
   one another

These phrases are marked by an intonational break, and so they cannot be compared with ordinary attributive modifiers. Eventually they must be incorporated into the Agreement Hierarchy – perhaps between attributive and predicate positions. However, examples are very hard to find; in our corpora there were only eight examples of postposed modifiers to conjoined noun phrases, of which six showed plural agreement.

2. In Chapter 8, note 1, we considered the suggestion of Nichols *et al.* (1980) that the effect of word-order could be understood as a consequence of whether the controller is the topic or not. They define topic as pre-verbal, so for predicate agreement it makes no difference whether one speaks of 'preceding the target' or 'topic', because on this definition of topic the two are equivalent. However, for other positions on the Agreement Hierarchy the two claims are distinct. When acting as the target of conjoined noun phrases, singular personal and relative pronouns are rare, and so finding sufficient data is difficult. The examples found suggest no correlation between the use of singular agreement and the controller being a non-topic. When we turn to attributive agreement the picture is much clearer. We have a reasonable number of examples of both singular and plural agreement. In addition, though the word-order is the same in all the examples from our corpus (the target precedes the controller), the noun phrases involved may be topic or non-topic. If the topic analysis is correct, it should be evident in this case. In Table 9.i the controllers are cross-clarified as animate/inanimate and topic/non-topic. This table is interesting because it shows that, in the majority

Table 9.i: Attributive Agreement with Conjoined Noun Phrases

	animate			inanimate		
	sg	pl	%pl	sg	pl	%pl
topic	0	0	–	9	1	10
non-topic	1	3	75	26	2	7

of cases, conjoined noun phrases which take attributive modifiers are inanimate and occur in non-topic position. However, Table 9.i does not prove any effect of the topic on the agreement found: there are insufficient examples to allow us to attach any significance to the difference between the ten per cent and seven per cent figures here. On the other hand, we saw that word-order does have a significant effect, as in example (5). In (5) we have plural agreement because the adjective is postposed, and furthermore the noun phrases which control the agreement are not in topic position. Unless new evidence comes to light, it appears that for analysing agreement we should think of word-order in terms of the controller preceding its target (precedence) rather than in terms of the topic notion.

3. This accounts for the difference in the totals between Table 9.1 and those

in Chapter 7 on the one hand, and Table 9.4 and later tables on the other. The two sentences with a plural verb and a singular noun predicate (examples (15) and (16)) are counted as plural examples in the former and singular in the latter, where they appear in the noun column.

4. It was scanned before the possibility of a difference between the verb and the participle in -*l* had been seriously considered. However, this corpus would have added little to Table 9.5 as all the examples of verbs, including the participle in -*l*, show singular agreement.

5. There is interesting variation between the spoken and written language. In the written language, the singular is favoured in the verb and short-form adjective, while both forms are about equally acceptable for long-form adjectives and nouns. Informants, however, accept singular and plural forms for the verb and short-form adjective; are very reluctant to accept singular long-form adjectives; and reject singular nouns. This variation is summarised in Table 9.ii. The

Table 9.ii: Agreement with Relative *kto*: Varying Norms

	verb		short-form adjective		long-form adjective		noun	
	sg	pl	sg	pl	sg	pl	sg	pl
written sources	✓	(✓)	✓	(✓)	✓	✓	✓	✓
informants	✓	✓	✓	✓	?*	✓	*	✓

informants show a regular shift in favour of plural (semantically justified) agreement as compared to the literary norm. Both variants are in accord with the requirements of the Predicate Hierarchy.

6. Past passive participles are included here: our data on conjoined noun phrases do not give grounds for treating them separately (cf. Chapter 3, note 5).

7. The totals of the subject-predicate inanimate section differ by two from figures given in Chapter 7 for the reason given in note 3. In addition, sentences with subjects consisting of a mixture of animates and inanimates are necessarily excluded from this table, which is why it includes eight fewer examples than Table 9.7.

8. Verb percentages add up to 101, owing to rounding of percentages.

Earlier in the book we investigated the target factors which influence agreement. Then, by concentrating on one type of target, the predicate, we were able to discover the controller factors at work. Having isolated target and controller factors, we analysed their interaction in Chapter 9. Throughout our study we have been careful to define the area in which factors are permitted to vary, to make sure that the effects observed have a single source. We can now allow controllers greater scope for variation than before. In this chapter we consider the full range of combinations of person, number and gender which can occur in the controller. And in Chapter 11 we survey the variety of agreements found with different quantifiers.

Resolution rules are one of the most interesting areas of Slavic syntax.[1] They apply in agreement with conjoined expressions. This is a subject we have already examined in some detail, but our analysis was deliberately restricted to agreement in number. However, there are other interesting problems, particularly when we have noun phrases which differ in gender. For example, those languages which preserve gender in the plural must have rules to specify the agreement with, say, a neuter plural and a feminine singular noun conjoined. The rules which determine the agreement form to be used in such cases may be termed 'resolution rules' as in Givón (1970); they fulfil the same function as Vanek's 'feature computation rules' (1970, 45-6). Resolution rules take their name from their ability to resolve clashes between noun phrases carrying different features; but in some instances they apply to noun phrases with the same features. For example, if two noun phrases in Russian are singular, the operation of the number resolution rule will produce plural agreement. When the resolution rules operate, there is agreement with all the conjuncts; therefore, the resulting agreement form always has greater semantic justification than that which appears if they fail to operate (when agreement is with one conjunct only). In these terms, our analysis of conjoined structures in Chapters 7, 8 and 9 was an investigation of the factors which made number resolution more or less likely to occur. We took for granted the use of the plural as the 'resolution form' – the form used for agreement with all conjuncts. In this chapter our main concern will be precisely with the question of the forms which are determined by the resolution rules. This involves another type of interplay of target and controller factors: the forms selected depend on the composition of the controller and on the morphological possibilities of the target.

Person resolution (§10.1) and number resolution (§10.2) operate in a similar fashion throughout the Slavic language family. Gender resolution shows considerable variety (§10.3) but we can identify common motivating factors at work (§10.4). We will concentrate on predicate agreement, where the greatest variation is found. In §10.5, however, we will discuss the operation of the resolution rules in general, including targets other than the predicate.

10.1 Person Resolution

When different persons are conjoined the rule, as Vondrák points out (1928, 432; following Miklosich, 1868-74, 763), is that the first person has priority over the second and the second over the third. In (1), first and second persons are conjoined:

(1) Sk: *Ja a   ty   sme* (1st pers pl) *bratia*
          I and you are   brothers
          (Bartoš and Gagnaire, 1972, 223)

The verb stands in the first person. The first person also results from the conjunction of first and third persons:

(2) OCS: отьсь *tvoi i   azz skrzbęšta iskaxově* (1st pers dual)
          father your and I   grieving   were seeking
          tebe
          you
          (Luke 2.48, quoted by Vondrák, 1928, 432)
(3) U: *Ale ščo   najcikaviše :   tak počuvajemo* (1st pers pl)
          But what (is) most interesting so   feel
          ne til'ky Mohyljans'kyj i   ja
          not only Mohyljans'kyj and I
          (Shevelov, 1963, 63)

When second and third persons are conjoined, we find second person agreements:

(4) SC: *Ti   i   Milan radićete* (2nd pers pl) *zajedno*
You and Milan will work   together
(Gudkov, 1969, 91)˙

(5) R: ... *vy   i   vaša sestrica kataetes'* (2nd pers pl) *na*
you and your sister   ride   on
velosipede ...
a bicycle
(Čexov, *Čelovek v futljare*)

The person resolution rules required may be stated as follows:

1. if the conjuncts include a first person, first person agreement forms will be used;
2. if the conjuncts include a second person, second person agreement forms will be used.

These rules are ordered – the second operates only if the condition on the operation of the first is not met. If neither rule operates, then third person forms are assigned by default. This results from a default condition which applies for any controller which is not marked as first or second person. Third person is best viewed as an absence of person marking; it is used for nouns and other elements, such as infinitives, which may function as subject.[2] Since this assignment of third person forms is brought about by a general default condition, there is no need for a separate resolution rule.

Most writers who deal with person resolution in Slavic state or imply that there must be agreement with all the constituents, in other words that the person resolution rules must apply. However, there are instances where person resolution need not operate. In Czech, agreement in person with the nearest conjunct only is perfectly acceptable, providing the verb precedes the subject, as in the sentence (from Trávníček, 1949, 433):

(6) Cz: *Půjdu* (1st pers sg) *tam   já a   ty*
Will go   there I and you

Here we see that the person resolution rules have not operated; the predicate agrees just with the nearer pronoun. The fact that this type of agreement usually occurs with predicate-subject word-order comes as no surprise in view of our discussion of precedence in §8.2. Occasional examples of agreement in person with the nearest conjunct are found in Russian; the following is particularly unusual as it has subject-predicate word-order:

(7) R: ... *ja i   ešče   odin iz nas možet* (3rd pers sg) *idti*
           I and another one of us can   go
           domoj ...
           home
           (Hertzen, quoted in Vinogradov and Istrina, 1954, 492)

Here again we have agreement with the nearer conjunct only.[3] Examples like this with no person resolution are rare in Russian. And in Slavic in general, person resolution usually applies. This is not surprising, as personal pronouns are animate and tend to precede the verb; thus both the main controller factors which favour semantically justified agreement are normally present.

When person resolution operates, the rules above cover all the cases. It is worth asking why these rules are of such general validity. The reason is that they correspond to the semantics of the personal pronouns. The first person plural pronoun can be used to mean 'speaker plus listener' or 'speaker plus another person', without any overt conjunction. These meanings are matched by the resolution rule which determines that a first person conjoined with a second or third person is resolved as first person. Similarly, the second person pronoun can on its own be used to indicate 'listener plus other person'; this is reflected in the rule which resolves second and third persons conjoined into the second person. Thus the person resolution rules have a clear semantic basis. They are also in accord with Givón's Topic Hierarchy (1976, 166) and they match Zwicky's Hierarchy of Reference, which constrains pronominal systems (1977, 718, 725).

10.2 Number Resolution

Most Slavic languages have only the singular and plural numbers. The dual survives in Slovene and Sorbian, though it is losing ground in the latter. The dual is used as a resolution form, providing the controller consists of two conjuncts, both of which are singular. Sentence (2) above is just such an instance in Old Church Slavic; (8) illustrates the same phenomenon in Slovene:

(8) Sn: *Tonček i   Igor sta* (dual) *prizadevna* (dual)
Tonček and Igor are   assiduous
(Lenček, 1972, 60)

Example (9) from Sorbian completes the set of languages where this rule applies:

(9) US: *Awto   a   motorske   stej* (dual) *važnej*
The car and the motor cycle are   important
komunikaciskej srĕdkaj (dual)
communication means
(Šewc-Schuster, 1976, 59)

In these languages, if there are two conjuncts of which one or both are not in the singular, then the plural is the resolution form. In example (10) we have singular and dual conjoined:

(10) Sn: *Marta in   njegova   brata* (dual) *bodo* (pl) *prišli* (pl)
Marta and his [Igor's] brothers   will   come
(Lenček, 1972, 61)

The next example has two duals conjoined (Šewc-Schuster, personal communication):[4]

(11) US: *Ruce* (dual) *a   noze* (dual) *mje bola* (pl)
Hands   and feet   me hurt
(My hands and feet hurt.)

If there are more than two conjuncts, then again the plural is used:

(12) Sn: *Tonček, Igor in   Jurček so* (pl) *prizadevni* (pl)
Tonček, Igor and Jurček are   assiduous
(Lenček, 1972, 61)

For further examples see (19)–(27) below. Finally, in the remaining Slavic languages, where the dual has been lost, when any elements[5] are conjoined the plural is the resolution form:

(13) P: *Na ulicy   Andrzej i   Amelia milczeli* (pl)
On the street Andrzej and Amelia were silent
(Gojawiczyńska, quoted by Kallas, 1974, 64)

We encountered many similar examples from Russian in Chapter 7. The number resolution rules required to cover these possibilities are as follows:

1. (for Old Church Slavic, Slovene and Sorbian only) if there are two conjuncts only, both of which are in the singular, then dual agreement forms will be used;
2. in all other cases, providing there is at least one non-plural conjunct, plural agreement forms will be used.

At first sight the restriction on the second rule appears superfluous; why should not instances where all the conjuncts are plural be covered by this rule? Subjects consisting only of plurals will, naturally, take plural predicates but there is no need for a resolution rule to be involved – the plural form results from agreement with the nearer conjunct. As we shall see below (§10.5.1) there are examples which prove that no resolution rule operates in such cases. A second complication with number agreement is that it frequently does not occur (as we saw in Chapter 7). Agreement is then with one conjunct only, normally the nearest, though agreement with the first, most distant, conjunct is also possible (§6.2.2). The option for agreement to be with all conjuncts (for the resolution rules to operate) or for agreement to be with one conjunct only (for the resolution rules not to operate) has already been examined. The target factors involved were discussed in §2.1.5 and §2.1.7, the controller factors in Chapters 7 and 8 and their interaction in Chapter 9. The main part of this chapter (the next two sections) is concerned with examples where resolution does occur.

The number resolution rules given above are similar in all the Slavic languages, apart from the provision for the dual in Old Church Slavic, Slovene and Sorbian. The reason why the rules have no variants is that they correspond to the semantics of the number categories. The plural number includes in its semantics the various types of conjoined structures. Thus 'entity plus entity plus entity' is a particular case of a plural. Similarly the dual is used of two entities, and again 'entity plus entity' is an example covered by the meaning of the dual. Both number and person resolution rules determine forms which correspond to the semantics of their respective categories; they therefore work in the same fashion in the different Slavic languages. Of course, grammatical person and number do not correspond exactly to real-world person and number (the use of honorifics like *vy* is a good example of a lack of correspondence). There is nevertheless a close relationship between the two, and this accounts in part for the simplicity of the resolution rules. The relationship between grammatical gender and the real world is much less clear; and gender resolution is considerably more complex than person and number resolution.

10.3 Gender Resolution

Gender resolution rules do not operate in all the Slavic languages. The East Slavic languages as well as Bulgarian and Macedonian of the South Slavic group do not distinguish gender in the plural; there is only one agreement form in the plural and so there can be no question of gender resolution. The languages that do require gender resolution – the West Slavic languages and Slovene, Old Church Slavic and Serbo-Croat in the Southern group – show interesting differences, and so will be dealt with individually. We begin with the South Slavic languages.

10.3.1 Slovene

In Slovene, the possible agreement forms in the predicate are as shown in Table 10.1 (*bil* is the past participle of the verb *biti* 'to be').

Table 10.1: Agreement Forms in Slovene

	masculine	feminine	neuter
singular	bil	bila	bilo
dual	bila	bili	
plural	bili	bile	bila

Let us first consider examples with a dual predicate; recall that the dual can result from the resolution rules only if two (and no more than two) singular nouns are conjoined. (All the examples in this section are from Lenček, 1972.)

(14) Sn: *Tonček* (masc) *i Marina* (fem) *sta*
Tonček   and Marina   are
prizadevna (masc dual)
assiduous

(15) Sn: *Tonček* (masc) *in to dekletce* (neut) *sta*
Tonček   and that little girl   are
prizadevna (masc dual)
assiduous

Here we see that when a masculine is conjoined with either a feminine (14) or a neuter (15), then a masculine dual predicate is found. Conjoining two feminines requires a feminine dual:

(16) Sn: *Marina* (fem) *in Marta* (fem) *sta prizadevni* (fem dual)
Marina and Marta are assiduous

Although the feminine and neuter dual forms are the same, it is not the feminine/neuter form which is used when a feminine and neuter singular are conjoined. Surprisingly, it is the masculine dual:

(17) Sn: *Ta streha* (fem) *in gnezdo* (neut) *na njej mi bosta*
That roof and the nest on it to me will
ostala (masc dual) *v spominu*
remain in memory
(i.e. will remain in my memory)

If two neuter singular nouns are conjoined, the same masculine dual agreement form is found:

(18) Sn: *To drevo* (neut) *in gnezdo* (neut) *na njem mi*
That tree and the nest on it to me
bosta ostala (masc dual) *v spominu*
will remain in memory

Thus the feminine form occurs only when both conjuncts are feminine – otherwise we find the masculine.

Our examples so far have had dual predicates. Let us look at examples where a plural predicate occurs. This may be because there are more than two conjuncts:

(19) Sn: *Tonček* (masc), *Igor* (masc) *in Marina* (fem) *so*
Tonček Igor and Marina are
prizadevni (masc pl)
assiduous

(20) Sn: *Tonček* (masc), *Igor* (masc) *in to dekletce* (neut)
Tonček Igor and that little girl
so prizadevni (masc pl)
are assiduous

(21) Sn: *Tonček* (masc), *Marina* (fem) *in to dekletce* (neut)
Tonček Marina and that little girl

so prizadevni (masc pl)
are assiduous

In each of these sentences there is at least one masculine conjunct, and we find masculine plural predicates. In our next two examples there are only two conjuncts, but we still find a plural predicate, because one of the conjuncts is not in the singular. Example (22) includes a dual conjunct:

(22) = (10) Sn: *Marta* (fem) *in njegova brata* (masc dual)
     Marta and his [Igor's] (two) brothers
     bodo prišli (masc pl)
     will come

In the following example we find a plural conjunct:

(23) Sn: *Igor* (masc) *in njegove sestre* (fem pl) *bodo*
   Igor and his sisters   will
   prišli (masc pl)
   come

In both of these sentences, as in (19)–(21), one of the conjuncts is masculine and the predicate is masculine plural. When all the conjuncts are feminine, then a feminine predicate is found:

(24) Sn: *Marina* (fem), *Marta* (fem) *in Marjanca* (fem)
   Marina Marta and Marjanca
   so prizadevne (fem pl)
   are assiduous
(25) Sn: *Marta* (fem) *in njene sestre* (fem pl) *bodo prišle* (fem pl)
   Marta and her sisters   will come

As in the dual, conjoining feminine and neuter leads to a masculine predicate:

(26) Sn: *Ta streha* (fem), *okno* (neut) *in gnezdo* (neut) *pod*
   That roof window and nest under
   njim mi bodo ostali (masc pl) *v spominu*
   it to me will remain in memory

The masculine also results when only neuters are conjoined:

(27) Sn: *To   okno* (neut), *drevo* (neut) *in   gnezdo* (neut)
          That window   tree   and nest
          v njem mi   bodo ostali (masc pl) *v spominu*
          in it   to me will   remain   in memory

The pattern of gender resolution for plural predicates is exactly the same as that which we observed for dual predicates. This means that the number resolution rules described earlier can determine the number required and that a single set of gender resolution rules can operate in all cases. Although the picture appears complex, the gender resolution rules can be stated simply:

1. if all conjuncts are feminine, then the feminine form is used;
2. otherwise the masculine form is used.[6]

10.3.2 Old Church Slavic

It is difficult to establish the situation in Old Church Slavic as most authorities pay scant attention to syntax. Moreover, resolution usually did not occur: agreement with the nearer conjunct was the norm (Xaburgaev, 1974, 371). However, Vaillant (1977, 13) discusses gender resolution briefly and states that when a masculine and a feminine are conjoined, masculine agreement forms are found, as is also the case when a feminine and a neuter are conjoined. His examples include the following:

(28) OCS: отьсь (masc) *ego i   mati* (fem) *ego*
          father   his and mother   his
          čudęšta (masc dual) *sę*
          being surprised
          (Luke 2.33)

In this example masculine and feminine singular conjuncts take masculine plural agreement. In the next sentence, a feminine and a neuter singular take the same form:

(29) OCS: slзnьce (neut) *bo i   luna* (fem) . . .
          sun   for and moon
          sзtvorena (masc dual) *jesta* (dual)
          made   are

(for sun and moon . . . were made)
(*Čudovskaja psaltyr'* 71.17)

Unfortunately, Vaillant does not mention conjoined feminines or conjoined neuters. The data available are consistent with the rules proposed for Slovene; until further evidence is found, we would not be justified in proposing a different analysis.

10.3.3 Serbo-Croat

The remaining South Slavic language with gender resolution rules, Serbo-Croat, is particularly interesting. It differs from Slovene, in having lost the dual, so there are fewer possible predicative endings.[7] These are illustrated by the past active participle of *biti* 'to be' in

Table 10.2: Agreement Forms in Serbo-Croat

	masculine	feminine	neuter
singular	bio	bila	bilo
plural	bili	bile	bila

Table 10.2. The agreements appear to be as in Slovene; thus we find a masculine predicate when one of the conjuncts is masculine:

(30) SC: *Plač* (masc) *i   kletve* (fem pl) *roditelja i   sva*
The crying and curses   of parents and all
nastojanja (neut pl) *sarajevskih   fratara nisu*
the efforts   of the Sarajevan monks did not
ništa   pomagali (masc pl).
anything help
(Andrić, *Kod Kazana*)

Similarly, conjoining feminine and neuter gives a masculine:

(31) SC: *Znanje* (neut) *i   intuicija* (fem) *su   kod njega*
Knowledge   and intuition   have in   him
sarađivali (masc pl) *i   dopunjavali* (masc pl)
worked together   and supplemented
se . . .
each other
(Andrić, *Travnička Hronika*)

(32) SC: ... *i   kad   bi   sumnje* (fem pl) *i   pitanja* (neut pl)
            and when would doubts   and questions
            učestali (masc pl)...
            become frequent
            (Andrić, *Travnička Hronika*)

The following example shows two neuter singular nouns with a masculine plural predicate:

(33) SC: *Njegovo mesto* (neut) *u   razvitku   kasabe*
            His   place   in the development of the town
            i   njegovo značenje (neut) *u   životu kasabalija*
            and his   importance   in the life of the inhabitants
            bili (masc pl) *su onakvi* (masc pl) *kako   smo ih*
            were   such   as (we) have them
            napred ukratko opisali.
            before briefly   described
            (Andrić, quoted by Gudkov, 1969, 91)

As we would expect, conjoining feminine nouns can give a feminine predicate:

(34) SC: *Sve snage* (fem pl) *i   sva pažnja* (fem sg) *biće*
            All powers   and all attention   will be
            posvećene (fem pl) *toj   borbi*...
            dedicated   to this struggle
            (Andrić, *Travnička Hronika*)

(35) SC: ... *njegova duhovna   lenost* (fem) *i   moralna*
            his   intellectual laziness   and moral
            ravnodušnost (fem) *nagonile* (fem pl) *su ga*...
            indifference   forced   him
            (Andrić, *Travnička Hronika*)

(36) SC: *Opreznost* (fem), *suptilnost* (fem) *i   pedanterija* (fem)
            The discretion   subtlety   and pedantry
            tih   bezbrojnih   poruka   zbunjivale (fem pl)
            of these innumerable assignments perplexed
            su mladića...
            the young man
            (Andrić, *Travnička Hronika*)

On the evidence so far we might reasonably conclude that the gender resolution rules are the same as those of Slovene: the predicate is feminine when all conjuncts are feminine, and masculine otherwise. There is, however, an interesting complication. Note that the feminine nouns in (36) are of two different types. *Pedanterija*, like the majority of feminine nouns in Serbo-Croat, ends in *-a* in the nominative singular (the *-a* declension). There is also a sizeable group of nouns like *opreznost* and *suptilnost* which have no inflection in the nominative singular (the *-ø* declension). These decline rather differently from nouns like *pedanterija* (they also decline differently from masculine nouns, the majority of which also have no inflection in the nominative singular). Though morphologically dissimilar, the two types of feminine noun generally behave in the same way for agreement purposes, which is of course why they are assigned to the same gender. The complication arises in gender resolution. As Gudkov (1965) points out, a masculine predicate is possible, even though all the conjuncts are feminine, providing that at least one of them belongs to the *-ø* declension, as does *lakomislenost* in (37):

(37) SC: *Vređali* (masc pl) *su ga   nebriga* (fem)   *i*
Offended   him the carelessness and
lakomislenost (fem) *Tahir-begova.*
capriciousness   of Tahir-beg
(Andrić, *Travnička Hronika*)

This type of agreement is not obligatory, as can be seen from (36), which has a feminine plural predicate even though the subject contains two nouns of the *-ø* declension, as well as one of the *-a* declension. Indeed, examples like (36) are more common than those like (37). The masculine agreement in (37) does not depend on a mixture of types, as has been claimed (Stevanović, 1974, 129). This is demonstrated by the following example, which shows no less than five femininines all of the same declensional type (the *-ø* declension), but still with a masculine plural predicate:

(38) SC: *Vezirova   potpuna   ukočenost* (fem), *njegova*
The vizir's complete inflexibility   his
ispravnost (fem) *u   novčanim pitanjima, i   zatim*
correctness   in financial questions and then
Tahir-begova umešnost (fem), *umerenost* (fem) *i*
Tahir-beg's skilfulness   moderation   and

> *širokgrudnost* (fem) *u upravljanju   zemljom,*
> generosity   in administering the country
> *stvarali* (masc pl) *su* . . .
> created
> (Andrić, *Travnička Hronika*)

Once again the feminine plural is more common, as in (35). The formulation of the agreement rule is difficult. Normally agreement rules refer
to syntactic or semantic categories, but here it seems that the relevant
factor is morphological — the declensional class of the noun.

Alternatively, one could look to a syntactic and phonological
condition, referring to feminine nouns which end in a consonant in the
nominative singular. This phonological similarity to masculine nouns
may well be a contributory factor in the development of the unusual
masculine agreements. However, the condition just suggested is inadequate for the following reason. Final *o* in Serbo-Croat may alternate
with non-final *l*. Thus *misao* 'thought' has the genitive singular *misli* (the
a occurs only in the nominative). This alternation accounts for the form
bio in Table 10.2. In nouns, however, it is not predictable: there are
nouns like *misal* 'missal' where the *l* is retained when final, and others
like *biro* 'office' (genitive *biroa*) where the *o* is retained non-finally.
Misao is a feminine noun of the -ϕ declension. It would not be covered
by the phonological condition above, since it ends in a vowel. However,
misao and similar nouns can give rise to masculine resolved forms:

(39) SC: . . . *ono crno i   strašno   u   što   su*
            that black and terrible (thing) into which had
         se odavno u njemu pretvorili (masc pl) *misao* (fem)
            long ago in him   turned   the thought
         na Krstino ubistvo i   želja (fem) *za sopstvenom*
            of Krsta's murder and the desire for his own
         smrću
         death
         (Andrić, *Anikina Vremena*)

Given that a non-predictable consonant alternation is involved, the
phonological condition loses any possible advantage, which makes the
morphological condition preferable. The resolution rule must refer to
the morphological feature which marks nouns like *opreznost*, *suptilnost*
and *misao* (say + declension IV). We shall continue to refer to them as
nouns of the -ϕ declension.

Having accepted the need for a morphological condition, we can adopt similar resolution rules to those required for Slovene, but we must allow for the first rule to be optional under certain conditions:

1. if all conjuncts are feminine, then the feminine form will be used; if at least one of the conjuncts is a noun of the -ϕ declension, then this rule is optional;
2. otherwise the predicate will be in the masculine.

The first rule, with its unusual morphological condition, is being further weakened. Gudkov (1974, 61) gives some remarkable examples in which the verb is masculine plural though all the conjuncts consist of feminine nouns of the -*a* declension:[8]

(40) SC: *Štula* (fem)   *i*   *štaka* (fem) *bili* (masc pl) *su sve što*
A wooden leg and a crutch   were   all that
je tadašnja   medicina mogla da mu   pruži.
of that time medicine could   to him offer
(M. Popović)

(41) SC: *Krošnja* (fem)   *i*   *grane* (fem pl) *zahvatili* (masc pl)
The crown (of tree) and branches   occupied
su čitavo   nebo . . .
the whole sky
(B. Ćosić, both quoted by Gudkov, 1974, 61)

These examples suggest that the first rule is becoming optional in certain cases even when both feminine nouns are of the -*a* declension. Thus Serbo-Croat has the same basic rules as Slovene, but the position of the first is being undermined so that the use of the masculine plural as the resolution form is becoming more frequent. We shall return to this development and the motivation for it in §10.4 below. In §10.5.1 we shall consider conjoined neuter plurals, which are not subject to the resolution rules. First, however, let us examine the gender resolution rules found in the West Slavic languages.

10.3.4 Czech

In the West Slavic languages, masculine nouns are divided into two categories in the plural. In Czech they are divided into animates and inanimates. The agreement forms are given in Table 10.3, and the past participle is again used for illustration. It can be seen that the masculine inanimates share an agreement form with the feminines, but

Table 10.3: Agreement Forms in Czech

	masculine animate	masculine inanimate	feminine	neuter
singular	byl		byla	bylo
plural	byli	byly		byla

not with the neuters. In spoken Czech, these gender distinctions in the plural have been lost: the vowels *i* and *y* are phonetically equivalent, and this ending is also used for the neuter plural, rather than the ending *-a*. The spoken language is therefore of little interest from the point of view of gender resolution. However, Standard Written Czech is worth study. It differs considerably from spoken Czech, and preserves the earlier, very interesting situation. All our examples are taken from this variety; they are quoted from Bauernöppel *et al.* (1976, 163-4; examples (42), (43), (45) and (47)); Širokova (1977, 166; example (44)); and Trávníček (1949, 432; example (46)).

Let us first consider sentences which include masculine animates conjoined with other genders:

    (42) Cz: *Člověk* (masc anim) *a   stroj* (masc inan)
                 The man   and the machine
                 pracovali (masc anim)
                 were working
    (43) Cz: *Bratr* (masc anim) *a   sestra* (fem) *přišli* (masc anim)
                 Brother   and sister   came

Example (42) shows a masculine animate conjoined with a masculine inanimate, and (43) shows a masculine animate conjoined with a feminine; in both cases a masculine animate plural verb form is used. The next sentence shows masculine and neuter conjoined, both plurals in this instance:

    (44) Cz: *Chlapci* (masc anim pl) *a   děvčata* (neut pl) *se*
                 Youths   and girls
                 vydali (masc anim) *na cestu*
                 set out   on the way

Once again the masculine animate form is found in the predicate. We conclude that if there is a masculine animate in the subject, then a masculine animate predicate will result (bear in mind that resolution is not always obligatory, as discussed above). Now suppose that there is no masculine animate in the compound subject:

(45) Cz: *Matka* (fem) *a*   *dítě* (neut) *čekaly* (masc inan/fem)
         The mother and child   waited

The conjunction of feminine and neuter, as in (45) leads to a masculine inanimate/feminine plural verb. Let us now consider neuter nouns:

(46) Cz: *Srbsko* (neut) *a*   *Bulharsko* (neut) *byly* (masc inan/fem)
         Serbia   and Bulgaria   were
         osvobozeny (masc inan/fem)
         liberated
(47) Cz: *Města* (neut pl) *a*   *jejich okolí* (neut sg) *nám*
         The towns   and their surrounding   to us
         byly (masc inan/fem) *dobře známé* (masc inan/fem)
         were   well   known

Example (46) demonstrates that conjoining neuter singular nouns produces not the neuter plural verb that we might expect, but a masculine inanimate/feminine plural form. This occurs when at least one of the nouns is singular, as in (47). If both were plural then, as in Serbo-Croat, no resolution would be possible and a neuter plural would result; such sentences will be analysed in §10.5.1. The situation appears complex; however, the gender resolution rules are comparatively simple:

1. if the conjuncts include at least one masculine animate form, the masculine animate form is used;
2. otherwise the masculine inanimate/feminine form is used.

Note that the neuter plural ending *-a*, which is preserved in Standard Written Czech for agreement with neuter plural nouns, never occurs as a result of the operation of the resolution rules. The same was true of the South Slavic languages; we shall consider why this should be so in §10.4.

10.3.5 Slovak

In Slovak the past tense verb has lost all gender distinctions in the plural (de Bray, 1980b, 205). However, the adjective preserves just one distinction, as shown by the forms of *zdravý* 'healthy'. Table 10.4

Table 10.4: Agreement Forms in Slovak

	masculine personal	non-personal	feminine	neuter
singular	zdravý		zdravá	zdravé
plural	zdraví		zdravé	

illustrates two ways in which Slovak and the other West Slavic languages differ from Czech: first, the masculines are divided into personals (i.e. those referring to humans) and non-personals; second, the non-personal form is shared with the feminines and neuters (there is no separate neuter plural form).

If the subject includes a masculine personal form then the predicative adjective will be masculine personal (Stanislav, 1977, 185–6); see also Pauliny *et al.*, 1968, 370):

(48) Sk: *Otec* (masc pers)*, matka* (fem) *a   diet'a* (neut) *sú*
Father   mother   and child   are
zdraví (masc pers)
healthy

In the absence of a masculine personal conjunct (even if the conjuncts are of mixed gender), the non-masculine personal form (= feminine/ neuter plural form) is used:

(49) Sk: *Naše mestá* (neut pl) *a   dediny* (fem pl) *sú   čoraz*
Our towns   and villages   are ever
krajšie (non-masc pers)[9]
more beautiful

The gender resolution rules are as follows:

1. if there is at least one masculine personal conjunct, the masculine personal form is used:
2. otherwise the non-masculine personal form is used.

10.3.6 Sorbian

Sorbian differs from the other West Slavic languages in preserving the dual number, though not in all dialects. Lower Sorbian, however, has lost gender distinctions both in the dual and in the plural and so will not be considered further. Upper Sorbian distinguishes masculine personal and non-masculine personal. The full range of possibilities is given in Table 10.5, the past active participle forms of *dźělać* 'to do, to work'. The resolution rules are as in Slovak: if there is at least one

Table 10.5: Agreement Forms in Upper Sorbian

	masculine personal	masculine non-personal	feminine	neuter
singular	dźělał	dźělał	dźělała	dźělało
dual	dźělałoj	dźělałej	dźělałej	
plural	dźělali	dźělałe	dźělałe	

masculine personal conjunct, the masculine personal form is used, otherwise the non-masculine personal form. This can be seen in the following examples (from Šewc-Schuster, 1976, 58-9):

> (50) US: *Wuj* (masc pers) *a   ćeta* (fem) *chcetaj* (masc pers dual)
>   Uncle   and aunt   want
>   *dar   nam   dać.*   (Winger)
>   a gift to us to give
> (51) = (9) US: *Awto* (neut) *a   motorske* (neut)
>   The car   and the motorcycle
>   *stej* (non-masc pers dual) *ważnej   komunikaciskej*
>   are   important communication
>   *srědkaj* (dual)
>   means

The finite verb (second and third persons dual) has the opposition of *-aj* for masculine personal and *-ej* for non-masculine personal agreements (as in (50) and (51)). The distinction between *-oj* and *-ej* in the past participle is largely lost (the masculine personal form *-oj* being used in all cases); in the dialects the distinction is also being lost in the finite verb forms and the ending *-ej* is then used for both genders. In the plural there is no distinction in the present tense, and most dialects have lost the *li~łe* opposition in the past participle (the masculine personal forms in *li* being generalised). However, north-western dialects preserve the opposition, as in the following sentences:[10]

> (52) US: *Nan* (masc pers), *mać* (fem) *a   bratr* (masc pers) *su*
>   Father   mother   and brother   have

> *mje wopytali* (masc pers)
> me visited

(53) US: *Kniha* (fem), *list* (masc) *a   wołojnik* (masc) *su   na*
> A book   a letter   and a pencil   were on
> *blidźe   leżałe* (non-masc pers)
> the table lying

Example (52) contains a masculine personal conjunct – and so the verb is masculine personal; (53) includes two masculine conjuncts but neither is personal and so a non-masculine personal verb results. The situation in the dialects is certainly complex.[11] Nevertheless, gender resolution always follows the same principle: whenever there is an opposition masculine personal ~ non-masculine personal, the masculine personal form is used providing there is at least one masculine personal conjunct. Together with the number resolution rules, the same gender resolution rules as were proposed for Slovak are sufficient to account for the data.

10.3.7 Polish

Like Slovak and Upper Sorbian, Polish has just two agreement possibilities in the plural. This distinction is found in the past tense, as illustrated by the verb *być* 'to be' in Table 10.6. Note that the two plural

Table 10.6: Agreement Forms in Polish

| | masculine | | feminine | neuter |
	personal	non-personal		
singular	był		była	było
plural	byli		były	

forms are clearly distinguished by the consonant alternation *ł ~ l*, as well as by different vowel quality. Feminine nouns, including those referring to humans, take the non-masculine personal form:

(54) P: *Siostry* (fem) *i   matka* (fem) *czytały* (non-masc pers)
> Sisters   and mother   were reading

However, the addition of a masculine personal noun produces masculine personal agreement (both examples are from Kulak *et al.*, 1966, 249):

(55) P: *Brat* (masc pers), *siostry* (fem) *i*   *matka* (fem)
Brother   sisters   and mother
czytali (masc pers)
were reading

It appears that the gender resolution rules given for Slovak are adequate for Polish: that is, if the subject includes a masculine personal conjunct, the predicate will be in the masculine personal form; and otherwise the predicate will be in the non-masculine personal form.

Examples like (54) and (55), together with rules which are equivalent to those given, can be found in numerous sources. There are however, interesting complications; Doroszewski (1962, 237) discusses the following example:

(56) P: *Hania* (fem) *i*   *Reks* (masc) *bawili* (masc pers)
Hania   and Reks   played
się piłką
with a ball

Hania is a girl's name, while *Reks* (Rex) is a dog. There is no masculine personal conjunct in this sentence, and so the rules would require the non-masculine personal form. The status of such sentences has aroused some discussion. Doroszewski gives no alternative, but Klemensiewicz (1967, 44-5) reports that speakers hesitate over the use of the masculine personal or non-masculine personal form in similar sentences (see also Brooks, 1973, 61-2; Rothstein, 1973, 313); Informant work suggests that the masculine personal form is strongly preferred,[12] while Buttler *et al.* (1971, 332) state that in such sentences it is the required form. The most informative study to date is that of Zieniukowa (1979); she describes responses to a questionnaire by 31 schoolchildren in their upper teens. In the following sentence, comparable to (56), the majority.. used the masculine personal form:

(57) P: *Basia* (fem) *i*   *piesek* (masc) *bawili* (masc pers)
Basia   and the dog   played
się w kuchni
in the kitchen

Zieniukowa reports (1979, 124) that only two informants used the non-masculine personal form in this sentence (and one used a different construction). In a sentence like (57), but with a second noun referring

to a female human added, all informants except one chose the masculine
personal form (1979, 124). Thus the masculine personal form is strongly
favoured in sentences like (56) and (57), but is not the exclusive form
as it is in (55).

According to Doroszewski, the masculine personal results from the
combination of subject nouns. Clearly the presence of the female human
conjunct in (57) cannot of itself produce the masculine personal
predicate, as example (54) shows. Nor, according to Doroszewski, is
a masculine animate conjunct sufficient on its own. He claims that
when there are only masculine animates in the subject, then the non-
masculine personal form is required (1962, 237):

(58) P: *Reks i   Burek pogryzły* (non-masc pers) *się*
          Reks and Burek bit   each other

For speakers like Doroszewski, a combination of feminine human and
masculine animate conjuncts results in a masculine personal predicate.
In sentences like (56) and (57) the subject is masculine personal 'on
aggregate'. Note that it is necessary to refer not only to the syntactic
gender of the nouns involved but also to semantic features (feminine
personal is not a syntactic category in Polish).

Doroszewski admitted only the non-masculine personal form in
sentences like (58), which have all masculine animate conjuncts. Klem-
enziewicz too (1967, 43-4) gives no alternative to the non-masculine
personal form. However, Zieniukowa found only seven informants
who agreed with Doroszewski; thus in example (59) the majority of
her 31 informants preferred the masculine personal form (1979, 123):

(59) P: *Pies* (masc) *i   kot* (masc) *jedli* (masc pers) *na podwórzu*
          The dog   and the cat   were eating   in the yard

Zieniukowa also tested two sentences with one masculine animate and
one masculine inanimate; in both cases the masculine personal form was
preferred. Clearly, then, the presence of a masculine animate form
makes the use of the masculine personal predicate possible; this is not
as likely as it is when there is also a conjunct referring to a female
human.

When the subject includes a masculine inanimate and a female
human, then again the masculine personal is possible. Zieniukowa
(1979, 124-5) reports that her informants were equally divided between
the following options (one informant chose neither):

(60) P: *Mama* (fem), *córeczka* (fem) *i   wózek* (masc)
      Mother   daughter   and pram
      ukazali (masc pers) *się nagle*
      appeared   suddenly
(61) P: *Mama* (fem), *córeczka* (fem) *i   wózek* (masc)
      Mother   daughter   and pram
      ukazały (non-masc pers) *się nagle*
      appeared   suddenly

In a similar sentence (but with only one feminine noun) the masculine personal form was favoured. Finally, there are examples where a minority of informants used a masculine personal form for two masculine inanimates, or for two feminine humans. Zieniukowa dismisses these as mistakes, but they may indicate that the masculine personal is further extending its scope.[13]

There are several other examples which show the need to extend the basic rules given above, but which were not included in Zieniukowa's questionnaire. The masculine personal form can be used when none of the nouns is syntactically masculine, as in the following example (Brooks, 1973, 61):

(62) P: *Pani* (fem) *i   dziecko* (neut) *szli* (masc pers)
      Lady   and child   went
      ulicą
      along the street

Here *dziecko* can refer to a male, even though syntactically it is neuter. Buttler *et al.* (1971, 332) give a similar sentence, but allow two possibilities in this case:

(63) P: *Dwoje dzieci* (neut) *i   kobieta* (fem) *uratowali* (masc pers)
      Two   children   and a woman   were saved
      się z   płonącego domu
      from the burning house
(64) P: *Dwoje dzieci* (neut) *i   kobieta* (fem)
      Two   children   and a woman
      uratowały (non-masc pers) *się z   płonącego domu*
      were saved   from the burning house

Rothstein (1976, 250) quotes an example where both nouns refer to male persons, though neither is masculine syntactically:

(65) P: *Wszystka młodzież* (fem) *i   biedactwo* (neut) *nie*
     Every   youth   and poor fellow   did not
     dali (masc pers) *za wygraną*...
     give   for win (i.e. did not give up)
     (Łusakowski)

We have seen that the masculine personal form can be used when the features masculine and personal are present in the subject, even though not in a single conjunct. Furthermore, these features may be either syntactic or semantic; thus in (60) there is a conjunct which is syntactically masculine and two conjuncts which are semantically personal (human), while in (65) the features masculine and personal are both semantic.

The evidence available indicates that the two rules often given for resolution in Polish need to be supplemented by two optional rules, as follows:

1. if there is at least one masculine personal conjunct, the masculine personal form is used;
2. if the conjuncts include the features masculine and personal, whether these are syntactic or semantic, the masculine personal form may be used;
3. if there is at least one masculine animate conjunct, the masculine personal form may be used;
4. otherwise the non-masculine personal form is used.

The first rule, which accounts for the form used in (55), requires no further comment. Rules 2 and 3, which are optional, both represent plausible weakenings of rule 1: in rule 2 the conditions apply to the controller as a whole rather than to a single conjunct and, more surprisingly, they allow semantic or syntactic features or a combination of these. Rule 3, on the other hand, retains the restriction to a single conjunct but reduces the requirement from personal to animate. Speakers like Doroszewski have rule 2 but not rule 3 (see discussion of example (58)) but many of the speakers in Zieniukowa's survey have both rules. Rule 2 accounts for the forms in sentences (60), (62), (63), (65). Rule 3 has operated in (59). It is significant that when both rule 2 and rule 3 can apply, then for Zieniukowa's informants the masculine personal form is almost obligatory (this is the situation in sentences (56) and (57)). When none of these rules apply, the non-masculine personal form is assigned by rule 4, as in sentences (54), (58), (61) and (64).

The resolution rules which operate in Polish require both syntactic and semantic conditions. A second point of interest is that the favoured resolution form is extending its scope (we noted some evidence for extension even beyond that reflected in the four rules above); in this respect the situation is similar to that which we observed in Serbo-Croat.

10.4 Strategies for Gender Resolution

We have investigated the rules for gender resolution in all the languages which require them. We noted that while person and number resolution are broadly the same in the various Slavic languages (apart from the additional factor of the dual in some instances), gender resolution rules differ. Within South Slavic and within West Slavic the differences are not great, but between the two groups there is a marked contrast. The different rules are presented in simplified form (ignoring complicating factors for the moment) in Table 10.7.

Table 10.7: Two Types of Gender Resolution

South Slavic	West Slavic

1. all conjuncts feminine
    → feminine predicate
	1. one conjunct masculine personal
	    → masculine personal predicate

2. otherwise masculine	2. otherwise non-masculine personal

The two groups appear to adopt opposing strategies. In the South Slavic group, the first rule picks out homogeneous controllers of a certain type. All 'mixed' controllers, as well as some other homogeneous ones, are assigned to the 'catch-all' category in rule 2. In the West, the presence of one conjunct of a certain type[14] is a sufficient condition for the operation of the first rule; clearly, many controllers containing mixed conjuncts will meet the condition on rule 1. While the rules are formulated differently for the two groups, the effect produced is largely the same — the masculine/masculine personal forms are favoured at the expense of the other forms. We must ask why this should be so.

In our discussion of person and number resolution, we explained the similarity of the rules in the different Slavic languages by appealing to a common semantic justification. It is natural to attempt a similar explanation for gender resolution. Let us consider first the instances where gender itself has a semantic basis, that is in nouns referring to humans. When a noun refers to both sexes simultaneously, the masculine form is used. For example, Serbo-Croat *Amerikanci* 'Americans' (the plural of *Amerikanac* 'American') can refer to American men and women. *Amerikanke* (the plural of *Amerikanka* 'American woman'), however, indicates that only women are included. When it refers to both sexes, *Amerikanci* and the numerous forms like it must take masculine plural agreements.[15] Similarly, Polish *państwo* 'Mr and Mrs' refers to both sexes; it has the appearance of a neuter singular noun but it takes masculine personal plural agreement forms.

We have established that the masculine is used to refer to both sexes with single nouns – independently of our resolution rules. This indicates that the semantics of the masculine gender include reference to both sexes. Thus we have a semantic basis for the resolution rules which require a masculine/masculine personal form for agreement with conjoined masculines and feminines, providing that these masculine and feminine nouns refer to humans. Let us now consider instances where gender has no semantic basis. When inanimates are involved, gender depends on morphological factors rather than on semantics (see Corbett, 1982b, for an account of how gender can be predicted in Russian). If the gender of the nouns themselves has no semantic basis, the resolution rules cannot assign a form whose gender will be semantically justified. It is understandable, therefore, that the resolution rules in this case should copy those which apply when gender is semantically based. Thus a combination of masculine and feminine is resolved as masculine. This is no more – and no less – surprising than the fact that nouns like Russian *stol* 'table' and *otec* 'father' take the same predicate agreement forms.

We have demonstrated that gender resolution is in part based on semantics. Two problems remain: the first is the impossibility of using the neuter plural as a resolution form, and the second is the extension of the scope of the masculine/masculine personal forms. In Slovene, Serbo-Croat and Written Standard Czech, there is a neuter plural form, but it cannot result from the operation of the resolution rules.[16] This seems particularly strange when all the conjuncts are neuter singular; whatever the semantic status of the neuter, it is surprising that it cannot serve as the agreement form when all the conjuncts are of that gender. Clearly we must look beyond the semantics of gender for for an explanation.

We have established that a motivating factor for the choice of the form to be favoured by the resolution rules is the *use of semantically justified gender forms.* A survey of a wide range of languages (Corbett, forthcoming b) reveals that this is the major factor which determines gender resolution. There is a second motivating factor at work: *clear marking of number.* As we have already seen, when the gender of the nouns involved in resolution has no semantic justification (when the nouns are inanimate) then no resolution form will be semantically justified in terms of gender. In this instance the resolution rules will operate to ensure that the resolution form clearly signals the appropriate number in as many instances as possible. This is a functional factor. However, as was noted earlier, grammatical number usually corresponds to number in the real world. Therefore the marking of duality or plurality will fulfil a semantic function, even if the particular form chosen is not justified in terms of gender. Thus this factor also has a semantic basis. With the two factors in mind, let us give further consideration to the agreement forms available, starting with Slovene as an example of a South Slavic language: Table 10.8 gives the relevant data.

Table 10.8: Agreement Endings in Slovene

	masculine	feminine	neuter
singular	ϕ	a	o/e
dual	a		i
plural	i	e	a

Note: Table 10.8 is slightly more complex than Table 10.1 as it includes the neuter ending -*e* which is taken by certain adjectives. These can occur in the predicate, but they did not appear in any of our examples.

Suppose the subject consists of two inanimate singular nouns; the number resolution rules specify the dual. The gender resolution rules cannot specify a form which would be semantically justified in terms of gender; we claim, therefore, that they will mark number as clearly as possible. Neither dual ending is unambiguously dual: the -*a* ending is found also in the singular, and the -*i* ending in the plural. However, the finite verb forms end in -*a* for all genders; for this reason -*a* is a clearer marker of duality than -*i* and so is favoured by the resolution rules (it is used except when there are two feminine conjuncts). Now let us consider instances where the gender resolution rules are to mark the predicate clearly as plural. Then the neuter ending -*a* would not be favoured because it coincides with the feminine singular and, though this is probably of less importance, with the masculine dual. Of the remaining alternatives, the feminine plural -*e* also occurs in the singular while the masculine -*i* is found in the dual as well as in the plural. In terms of marking plurality, a case can be made for the masculine and for the feminine, but the neuter ending would be avoided.

We can now assess the relative merits of the different forms. The masculine forms (dual and plural) are semantically justified in some cases (when the conjuncts refer to male persons or to persons of both sexes). In the dual, the masculine marks number more clearly than the alternative, and in the plural it marks number as clearly as or more clearly than the alternatives. As a result of these two factors, the masculine is favoured by the resolution rules. The feminine is also semantically justified in some instances (when the conjuncts refer to female persons); the feminine/neuter dual form marks number less clearly than the masculine, but in the plural, the feminine form marks number more distinctly than the neuter would. The feminine occurs as a resolution form, but is more restricted than the masculine. The neuter has no semantic backing and does not mark number clearly; it is there-fore excluded from the output of the resolution rules.

We have proposed a solution to our first problem – the fact that the neuter plural cannot result from the resolution rules. We are also well on the way towards understanding the second – the extension in the use of the masculine form. This will become clear when we turn to Serbo-Croat. The forms are as for Slovene, except that there are no dual forms. The same analysis will still apply; however, as there is now no -*i* form in the dual, the advantage of the masculine -*i* form as a clear plural marker is even greater. It may well be no accident that it is precisely in Serbo-Croat that the extension of the use of the masculine plural has been observed. As we saw in §10.3.3, there are examples where masculine plural agreements are found even when all the con-juncts are feminine. This occurs most commonly when one of the conjuncts is a noun of the -ϕ declension. This morphological condition appears damaging to our claim that gender resolution rules have a semantic motivation. However, the -ϕ declension includes a large proportion of abstract nouns, and few animates. When one collects examples of conjoined noun phrases it is striking that the overwhelming majority involve conjunctions of nouns of the same semantic type, that is to say all animate or all inanimate (cf. Table 7.3). Thus when a feminine noun ending in a consonant is one of the conjuncts then there will normally be no animates in the subject. This means, in turn, that the use of the feminine agreement form will have no semantic justifi-cation (unlike its use with animate conjuncts which refer to females).

What is happening is that Serbo-Croat is moving towards a set of gender resolution rules where the semantic motivation is reflected more directly in the conditions on the rules. This new system would take the following form:

1. if all the conjuncts refer to females, the feminine form is used;
2. if all conjuncts are feminine, the feminine form may be used;
3. otherwise the masculine form is used.

The fact that the feminines of the -ϕ declension are affected first is to be explained, therefore, by the fact that the nouns involved are almost exclusively inanimate. The suggestion that the language is moving towards rules of the type just given is borne out by sentences (40) and (41), in which the masculine is used even though all the conjuncts are of the -*a* declension. No examples have been found of masculine agreement with feminine nouns referring to persons. When the feminine form is semantically justified, therefore, it must be used, but it is becoming optional in other cases. Serbo-Croat has replaced a set of rules like those of Slovene (in which the conditions on the rules are syntactic in nature, referring only to syntactic gender), with the set in §10.3.3, which includes a morphological condition. The language is now moving towards the set just given, which has both syntactic and semantic conditons. Though the conditions on the rules differ, the basic motivation for each set is semantic. The combinations of conjuncts which have been affected by these developments are those where gender is not semantically justified and the changes have had the effect of marking number more clearly in these instances.

If we now turn to the West Slavic languages, Written Standard Czech is the only one with a neuter plural form. Its exclusion from the resolution rules can be explained in a similar fashion to that used for the South Slavic languages. In the remaining West Slavic languages, which have only two plural forms, the masculine personal enjoys all the advantages. The most complex case is Polish, so we will again consider the endings available (see Table 10.9: adjectival endings are included, so this table is more detailed than Table 10.6).

There appears to be little to choose between the masculine personal and the non-masculine personal endings since all the available endings occur also in the singular. But there is a crucial difference: the masculine personal endings require a mutation of consonant in the case of a large number of adjectives and, most importantly, in the past active participle. The masculine personal forms are therefore particularly

Table 10.9: Agreement Endings in Polish

	masculine personal	masculine non-personal	feminine	neuter
singular	ϕ/y/i		a	o/e
plural	i/y		y/e	

clearly marked as plural in Polish, and so are favoured for use in cases of gender resolution. As we observed in § 10.3.7, the masculine personal form has extended its scope considerably. It enjoys the double advantage of being the form which is more often semantically justified (when the conjuncts refer to male persons only, or to persons of both sexes) and also the form which is the more clearly marked for number. These advantages account for its encroachment on the preserve of the non-masculine personal form.

There is a further reason for the advance of the masculine/masculine personal form (though unlike our previous arguments this does not apply specifically to Serbo-Croat and Polish). We have seen that animacy is a major factor in determining whether or not the resolution rules will apply – resolution is much more likely to apply with an animate than with an inanimate controller. A large proportion of the controllers consisting of animate noun phrases will include at least one masculine noun. Given that the resolution rules are loaded in favour of the masculine or masculine personal form (in a 'mixed' subject is has priority in rules of both types), this means that the masculine/masculine personal form enjoys a dominant position simply in terms of frequency. There is no strong motivation for retaining the competing forms and so the frequently occurring form is likely to extend its scope.

So far we have been concerned with the extension of the masculine/ masculine personal form as the resolution form. However, in our discussion of West Slavic we noted a more general expansion of its use. Spoken Czech has lost gender agreement forms in the plural; Slovak preserves two plural forms in adjectives only. And in Sorbian too, gender distinctions are being lost. What is significant is that in almost every case the form favoured by the resolution rules is the one which is bidding to take over as the sole form.[17] This is not as a result of being favoured by the resolution rules – conjoined structures are not sufficiently common to bring about such a change. Rather it shows that the resolution rules 'back the right horse': they favour the form most clearly marked for number, which is also the one which survives when gender distinctions are lost.

Let us now return to our two rule types – the South Slavic variant, which first isolates homogeneous conjuncts, and the Western variant, which first scans for the presence of one conjunct of a particular sort. The older rule type, probably going back to Common Slavic (as the Old Church Slavic data suggest), is found in the South Slavic group. The West Slavic group has developed a new morphological category, the masculine personal category (masculine animate in Czech), and so has reshaped its resolution rules accordingly. Thus both groups have resolution rules designed to make best use of the morphological form which most often is semantically justified and which indicates number most clearly. The difference between the two types is based upon a difference in morphology. However, the basic factors which favour one resolution form over the others are the same. These are: semantic justification in terms of gender; and clear marking of number.

10.5 The Operation of the Resolution Rules

In the last two sections attention has been centred on gender resolution, the most complex type of resolution. We must now take a broader view of the three types of resolution rule and consider their interaction with each other, and with factors discussed earlier in the book.

10.5.1 Interaction of the Three Types of Resolution Rule

One interesting conclusion to be drawn from our analysis is that the three types of resolution rule are independent, in the sense that each refers to one category only. As an illustration, one of the person resolution rules specifies that if the conjuncts include a first person, then the resolution form will be the first person. The rule does not refer to the number or gender of the conjuncts. Nor, indeed, does it specify the number or gender of the resolution form. In examples (1) and (3) the resolution form was the first person plural, but in (2) it was a first person dual. This less familiar possibility deserves further illustration:

(66) Sn: *Jaz in   Tonček sva* (1st pers dual) *prizadevna* (dual)
      I   and Tonček are   assiduous
      (Lenček, 1972, 61)

Here the person resolution rule specifies first person; it operates in exactly the same fashion whether the predicate is to be dual or plural, and irrespective of its gender. Similarly, the number and gender resolution rules involve only a single category (cf. §10.3.1). There are no special rules for, say, feminine plurals or second person masculines. In this sense the resolution rules are independent of each other. From a different viewpoint they are, however, interrelated in two ways. First, as we saw in §10.4, gender resolution is subservient to number resolution: particular gender forms are favoured because they mark number clearly. This relationship is a clear consequence of the greater congruence between real world and grammatical number. The second type of interdependence is more direct. While there is often the option to apply the resolution rules or not (and then to have agreement with one conjunct only), there is no possibility of choosing from among the rules. Given a subject consisting of a feminine singular and a neuter singular noun, it is not possible to apply gender resolution (to give a masculine) but at the same time fail to apply number resolution, and so have a masculine singular predicate. If resolution is applied, then all three sets of rules must be applied where possible.

There are some examples which we must consider further, in order to demonstrate that our account is adequate. They were mentioned briefly in the sections on Serbo-Croat and Czech, and contain conjoined neuter plural nouns:

(67) SC: . . . *ta   sećanja* (neut pl) *i   razmatranja* (neut pl)
          those memories   and reflections
          sve   su   više   ustupala (neut pl) *mesto novim*
          ever have more yielded   place to new
          utiscima . . .
          impressions (i.e. made way more and more to new impressions)
          (Andrić, *Travnička Hronika*)

In such sentences the resolution form cannot be used (the masculine plural **ustupali* is unacceptable). Intuitively the reason is obvious: both conjuncts are neuter plural, which means that there is no feature clash to resolve, and so a neuter plural verb is required. However, it is not immediately clear how the rules given above can block the ungrammatical form. We cannot claim that gender resolution rules operate only when the conjuncts are of different gender because conjoined neuter singular nouns in Serbo-Croat take a masculine plural verb (as in (33)) through the operation of the resolution rules. Another possibility is to suggest that gender resolution operates only as a consequence of number resolution. This suggestion is shown to be inadequate by sentences such as (32), where the subject consists of a feminine plural and a neuter plural noun and the predicate is masculine plural. There is no need for number resolution in such sentences, but clearly gender resolution has operated. The correct generalisation appears to be as follows. Gender resolution can be triggered in two ways — either by the operation of number resolution (if one resolution rule operates, all must operate if possible), or by the presence of different genders in the subject. Sentence (67) does not meet either condition, and so gender resolution cannot operate. It is this generalisation which requires the formulation of the number resolution rules (§10.2) to refer to the presence of a non-plural conjunct. The logical conclusion is that sentences with conjuncts which are all plural and all of the same gender (like (67)) do not undergo number resolution.

10.5.2 Interaction of the Resolution Rules with Target and Controller Factors

We have concentrated on the operation of the resolution rules in predicate agreement. However, the resolution rules apply throughout the agreement system. The forms which they determine are the same; the frequency with which they apply will differ. We had a clear instance of this phenomenon in §9.1, where we investigated agreement with conjoined noun phrases in Russian. In the different positions on the Agreement Hierarchy, the resolution form was the plural in each case. Number resolution is rare in attributive position in Russian (some other Slavic languages do not permit it at all)[18] but it is much more common in the predicate; the relative pronoun usually, but not always takes the resolution form (the plural), while the personal pronoun is almost bound to be plural. In §2.1.5 we saw the effect of the Agreement Hierarchy on gender resolution in Serbo-Croat. Those data are worth reconsidering, now that the resolution rules for Serbo-Croat have been established. The examples all include feminine plural and neuter plural nouns and so the only resolution rule which can apply is gender resolution. In attributive position, agreement is with the nearer conjunct only (sentence (70) is from *Anikina Vremena* by Andrić; the rest are from the same author's *Travnička Hronika*):

> (68) SC: . . . *najsvirepije* (fem pl) *kazne* (fem pl) *i*
>   the cruellest   punishments   and
>   *mučenja* (neut pl) . . .
>   tortures

In this position, the resolved form *najsvirepiji (masc pl) is ungrammatical. In the predicate, however, agreement may be with the nearer conjunct only, as in (69), or gender resolution may operate (70):

(69) SC: *Toj   službi su bile* (fem pl) *posvećene njene*
To this job   were   devoted   her
misli (fem pl) *i   njena osećanja* (neut pl). . .
thoughts   and her   feelings

(70) SC: *Sve njegove molbe* (fem pl) *i   uveravanja* (neut pl)
All his   prayers   and assurances
nisu   pomagali (masc pl) *ništa.*
did not help   at all

Similarly, the relative pronoun may either agree just with the nearer conjunct (71), or it may show the resolution form (72):

(71) SC: *U svetlosti filozofskih   istina* (fem pl) *i   verskih*
In the light of philosophical truths   and religious
nadahnuća (neut pl), *koja* (neut pl) *su se manjala* . . .
inspirations   which   changed

(72) SC: *Dok sve one   mučne sumnje* (fem pl) *i*
While all those painful doubts   and
kolebanja (neut pl) *koje* (masc pl acc) *je pobeda rasprsĩla* . . .
hesitations   which   victory dispersed

The personal pronoun must be masculine plural. Thus resolution does not occur in attributive position in this construction in Serbo-Croat; it may or may not operate in the predicate and the relative pronoun, but the personal pronoun must take the resolved form. The Russian construction examined in §9.1 was a case of number resolution being constrained by the Agreement Hierarchy; our Serbo-Croat data illustrate the hierarchy's similar effect on gender resolution. Given the interrelationship of these rules, we would expect them to be equally subject to the hierarchy. The distribution of forms which it requires confirms the claim that resolution forms have greater semantic justification than non-resolution forms. In the Serbo-Croat examples we have just discussed, the masculine form has of itself no greater semantic justification than the others; however, this is the form (favoured for reasons discussed in §10.4) which indicates that there is agreement with all the conjuncts. It is the fact of marking agreement with all the conjuncts which means that resolution forms have greater semantic justification than non-resolution forms. Given that the resolution rules are constrained by the Agreement Hierarchy, we would expect them to be bound also by the Predicate Hierarchy[19] – the two hierarchies being linked as we saw in Chapter 9. Indeed the test case which we used to demonstrate the link was precisely number resolution in Russian. And just as resolution or non-resolution is influenced by the Target Hierarchies, so also the controller factors established in Chapter 7 play their part. Resolution is more likely with animate controllers than with inanimates, and controllers preceding the target are more likely to take resolution forms than those following (see sentences (69) and (70)). There are insufficient data available to demonstrate the effect of the Target Hierarchies and of the controller factors on all the instances of resolution. However, it can be seen that by claiming that all resolution forms have greater semantic justification than non-resolution forms, and that they are therefore subject to the target and controller factors we have identified, we are making very strong claims about the possible distributions of agreement forms.

We have demonstrated that the resolution rules are interrelated; they all apply, where appropriate, or fail to apply as a set. Whether or not they apply is determined by the target and controller factors which we have already established.

10.6 Conclusion

Person and number resolution operate in a similar fashion in the various Slavic languages. Gender resolution, on the other hand, shows greater variety. The reason for the difference is that person and number resolution produce forms which are semantically justified, and this is not always possible for the gender resolution rules. This problem is a consequence of the semantics of gender itself. The gender resolution rules are nevertheless based on semantic principles. They operate so as to produce forms which are justified in terms of 'real world' gender where possible, or failing this they mark number (which has a semantic basis) as clearly as possible. The variation in gender resolution rules stems largely from the differences in the morphological resources available in the various languages. Thus resolution depends on the composition of the controller (the types of noun phrase involved) and the morphological possibilities of the target. Since resolution forms mark agreement with all the conjuncts, they have greater semantic justification than non-resolution forms. The distribution of the two types of forms is constrained both by the Target Hierarchies and by the controller factors established earlier.

Notes

1. This chapter is a substantially revised version of Corbett (1982a). If the number of a conjunct is not given it is singular; predicates are plural unless otherwise specified.

2. For these, special 'neutral' agreement forms may be available (Corbett, 1980a).

3. Note that we have an example where animate noun phrases precede their target and where agreement is still with the nearer only. In all our literary corpora in Chapter 7 – including those from the last century – we found no such examples, though there were examples in the dialect data.

4. If agreement is with the nearer conjunct only in such a case, then of course the dual is used; see Faska (1959, 59) for an example.

5. Providing the conjuncts are not unspecified for number; see Chapter 7, note 4.

6. We have followed Lenček (1972), who gives by far the clearest and fullest account of the problem. However Bajec (1955-6, 13) claims that, given two nouns of the same gender, the predicate will stand in that gender. This differs from Lenček's description only for the neuter. Bajec gives the following sentence:

(i) Sn: *Žrebe* (neut) *in   šcene* (neut) *sta razposajeni* (neut dual)
     The foal   and the puppy   are frolicsome

He admits that *razposajena* (masc dual) would probably also be heard, but says that it cannot be recommended for the literary language. It is difficult to interpret normative statements of this type. Often they are attempts to preserve a previous state of the language. If the agreements Bajec describes were once found regularly, then a very interesting picture emerges. In the earlier state, the language had an additional rule: '1(a) If all conjuncts are neuter, then the neuter form is used.' The three rules including 1(a) cover the former situation, and the loss of rule 1(a) in the development to the present situation is easy to understand, as conjoined neuter nouns occur surprisingly rarely in Slavic. While this analysis is attractive, we must await further evidence before adopting it. We might look to Old Church Slavic for an insight into the earlier state; unfortunately, the few data available, presented in §10.3.2, are consistent with either set of rules.

7. There is only one form in the masculine singular; the alternative form in Table 5.1 is for attributive adjectives and the relative pronoun. The existence of this alternative in other positions does not affect the discussion in §10.4 below for the following reasons: first, the predicate is the most important position for resolution simply in terms of frequency of occurrence; second, resolution in attributive position practically never occurs in Serbo-Croat (see note 18) and so this position is not relevant to the argument in §10.4; third, the relative pronoun has no form which marks number clearly (the nominative singular forms are *koji, koja, koje* and the plural forms *koji, koje, koja*) so it too does not affect the analysis in §10.4.

8. For more examples of this type, and for a fine account of the whole problem in Serbo-Croat, see Megaard (1976, 69-107).

9. This ending is short in comparative adjectives.

10. I am grateful to Professor H. Šewc-Schuster for examples (52) and (53) and for other information used in this section.

11. The dialect of Rodewitz is particularly interesting in this respect. As Jentsch (1980, 95, 134) reports, this dialect has lost the dual number, but preserves the masculine personal ~ non-masculine personal opposition in the plural. However, the masculine personal form has encroached on the preserve of the

non-masculine personal form and is used in approximately half the cases when the subject is non-masculine personal, while the non-masculine personal form is used solely with non-masculine personal subjects. In cases of gender resolution, when there is a masculine personal conjunct the masculine personal form is used.

12. Gerald Stone reports that his informants say the masculine personal is the correct form in such sentences, but that there is social and regional variation. Rothstein (1973, 313) discusses vacillation over the use of the masculine personal form *biegli* and the non-masculine personal form *biegły* in the following sentence:

(ii) P: *Chłopcy* (masc pers pl) *i   psy* (non-masc pers pl) *biegli/biegły*
    Youths   and dogs   ran

This is simply an example of gender resolution applying or failing to apply. The form *biegły*, for those speakers who accept it, occurs if the gender resolution rules do not operate; the verb then agrees with the nearer noun only. For data see Zieniukowa (1979, 125–7).

13. One of my informants even accepted the use of the masculine personal in a sentence with two feminine conjuncts, one referring to a human and one to a non-human animate:

(iii) P: *Hania* (fem) *i   kotka* (fem) *bawili* (masc pers) *się piłką*
     Hania   and the cat   were playing   with a ball

However, she preferred the non-masculine personal *bawiły*.

14. Note that we cannot formulate the West Slavic rule 1 as: 'if all conjuncts are non-masculine personal, then the non-masculine personal form is used'. The reason is that there is no independent motivation for nouns to be labelled 'non-masculine personal'; rather, they are labelled as feminine, neuter, masculine inanimate (see Corbett, forthcoming a); when in the plural, such nouns take the non-masculine personal plural form.

15. See Schane (1970, 286–94) and Lenček (1972, 56–7). Note, however, that it is insufficient to claim simply that it is the unmarked form which will be favoured by the resolution rules. First, in syntactic terms, it is not clear which of the genders is the unmarked one. The argument above would suggest the masculine, but the fact that infinitives, clauses and other elements with no inherent gender take forms which normally coincide with neuter forms would suggest that the neuter is the unmarked gender. Second, the person and number resolution rules favour the first person and the plural, both of which are marked categories; it would therefore have to be argued that gender resolution operates in a quite different way from person and number resolution. Nor does it help to appeal to morphology: the masculine plural is not unmarked in relation to the other genders – on the contrary, in Polish the mutation of consonant makes the masculine personal marked in morphological terms.

16. This may be true of Old Church Slavic but the position is uncertain. See also note 6.

17. The exception is the generalisation of the *-ej* ending for the dual of finite verb forms in Sorbian. Here, however, both forms are clear markers of the dual number.

18. Resolution in attributive position is possible in Czech (see sentence (9) in §4.1) and Ukrainian (Shevelov, 1963, 22). Examples occur in Bulgarian, but according to Popov (1964, 100) these are not characteristic of Bulgarian but result from foreign influence. The phenomenon is highly restricted in Serbo-Croat; there were no examples in the corpus described in §6.2.2. It is impossible in Sorbian; indeed, the use of a single modifier with more than one noun is felt to

be unnatural – the modifier would normally be repeated (Šewc-Schuster, personal communication).

19. There are instances of compound predicates which include both resolution and non-resolution forms. If the Predicate Hierarchy operates as a sentence level constraint (§4.2), then such instances must conform to it. The following example (similar to (28) but quoted from different manuscripts) is significant in this respect:

(iv) OCS: *bě* (3rd sg) *Iosifz   i   mati   ego čudęšta* (masc dual) *sę*
was   Joseph and mother his wondering
(Luke 2.33, Zographensis and Marianus Codices, quoted by
Xaburgaev, 1974, 371)

In this example the verb *bě* agrees with the nearer conjunct only, but the participle agrees with both conjuncts – it stands in the masculine dual as the result of the gender and number resolution rules. Thus the verb fails to undergo number resolution while the participle (further to the right on the hierarchy) shows the resolution form. As the resolution form has greater semantic justification, the requirement of the Predicate Hierarchy is met.

Normally the difference between the positions on the Predicate Hierarchy is insufficient to produce different agreements in compound predicates when they agree with conjoined noun phrases. In (iv), however, the difference between the two positions is heightened by the controller factor of precedence; the participle is more likely to take semantically justified agreement than the verb both because of their respective positions on the Predicate Hierarchy, and because the controller precedes it (while the controller follows *bě*). Professor B. Koenitz informs me that similar sentences occur in Czech:

(v) Cz: *Včera   byl* (masc sg) *Jan a   Marie pro svou výtržnost*
Yesterday was   Jan and Marie for their misbehaviour
biti (masc anim pl)
beaten

Here again the combination of target and controller factors accounts for the different agreement forms.

11 QUANTIFIED EXPRESSIONS

In this chapter, as in the previous chapter, we compare a set of constructions in different Slavic languages. While in Chapter 10 some languages were excluded, as they did not show agreement of the type under discussion, in this chapter we will consider data from all the Slavic languages. We have already examined quantified expressions in Chapter 8, where we demonstrated the effect of animacy and precedence upon agreement. We also noted the differences in agreement caused by the quantifiers themselves. While our concern then was to try to exclude this complication, in order to focus on the more general controller factors of animacy and precedence, we will now attempt to cover the full range of variation which stems from differences between quantifiers.[1] Once again, we will concentrate on predicate agreement, since this is the position where there is the greatest variation and for which most information is available. But we will also show the way in which agreement in other syntactic positions fits with claims made earlier in the book. Of the quantifiers themselves we give pride of place to cardinal numerals: these show the full range of variation found in Slavic and deserve preference as they allow the most direct comparisons between the different languages.

Numerals, and indeed all the quantifiers, pose a new problem. Whereas in Chapter 10 we had to contend with agreement being with one conjunct or with all conjuncts − in other words different elements could act as the controller − with quantified expressions it is not at all obvious which element controls the agreement. For this reason we begin our investigation with an analysis of the structure of quantified expressions (§11.1). In the course of this analysis we look into agreement in different syntactic positions. We then consider the variation in predicate agreement between languages and between different quantifiers (§11.2). The variation between quantifiers can be correlated with other syntactic properties which show their relative degrees of similarity to nouns (§11.3). As these other properties have changed in the course of time, we consider briefly the historical perspective (§11.4). Our conclusion highlights the wide range of variation found in quantified expressions, together with the basic unifying factors (§11.5).

11.1 Quantified Expressions as Controllers

In this section we consider a typical quantifier, the numeral 5, in order to establish a general outline of the way in which agreement operates with quantified expressions. We will then be able to tackle the variety in agreement which depends on differences between quantifiers. Let us start from the Russian phrase:

(1) R: *pjat'* (nom) *devušek* (gen pl)
      five   girls

The question arises as to which element is the head of this phrase. In semantic terms the head is *devušek*, for the appropriateness or otherwise of the predicate depends on its compatibility with this noun. In syntactic terms, however, the fact that *devušek* stands in the genitive case makes it seem much less likely that it is the head.

We shall see, however, that it is indeed the noun which is the head of quantified expressions like (1), and so is the agreement controller. To validate this claim we will have to look at agreement of different types and in doing so we will be able to check that agreement with quantifiers is consistent with our general claims about constraints on agreement.

We begin with attributive modifiers, two of which have been incorporated into our original phrase to give the next example:

(2) R: *èti* (nom pl) *pjat'* (nom) *krasivyx* (gen pl) *devušek* (gen pl)
      these   five   beautiful   girls

The modifier *krasivyx* presents no problem – it agrees in number and case with *devušek*. But *èti* is more difficult as it is not clear what it agrees with. An obvious suggestion is that it agrees with *pjat'*. This view is untenable for two reasons. The first is that when a numeral represents an abstract quantity and so is not followed by a noun, then the agreement with it is neuter singular (Suprun, 1959, 80):

(3) R: *krugloe* (neut sing) *pjat'*
      a round   five

This type of agreement is best analysed as a 'default' form: the neuter singular is used when agreement is required with an element which lacks the features necessary for agreement (such elements are infinitives, interjections and so on). The second reason why *èti* in (2) cannot be taken as agreeing with *pjat'* concerns animacy. The category of animacy affects the morphology and syntax of the Slavic languages to varying degrees. In Russian, where animacy is particularly well established, it determines the accusative case forms of most nouns which are masculine and animate, and of all nouns which are animate and plural. The effect is that for animates the accusative case matches the genitive, as illustrated in Table 11.1.

Table 11.1: Russian Accusative Case Forms in the Plural

	devuški 'girls' (animate)	*knigi* 'books' (inanimate)
nominative	devuški	knigi
accusative	devušek	knigi
genitive	devušek	knig

Animacy also has a role as an agreement category. If a noun in the accusative is animate, and is masculine or plural, then its modifiers will show agreement in animacy by taking the genitive form:

(4) R: *Ja videl ètix* (acc=gen) *devušek* (acc=gen)
      I   saw   these   girls

The verb *videt'* 'to see' takes the accusative; *devuški* 'girls' is animate and so stands in a form which matches the genitive, and the modifier *ètix* similarly stands in a form like that of the genitive. Let us now return to our quantified expression; if it occurs in direct object position the required form is as follows:

(5) R: *ètix* (acc=gen) *pjat'* (acc=nom) *krasivyx* (gen)
        these   five   beautiful
        devušek (gen)
        girls

While *pjat'* is not affected by animacy in Modern Russian, the modifier *ètix* is. We are forced to conclude that it agrees with the noun *devušek* in animacy. It is then logical to assume that in our original nominative phrase (*èti pjat' krasivyx devušek*) it agrees in number with the noun *devušek*, though it does not agree in case. This means that, for agreement purposes at least, it is the noun which is the head of the quantified expression. The nearer attributive modifier agrees with it fully, in number and case. The further modifier *èti* agrees in number but not always in case (in the oblique cases it does agree in case, as in (33) below). This interesting situation is a special case of stacking, which we discussed in §4.3.1. Once again the nearer modifier shows full syntactic agreement, while the further takes agreement which has greater semantic justification (*devušek* is functioning as a subject and so the nominative case has the greater semantic justification). What is special about this is that the numeral *pjat'* is treated as a modifier: it marks the boundary between modifiers showing full agreement and those in the nominative, as in the following phrase:

(6) R: *vse* (nom) *èti* (nom) *pjat'* (nom) *krasivyx* (gen)
        all   these   five   beautiful
        makedonskix (gen) *devušek* (gen)
        Macedonian   girls

According to our constraint, if stacked modifiers show different agreement forms, it must be the further modifiers which show the semantically justifiable form. If *pjat'* is counted as a modifier, then this accounts for the case form of the preceding modifiers.[2] However, the main point we have established is that it is the noun which is the head of the quantified phrase. This can be seen clearly in Serbo-Croat, where all modifiers agree with the noun fully, even when the phrase functions as subject:

(7) SC: *ovih* (gen pl) *pet* (nom) *devojaka* (gen pl)
          these   five   girls

There is no question but that *ovih* agrees with *devojaka*. In Polish, modifiers preceding the numeral may be nominative plural or genitive plural:[3]

(8) P: *wszystkie* (nom pl) *pięć* (nom) *pociągów* (gen pl)
         all   five   trains
(9) P: *wszystkich* (gen pl) *pięć* (nom) *pociągów* (gen pl)
         all   five   trains

While the data on attributive agreement with the 'average' quantifier 5 show that the noun is the head, the status of the quantifier is ambiguous. In Serbo-Croat it does not enter the agreement relationships within the quantified phrase. In Russian it counts as a modifier, so that the phrase is subject to the constraint on stacked modifiers. In Polish the quantifier may be treated as a modifier or not, with results similar either to those found in Russian or to those in Serbo-Croat.

Let us now turn to predicate agreement and the problem of agreement with a head noun standing in the genitive. Normally in Slavic the subject must be in the nominative if it is to take full predicate agreement. Subjects may stand in the genitive, particularly with negated existential verbs. When this occurs, then predicate agreement is 'by default' — the third person singular neuter form is used:

(10) R: *Ivana* (gen) *ne bylo* (neut sg) *tam*
      Of Ivan   not was   there
      (Ivan was not there)

Here *Ivana* is the subject, but as it is in the genitive, the verb is neuter singular rather than masculine singular. This is the default form of agreement which occurs when normal agreement is impossible. The same type of agreement may be found with quantified expressions:

(11) R: *vošlo* (neut sg) *pjat' devušek*
      came in   five girls

But as we have seen previously, plural agreement also occurs:

(12) R: *vošli* (pl) *pjat' devušek*
      came in five girls

Here the plural form results from agreement with the head noun; naturally, plural agreement as in (12) has greater semantic justification than singular agreement (11). The reason why agreement with the noun is possible in (12) but not in (10) is that in (12) part of the subject noun phrase is in the nominative, while in (10) there is no nominative, and so subject-predicate agreement is ruled out. We can see that plural agreement is indeed agreement with the noun by turning to Serbo-Croat: when such phrases take plural agreement, which is the less usual alternative (cf. Table 8.4), certain types of predicate show gender agreement:

(13) SC: *pet devojaka su* (pl) *došle* (fem pl)
       five girls   have   come

The gender of the past active participle *došle* indicates clearly that it agrees with the feminine noun *devojaka*. A further argument which confirms that plural agreement represents agreement with the noun stems from the fact that quantified expressions which include animate nouns are more likely to take plural agreement than are those with inanimates; this claim was amply supported in §8.4.1. In such phrases animacy is a feature of the noun rather than of the quantifier. However, before we become too involved in the factors which influence the choice of agreement, let us first consider the simple fact that alternative agreements are possible, and check that our previous claims on agreement options are valid. We noted that in attributive position there is full syntactic agreement with the head noun. Further modifiers may show agreement with greater semantic justification according to the stacking constraint (depending on the status of the quantifier in the particular language). In the predicate, the syntactic form of agreement (equivalent to the genitive plural in attributive position) is the default form. This form occurs, but the plural is also possible. As this option occurs in the predicate, the requirement of the Agreement Hierarchy is met. There is also evidence to show that the requirements of the Predicate Hierarchy are met: see Corbett (1979a, 57-93) for a compilation of the data in Russian, and §5.4 for a discussion of Serbo-Croat. When we return to the remaining positions on the Agreement Hierarchy, the relative and personal pronouns, we find that the plural is used in the overwhelming majority of instances:

(14)   R: *pjat' devušek, kotorye* (pl) . . . *oni* (pl) . . .
            five girls   who   they

Singular (default) agreements are theoretically possible but exceptionally rare (see Corbett, 1979a, 60, for Russian data). In our Serbo-Croat corpus (detailed in §6.2.2), all relative and personal pronouns referring to quantified expressions are in the plural. Thus the requirements of the Agreement Hierarchy are met. The position in which quantified expressions give rise to the most interesting variation is the predicate, so we will now concentrate on this area.

11.2 Variation in Predicate Agreement

In Chapter 8 we saw that the choice of the agreement form in the predicate is strongly influenced by the animacy of the subject and by the subject's position relative to the predicate. We noted that the quantifier involved has a substantial influence, but in §8.4 we minimised this effect by using a large corpus or by restricting attention to an individual quantifier. We now consider the influence of the different quantifiers in more detail. We are concentrating on numerals, as these can be directly compared in different languages, and we will deal with the simple cardinal numerals. Table 11.2 gives details of predicate agreement with phrases

Table 11.2: Predicate Agreement with Numeral Phrases

	2	3	4	5-10	100
Bulgarian	pl	pl	pl	pl	pl
Macedonian	pl	pl	pl	pl	pl
Slovak	pl	pl	pl	sg/pl	sg
Sorbian	dual	pl	pl	sg/pl	sg
Old Church Slavic	dual	pl	pl	sg/(pl)	
Polish	99% pl (N = 123)	91% pl (N = 43)	100% pl (N = 15)	7% pl (N = 68)	
Serbo-Croat	97% pl (N = 735)	89% pl (N = 249)	83% pl (N = 133)	7% pl (N = 1161)	
Czech	pl	pl	pl	sg	sg
Slovene	dual	pl	pl	sg	sg
Belorussian	92% pl (N = 219)	78% pl (N = 67)	63% pl (N = 16)	39% pl (N = 49)	50% pl (N = 2)
Russian	86% pl (N = 541)	77% pl (N = 247)	76% pl (N = 68)	50% pl (N = 220)	
Ukrainian	83% pl (N = 208)	79% pl (N = 150)	74% pl (N = 34)	38% pl (N = 45)	21% pl (N = 14)

including the simple cardinal numerals 2, 3, 4, 5-10 and 100 in all the Slavic languages. When an entry in Table 11.2 consists of a single abbreviation (e.g. 'pl'), this indicates that the form given is used in the majority of cases, though not necessarily all. Thus in Slovene, the plural is normal with 3 and 4, but the singular may be used in expressions of time. In the absence of precise data, these few exceptions are ignored (time expressions also account for some of the singular forms with 2, 3 and 4 in other languages). The languages are ordered roughly in order of decreasing use of the plural. A gap indicates a lack of data. A few more points about Table 11.2 require explanation before we discuss its implications.

The judgements and statistics presented are taken from Suprun (1969, 175-87) unless otherwise stated. In Slovak, with the numerals 5-10 the plural is used with masculine personal forms and otherwise the singular; exceptions to the rules as given occur in less than one per cent of the examples, according to Suprun. *Sto* '100' takes the singular (Ďurovič, personal communication). Sorbian preserves the dual number; otherwise agreements are broadly similar to those of Slovak (Suprun, 1963a). Old Church Slavic data are given in Suprun (1961, 81-6); for the 5-10 entry, he has ten examples of singular predicates, six of plural predicates and two where one source has singular agreement and another has plural. However, Večerka (1960, 197) says that in the Gospels the singular is used in the overwhelming majority of instances, hence the plural entry is bracketed. Suprun also gives an example with *szto* '100', one with *tysęšta* '1,000' and one with tьma '10,000' − all three with singular agreement. The Polish figures are calculated on the basis of examples given in Suprun (1963b).[4] The final Polish entry is for numerals of all types from 5 up to 999. There are also seven examples of agreement with *tysiąc* '1,000' − all singular. The Serbo-Croat statistics are taken from Sand (1971, 51-2, 73); this corpus was described in §8.4.2. The figure for *dva* 'two' includes examples with *oba* 'both'; 2-4 include compound numerals ending in 2-4 and the remaining figure is for all other numerals above 4. Judgements on Slovene are from Vincenot (1975, 196) as well as from Suprun (1969, 176). The final entry for Ukrainian includes examples with *sorok* '40' as well as *sto* '100'.

With these details dealt with, we can now turn to the basic patterns revealed by Table 11.2. Bulgarian and Macedonian differ from the other languages in using the plural with all numerals in almost all instances. Other Slavic languages use both singular and plural. The remaining South Slavic languages (Old Church Slavic, Serbo-Croat and Slovene) show a strong preference for plural (or dual) agreement for quantified phrases with the numerals 2-4, and for singular agreement − with varying degrees of tolerance towards the plural − with numerals from 5 upwards. In several languages the distinction between 2-4 on the one hand, and 5 upwards on the other, is fairly sharp. However, the statistics for Serbo-Croat and Polish show that here the division is not absolute. It is in these languages, together with those of the East Slavic group, where the situation is more fluid, that we find the most interesting data and so they will be highlighted in the next section. The overall picture is clear: the higher the numeral the more likely is singular agreement. The form which is semantically justified becomes more likely the lower the numeral. This is clearly true in the straightforward cases like Slovak. The statistical data too support this claim, apart from two minor inconsistencies: the 100 per cent plural figure for 4 in Polish, and the 50 per cent plural for 100 in Belorussian. These two cases need not concern us as the sample size for both numerals is small. Even apart from these two instances, it is not the case that there is a statistically significant difference between every pair of successive numerals in each language. What is important is that, apart from the two exceptions mentioned, the rank order of the numerals according to the frequency with which they take plural agreement is the same in the different languages and that this order is inversely related to numerical value. Thus languages of both types – those like Slovak where the numeral largely determines the agreement form to be used and those like Ukrainian where there is a greater degree of choice – all provide convincing evidence for the relationship between numerical value and agreement: the lower the numeral, the more likely it is to take semantically justified agreement.

In Table 11.2 as a whole, it is obvious that the particular quantifier used is a major determining factor in the choice of agreement form. In a language like Czech, where the plural is used with the numerals 2-4, and the singular with 5 and above, there is little more to be said. But in those languages where the choice is less clear-cut, we must ask how the choice of quantifier interacts with the other controller factors – animacy and precedence. Take, for example, the situation in Russian. We established in §8.4 that if the quantified subject is animate, or if it stands before the predicate, then the likelihood of plural agreement is increased. Suprun gives no figures for these two factors. It is therefore theoretically possible that the difference between the frequency of plural agreement with the numeral 2 (86 per cent) and with 5-10 (50 per cent) results solely from animacy and precedence. This would be the case if the numeral 2 occurred with animate nouns and stood before the predicate substantially more frequently than do higher numerals. There is no evidence to support this suggestion. It seems more likely that the following is the correct analysis: both 2 and the numerals 5-10 allow singular and plural agreement, but this is more favoured by 2 than by 5-10. Both are subject to the influence of animacy and precedence. Given the same quantifier, then both factors increase the likelihood of plural agreement. Equally, given a particular sentence type (e.g. animate subject standing after the predicate) then the plural is more likely with the numeral 2 than with a higher numeral. The large corpora on which Table 11.12 is based allow us to abstract away from the other controller factors and so to isolate the effect of the quantifier. In our next section we will ask why it is that quantifiers have such different agreement requirements.

11.3 The Syntax of Cardinal Numerals

We have established that plural agreement becomes less likely as the numeral becomes larger; in some languages there is a clear break at a particular point on the scale, in others it is less dramatic. We must now analyse the numerals involved to discover the reasons for this behaviour. Perhaps the most interesting set of languages in Table 11.2 is the East Slavic group, as all the numerals appear to behave independently here. We will investigate Russian as an example of this group (§11.3.1). Two other languages, one from each of the remaining groups, show interesting agreement patterns and are well documented; these will also be analysed − Serbo-Croat in §11.3.2 and Polish in §11.3.3. We will then turn to Old Church Slavic (§11.3.4), first as an example of a language with a clear distinction between 4 and 5, but also because it will give an historical perspective to our analysis.

11.3.1 Russian

We begin our investigation of the simple cardinal numerals of Russian with the smallest. *Odin* 'one' agrees with a following noun in gender:

(15) R: *odin* (masc) *žurnal* (masc)
          one   magazine
(16) R: *odna* (fem) *gazeta* (fem)
          one   newspaper
(17) R: *odno* (neut) *okno* (neut)
          one   window

Not surprisingly, numeral and noun stand in the singular. This in fact represents agreement in number, for when associated with nouns of the pluralia tantum category, *odin* stands in the plural:

(18) R: *odni* (pl) *sani* (pl)
          one   sledge

All the examples so far have involved the nominative case of both numeral and noun. *Odin* always agrees in case, as the following suggest:

(19) R: *odnim* (masc inst) *žurnalom* (masc inst)
     one   magazine
(20) R: *odnu* (fem acc) *gazetu* (fem acc)
     one   newspaper

The numeral *dva* 'two' also shows agreement in gender, but in a restricted way. It agrees in gender only in the nominative case (and in the inanimate accusative, which is equivalent to the nominative); furthermore, instead of the usual three-way agreement in the nominative, it distinguishes only feminine (*dve*) from masculine and neuter (*dva*):

(21) R: *dve gazety* (fem)
     two newspapers
(22) R: *dva žurnala* (masc)
     two magazines
(23) R: *dva okna* (neut)
     two windows

The form of the noun is interesting. In these sentences it is equivalent morphologically to the genitive singular. This is almost always true, but there are nouns which preserve a distinct form here:

(24) R: *dva časá*
     two hours
(25) R: *okolo čása* (gen sing)
     about an hour

The form used after *dva* in (24) is differentiated by stress from the genuine genitive singular, as in (25). The forms used with *dva* 'two' are generally taken to go back to dual forms now lost, though this is not certain. Even in the modern language they must be marked by an irregular syntactic marker (which will normally be interpreted in the morphological component as genitive singular). In the oblique cases, *dva* does not vary according to gender, and it is followed by a noun in the same case:

(26) R: *dvum* (dat) *gazetam* (dat pl)
     to two   magazines

Both *odin* and *dva* also agree in animacy. As we saw in §11.1, animacy is a morphological and syntactic category restricted to masculine and plural nouns. Animate nouns have their accusative as the genitive:

(27) R: *Ja videl odnogo* (masc acc=gen) *mal'čika* (acc=gen)
      I saw one   boy

(28) R: *Ja videl dvux* (acc=gen) *devušek* (acc=gen)
      I saw two   girls

In the following sentences the nouns are inanimate and the forms found are the same as those when the numeral phrase is in subject position:

(29) R: *Ja videl odin* (acc=nom) *žurnal* (acc=nom)
      I saw one   magazine

(30) R: *Ja videl dve* (acc=nom) *gazety* (gen sg)
      I saw two   newspapers

Tri 'three' and *četyre* 'four' behave like *dva* with respect to animacy: there are occasional examples of animates being treated as inanimates with these three numerals (Suprun, 1959, 83). In fact *dva*, *tri* and *četyre* show the same syntactic behaviour, with the single difference that *dva* shows a distinction in gender (*dva/dve*) which is not found in *tri* and *četyre*.

From *pjat'* 'five' upwards the numeral is not affected by animacy:[5]

(31) R: *Ja videl pjat'* (acc=nom) *mal'čikov* (gen pl)
      I saw five   boys

(32) R: *Ja videl pjat'* (acc=nom) *žurnalov* (gen pl)
      I saw five   magazines

As these sentences also illustrate, *pjat'* is followed by a noun in the genitive plural, when it stands in a direct case (nominative or accusative =nominative). In the oblique cases, numeral and noun agree in case:

(33) R: *pjati* (dat) *mal'čikam* (dat)
      to five   boys

Turning to higher numerals, we find that *sto* '100' is similar in its syntactic behaviour to *pjat'*. However, unlike *pjat'*, *sto* may also be used in the plural, but only in a few set expressions where it stands in an oblique case. On the other hand *tysjača* '1,000' and *million* '1,000,000' have full plural paradigms which may be used without restriction. These two can – though this is rare – take a determiner agreeing with them in gender and number:[6]

(34) R: *èta* (fem sg) *tysjača*
        this   thousand
(35) R: *ètot* (masc sg) *million*
        this   million

Other numerals require a plural determiner (agreeing in number with the noun), as we saw in §11.1 above. As for the case of the following noun, *million* requires the genitive plural, irrespective of the case of *million* itself:

(36) R: *million* (nom) *rublej* (gen pl)
        a million   roubles
(37) R: *o*   *millione* (loc) *rublej* (gen pl)
        concerning a million   roubles

Tysjača may behave in this fashion as in (38), or it may follow *sto* and *pjat'* in taking a noun in the same case, when it itself stands in an oblique case, as in (39):

(38) R: *o*   *tysjače* (loc) *rublej* (gen pl)
        concerning a thousand   roubles
(39) R: *o*   *tysjače* (loc) *rubljax* (loc pl)
        concerning a thousand   roubles

The features described are summarised in Table 11.3. *Četyre* 'four' behaves like *tri* 'three', 6-10 behave like *pjat'* 'five' and *milliard* 'thousand million' and other higher numerals follow *million*. We are not concerned with compound and complex numerals.

The numbered phrases down the left hand side of Table 11.3 may be thought of as tests which are applied to each of the numerals. Thus *odin* is the only numeral which agrees with its noun in number; the '+' indicates that it 'passes' the test while the other numerals 'fail'. Tests 1-4 are features we normally associate with the syntax of adjectives. These first four tests do not split the numerals into two clear groups (adjectives and non-adjectives). Instead they show that the numerals are adjectival to a greater or a lesser degree – the more adjectival being those to the left. Similarly, tests 5-7, which are features of the syntactic behaviour of nouns, show that some numerals are more noun-like than

Table 11.3: The Syntax of Russian Cardinal Numerals

	odin 1	*dva* 2	*tri* 3	*pjat'* 5	*sto* 100	*tysjača* 1,000	*million* 1,000,000
1. agrees with noun in syntactic number	+	−	−	−	−	−	−
2. agrees in case throughout	+	−	−	−	−	−	−
3. agrees in gender	+	(+)	−	−	−	−	−
4. agrees in animacy	+	+ (−)	+ (−)	−	−	−	−
5. has semantically independent plural	−	−	−	−	(+)	+	+
6. takes agreeing determiner	−	−	−	−	−	+	+
7. takes noun in genitive throughout	−	−	−	−	−	±	+

Note: parentheses indicate restriction: thus the (+) under *dva* shows that it agrees in gender but not fully; ± indicates an alternative; the combination $\frac{+}{(-)}$ indicates that the alternatives are most unequal: in this instance the failure to mark animacy is exceptional.

others. We may combine the two parts of Table 11.3 by adopting a single standard: syntactic characteristics shared with adjectives. This can be done by adding 'it is not the case that' to tests 5–7. The matrix which results is given as Table 11.4.

Table 11.4: Russian Numerals: Combined Table

		odin 1	*dva* 2	*tri* 3	*pjat'* 5	*sto* 100	*tysjača* 1,000	*million* 1,000,000
	1. agrees with noun in syntactic number	+	−	−	−	−	−	−
	2. agrees in case throughout	+	−	−	−	−	−	−
	3. agrees in gender	+	(+)	−	−	−	−	−
	4. agrees in animacy	+	+ (−)	+ (−)	−	−	−	−
it is not the case that the numeral	5. has semantically independent plural	+	+	+	+	(−)	−	−
	6. takes agreeing determiner	+	+	+	+	+	−	−
	7. takes noun in genitive throughout	+	+	+	+	+	±	−

The matrix given in Table 11.4 is 'well behaved': that is to say, the degrees of acceptability decrease monotonically along the rows and up the columns. *Odin* 'one' is the numeral which is most like an adjective (though it is not fully an adjective — it cannot, for example, occur in comparative constructions). Each succeeding numeral is less like an adjective and more like a noun, up to *million*, which is most like a noun. (Even this is not a true noun — it is limited, for example, in the modifiers it can take.) There is no point at which we can sensibly divide the numerals into two groups — rather they form a continuum which falls between the poles of adjective and noun. A matrix which is regular in the way we have described is what Ross calls a 'squish' (see Ross, 1972, 1973a, b, 1975 for explanation and examples). It is interesting to note that Table 11.4 arranges the numerals in order of increasing similarity to nouns, and that this is also their numerical order. While this may seem obvious, there is no logical reason why this pattern should occur. However, data from a wide range of languages (Corbett, 1978b) indicate that this correlation of 'nouniness' and numerical value is a universal.

Given that the cardinal numerals of Russian vary in their syntactic behaviour, from those which are most similar to adjectives to those which are most similar to nouns, we will now investigate how this variation affects predicate agreement. Consider first, in theoretical terms, what type of predicate agreement we would expect with a subject consisting of an unknown element X and a noun. If X is an adjective, then clearly we expect full agreement of the predicate with the noun:

(40) R: *Russkie   studenty* (pl) *priexali* (pl)...
      The Russian students   arrived

If, however, X is a noun (and the other noun is dependent on it), then we expect X to control predicate agreement:

(41) R: *Prijatel'* (masc sg) *studentov* (gen pl) *priexal* (masc sg)...
      The friend   of the students   arrived

But what of intermediate values of X? If it is almost equivalent to an adjective or to a noun, it may be treated as such. However, in the middle range of values, X may be insufficiently like a noun to control agreement, yet it may be sufficiently like a noun to block access to the features of the other noun for predicate agreement. If this occurs we will find the default agreement form (third person singular neuter) which we discussed earlier.

In practice we find that *odin* 'one' is sufficiently like an adjective to have no effect on predicate agreement – the predicate agrees with the noun. At the other end of the scale, *tysjača* '1,000' and *million* normally behave like nouns and control predicate agreement:

(42) R: *Dejstvitel'no, ljubaja tysjača   načal'nikov dannogo*
          Really   any   thousand chiefs   of a given
          ranga   ravnocenna (fem sg) *ljuboj drugoj*
          rank (is) equivalent   to any other (thousand)
          togo že   ranga.
          of the same rank
          (Zinov'ev, *Zijajuščie vysoty*)

However, data are hard to find. It is the intermediate range of numerals for which we have sound statistical evidence, given in Table 11.5.

Table 11.5: Predicate Agreement with Numeral Phrases in Russian

	2			3			4			5–10	
sg	pl	%pl	sg	pl	%pl	sg	pl	%pl	sg	pl	%pl
74	467	86	56	191	77	16	52	76	110	110	50

We can now account for these figures. The numeral 2 shares many properties with adjectives. Usually, but not always, it allows access to the features of the noun. The latter carries an irregular syntactic marker, mentioned earlier, which for agreement purposes is equivalent to a plural. The numerals 3 and 4, as we saw in Table 11.4 above, are less like adjectives than is 2; Table 11.5 shows that they also take plural agreement less frequently. The difference between 3 and 4 in Table 11.5 is not statistically significant, though a larger sample might reveal a significant difference, to match that of an independent syntactic test reported in Corbett (1979a, 72-4). However, the difference between 3 and 4 on the one hand and 5-10 on the other is quite clear. The numerals 5-10 are more like nouns in their behaviour and so they more often block access to the agreement features of the quantified noun.

We conclude that there are two interlinked patterns: as Russian numerals increase in numerical value so they become more like nouns; and the more noun-like the numeral is, the less likely this makes plural predicate agreement.

11.3.2 Serbo-Croat

Having discussed the syntax of Russian numerals in some detail, we can treat Serbo-Croat more briefly, as the tests we shall apply are the same. We will go directly to the matrix in which the tests for noun-like behaviour are negated, and so all tests are for adjective-like behaviour (Table 11.6). *Dva* 'two' agrees in gender in all cases: however, as in Russian, the agreement is limited to feminine (*dve*, etc.) versus masculine and neuter (*dva*, etc.). *Četiri* 'four' behaves like *tri* 'three'. While 2–4 may agree in case throughout, they are usually used in the nominative-accusative form after prepositions, and the oblique case forms are being lost elsewhere (for discussion see Rogić, 1955; Hamm, 1956-7). There are alternatives for 100; of these only *stotina* has plural forms. The ± signs against the agreeing determiner test indicate that some speakers accept agreeing determiners here while others find them unnatural.[7] It should be noted that we have found no test to distinguish *milion*, its alternative *milijun* and higher numerals from *hiljada* or *tisuća* '1,000'. More generally, it can be seen that Serbo-Croat numerals also form a squish, but that the tests must be arranged in a different order from Russian. There is a second difference which is particularly relevant to agreement: while in Russian the numerals 3 and 4 differ from 5–10 in one test only, in Serbo-Croat there is a clearer distinction as they differ in two tests.

Consider now the figures for predicate agreement, given in Table 11.7. The numerals 2–4, which are much more like adjectives than are the numerals 5 and above, show a markedly higher frequency of plural predicate agreement. This corresponds to the clear distinction between them shown in Table 11.6. Within the 2–4 group, there are also differences in agreement: that between 2 on the one hand and 3 and 4 on the other is expected from our previous tests. But here we also find a difference between 3 and 4. While this is not matched by any of the tests reported in Table 11.6, there is another phenomenon which reflects a distinction between 3 and 4. It is the agreement option discussed in §5.4: when phrases consisting of 2–4 plus masculine noun take plural agreement in compound predicates, there is then a choice between the endings -*a* (neut pl) and -*i* (masc pl) for forms which agree in gender. The masculine plural is the form with the greater semantic justification. The figures presented in Table 11.8 are taken from Sand (1971, 55–6): again *oba* is included with *dva* and compound numerals ending in 2–4 are also counted. These figures support the difference in behaviour between 3 and 4 shown in Table 11.7; the

Table 11.6: Serbo-Croat Numerals

	jedan	dva	tri	pet	sto/stotina	hiljada/tisuća	milion/milijun
	1	2	3	5	100	1,000	1,000,000
1. agrees with noun in syntactic number	+	−	−	−	−	−	−
2. agrees in animacy	+	−	−	−	−	−	−
3. agrees in gender	+	(+)	−	−	−	−	−
4. agrees in case throughout	+	(+)	(+)	−	−	−	−
5. takes noun in genitive throughout	+	+	+	+	−	−	−
6. has semantically independent plural	+	+	+	+	(+)	−	−
7. takes agreeing determiner	+	+	+	+	±	±	±

it is not the case
that the numeral { 5. 6. 7.

Table 11.7: Number Agreement with Numeral Phrases in Serbo-Croat

	2			3			4			5 and above	
sg	pl	%pl	sg	pl	%pl	sg	pl	%pl	sg	pl	%pl
22	713	97	27	222	89	23	110	83	1079	82	7

**Table 11.8: Gender Agreement with 2, 3 and 4 Plus
Masculine Noun in Serbo-Croat**

	2			3			4	
neut	masc	%masc	neut	masc	%masc	neut	masc	%masc
180	52	22	76	10	12	53	5	9

lower numeral is more likely to take the semantically justified agreement form.

11.3.3 Polish

The system of numerals in Polish is shown in Table 11.9. The (+) under *dwa* again indicates that gender is not fully distinguished. Different writers fail to agree on the forms available for certain gender/case combinations: this is one instance of the general variability which seems to pervade the Polish numeral system. *Cztery* 'four' again behaves

Table 11.9: Polish Numerals

	jeden 1	*dwa* 2	*trzy* 3	*pięć* 5	*sto* 100	*tysiąc* 1,000	*million* 1,000,000
1. agrees with noun in syntactic number	+	—	—	—	—	—	—
2. agrees in gender	+	(+)	—	—	—	—	—
3. agrees in case throughout	+	+	+	—	—	—	—
4. agrees in animacy	+	+	+	+	+	—	—
5. has semantically independent plural	+	+	+	+	+	—	—
6. takes agreeing determiner	+	+	+	+	+	—	—
7. takes noun in genitive throughout	+	+	+	+	+	(+)	—

(rows 5–7 bracketed: it is not the case that the numeral)

like *trzy* 'three'. The (+) under *tysiąc* indicates that while a noun in the genitive plural is the norm, examples with numeral and noun in the same case also occur (Buttler *et al.*, 1971, 347).

The figures for predicate agreement are given in Table 11.10, in

Table 11.10: Predicate Agreement with Numeral Phrases in Polish

2			3			4			5–999			1,000		
sg	pl	%pl	sg	pl	%pl	sg	pl	%pl	sg	pl	%pl	sg	pl	%pl
1	122	99	4	39	91	0	15	100	63	5	7	7	0	0

which there are two points which require comment. First, the 100 per cent plural figure for the numeral 4 breaks the pattern. This irregularity was commented on in the discussion of Table 11.2, and it was suggested that the small number of examples available means that we should not pay undue attention to this figure. The second point is the very considerable drop in plural agreement between 2–4 and the higher numerals. In Table 11.9, we see evidence for a difference in syntactic behaviour between 2–4 and the higher numerals; however, this is less marked than in Serbo-Croat, where the difference in predicate agreement is also large. There is a special factor at work in Polish – the highly developed masculine personal category. Numerals like 5 and 100, when quantifying masculine personal nouns, not only take an accusative form equivalent to the genitive, but also take this same genitive form when in subject position:

(43) P: *przyszło* (sg) *pięciu* (gen) *panów* (gen)
     came   five   men

Since there is no nominative subject, only singular (default) agreement is possible. As a result, the masculine personals, which we would expect to provide a large proportion of the plural predicate agreements, are in fact ruled out – they stand in the genitive and permit no agreement choice: only the singular is possible.

11.3.4 Old Church Slavic

Data on the syntax of numerals in Old Church Slavic are limited, but the evidence gathered by Suprun (1961) gives us a reasonable picture of the situation, presented in Table 11.11. *Dъva* 'two' agrees in gender in the nominative and the accusative cases, while trъje 'three' and

Table 11.11: Old Church Slavic Numerals

		jedinъ	*dъva*	*trъje*	*pętь*	*desętь*	*sъto*	*tysęšta*
		1	2	3	5	10	100	1,000
	1. agrees with noun in gender	+	(+)	((+))	−	−	−	−
	2. agrees in number	+	+	+	−	−	−	−
	3. agrees in case	+	+	+	−	−	−	−
it is not the case that the numeral	4. takes noun in genitive throughout	+	+	+	(+)	−	−	−
	5. takes agreeing determiner	+	+	+	±	?	?	?
	5. has semantically independent dual and plural	+	+	+	+	(−)	(−)	−

četyre 'four' agree in the nominative only. 1-4 all agree in number: *jedinъ* normally stands in the singular but takes the plural with nouns of the pluralia tantum class; *dъva* stands in the dual, *trъje* and *četyre* in the plural. The (±) sign under *pętь* indicates a particularly interesting situation. The norm here is the genitive plural, but it seems that it was possible for the numeral and noun to agree in the oblique cases (see Večerka, 1960; Corbett, 1978c, 70-1). The numerals 6-9 behave like 5. As regards the use of determiners with this group, Suprun (1961, 77-8) gives four examples with determiners agreeing fully with the numeral and two with plural determiners agreeing with the noun. '?' records a lack of data, though our knowledge of the early development of the Slavic languages suggests that agreeing determiners were the norm here. (−) indicates that while dual and plural forms existed, they were restricted in use to compound numerals. It is this test which separates 10 from 5-9 in Old Church Slavic. Finally *tъma* '10,000' behaved, as far as we know, like *tysęšta*. Once again we find a monotonic decrease along the rows and up the columns. Indeed, the matrices for all four languages are perfectly 'well behaved'; Ross (1975, 425) was pessimistic about the chances of finding such squishes.

In the case of Old Church Slavic, there is a much clearer division between 2-4 and 5 upwards than we have seen in the other languages. This division is reflected in predicate agreement. With 2, the noun stands in the dual, the numeral agrees with it and so does the predicate. With 3 and 4, the noun is plural, the numeral agrees and, again, so does the predicate. With 5-10, as described earlier, singular agreement is

more usual, but the plural is also found. Thus, up to 4, we have obligatory agreement with the noun: from 5 upwards there is a choice, with
the singular prevailing. This reflects the other differences in syntactic
behaviour between the lower and higher numerals, which were summarised in Table 11.11.

11.4 Diachronic Variation

Our investigation of the position in Old Church Slavic leads us to
consider the different paths of development of the numeral system.
The loss of the dual category in most of the Slavic languages (documented in Belić, 1932; see also Mayer, 1967, 300-4) led to a reorganisation
of the syntax of the lower numerals. In some instances this meant that
they became less like adjectives. A more general change has been that
higher numerals such as 1,000,000 have been added to the system, and
the numerals 5-10, 100, 1,000 have lost some of their noun-like properties;[8] this is evident when one compares Tables 11.4, 11.6 and 11.9 with
Table 11.11. However, for some languages there is still a relatively
clear break between 4 and 5, and this is reflected in the possibilities
for predicate agreement. In other languages, however, the old division
of the numeral system has been effaced, in the sense that there are now
no more factors dividing 4 from 5, than divide any other contiguous
pair of numerals. This latter line of development is found in East Slavic.
The consequence for predicate agreement is that most numerals allow
a choice of agreement. This is shown in Table 11.2, the relevant portion
of which is repeated below for convenience as Table 11.12.

In this table we see a monotonic decrease in plural predicate agreement as we move from 2 to 100. (The single exception, the 50 per
cent plural figure for 100 in Belorussian, is based on two examples only
and so may be disregarded.) It is quite clear that there is no longer the
sharp division between 4 and 5-10, which is still evident in some other
Slavic languages.

Thus, if we ignore Bulgarian and Macedonian, whose special development has led to the use of the plural with all numerals except 1, the
most innovative languages in this area have been the East Slavic group.
Here the division between 4 and 5, which remains in force in most of
the West and South Slavic languages, has been largely broken down.
However, while the general trend of development is clear, we must
not fall into the trap of assuming a gradual and continuous development. Data are available on predicate agreement in Russian from the

Table 11.12: Predicate Agreement in East Slavic

	2			3			4			5-10			100		
	sg	pl	%pl	sg	pl	%pl	sg	pl	%pl	sg	pl	%pl	sg	pl	%pl
Belorussian	18	201	92	15	52	78	6	10	63	30	19	39	1	1	50
Russian	74	467	86	56	191	77	16	52	76	110	110	50	not given		
Ukrainian	36	172	83	32	118	79	9	25	74	28	17	38	11	3	21

eighteenth century to the present day (from Suprun, 1969, 185, 188), and these show clearly that changes have not all been in one direction (see Table 11.13).

Table 11.13: Predicate Agreement in Russian: Eighteenth to Twentieth Centuries

	eighteenth century			nineteenth century			twentieth century		
	sg	pl	%pl	sg	pl	%pl	sg	pl	%pl
2–4	55	357	87	54	357	87	146	710	83
5–10	19	34	64	74	82	53	110	110	50
collectives (e.g. *dvoe* 'two')	25	41	62	23	82	78	35	255	88
complex numbers (e.g. *dvadcat'* '20')	48	26	35	71	62	47	103	65	39
compound numbers (e.g. *sorok pjat'* '45')	45	24	35	72	71	50	57	40	41
neskol'ko 'a few'	105	28	21	151	139	48	137	78	36
mnogo 'many', *skol'ko* 'how many', *stol'ko* 'so many'	42	0	0	not given			282	9	3
total (excluding *mnogo*, etc.)	297	510	63	445	793	64	588	1258	68

Table 11.13 shows that the overall change during the last two centuries has been relatively slight.[9] The increase in plural agreement shown under 'total' is rather misleading as it covers considerable fluctuations in particular quantifier types. Indeed, only quantifiers like *dvoe*, which have a limited range of usage, show a consistent increase in predicate agreement (probably caused by the fact that they are increasingly being restricted to use with animates). The slight overall increase from the nineteenth to the twentieth century is due largely to the different relative frequencies of the quantifiers; for example, there are over twice as many examples with 2–4 in the twentieth-century sample than in the nineteenth (which tends to boost the total percentage of plural agreement), while the number of examples with compound numerals is lower in the twentieth century than in the nineteenth. There are three types of quantifier which show a rise in plural agreement from the eighteenth to the nineteenth century, followed by a fall between the nineteenth and the twentieth century.

Besides proving that the development has not been straightforward and gradual, this type of variation reinforces the point that the individual quantifiers behave differently with respect to agreement.

We have concentrated on simple cardinal numerals, because of their frequency and because of the ease of comparison between languages. Table 11.13 reminds us that quantifiers of other types show similar variation. These too can be analysed in terms of their noun-like features (as in Corbett, 1979a, 77-8).

11.5 Conclusion

In this chapter we first investigated the way in which quantified expressions function as controllers. We established that they conform to the requirements of the Agreement and Predicate Hierarchies. Having found that the greatest variation was in the predicate, we concentrated on this position. We discovered that in predicate agreement with quantified expressions, there is considerable variation, both between languages and when we compare different quantifiers in individual languages. (The role of animacy and precedence in the choice of agreement form was established earlier.) Differences in agreement between quantifiers correlate with other features of their syntax. The more noun-like a quantifier is, the more likely it is to block access to the features of the quantified noun, and so the more likely singular agreement becomes. Conversely, the more like an adjective a quantifier is, the more readily it permits access to the features of the quantified noun and the more likely the semantically justified agreement form becomes.

Thus, while the range of variation between and within languages is great, it is constrained by the two Target Hierarchies, by the controller factors of animacy and precedence, and also by the nouniness of the quantifier.

Notes

1. Some of the claims made in this chapter rest on previous research which can only be referred to briefly. A more formal analysis of quantified expressions is given in Corbett (1978a, b, d, 1979a, 58-71). The postulated 'default' agreement forms mentioned in the discussion of (10) are justified in Corbett (1979a, 2-31, 58-64). Details of the morphological role of animacy (outlined in Table 11.1) can be found in Corbett (1981b).

2. An additional complication is described in Corbett (1979c); data there

(on *celyx* 'whole') show that the numeral is not always treated as a modifier, even in Russian. Note that if there is an attributive modifier in the nominative plural, as in (6), then the predicate must be plural. This may be taken as another example of the Agreement Hierarchy operating as a sentence-level constraint (§4.1).

3. See Klemensiewicz (1930, 122), Grappin (1950, 83–4), Decaux (1964, 70–1) and Bogusławski (1973, 30–1). The alternatives in Polish have been analysed as resulting from two different rule orders, one of which is obligatory in Russian, and the other in Serbo-Croat (Corbett, 1978a, 10).

4. Instances where the numeral itself is in the genitive (even though the quantified phrase is in subject position) are excluded here (see example (43)). For discussion of these forms see Schenker (1971), Corbett (1978a, 10–11), and for the history of the construction see Grappin (1950, 102–16).

5. In certain seventeenth- and eighteenth-century documents there are examples of numerals like *pjat'* 'five' agreeing in animacy (Drovnikova, 1962; Titova, 1964; Elenskij, 1978). This possibility was later lost. The important thing is that 5 could agree in animacy only when 1–4 already did so.

6. Determiners are usually avoided. It appears that, besides the singular form, which is the norm when a determiner is used, the plural is beginning to occur here; Iomdin (1979, 20) gives the following phrase without comment:

(i) R : *èti* (pl) *million dollarov*
     these   million dollars

My informants reject this example, but if such examples are confirmed, this will require us to reorder test 7 above test 6 in Tables 11.3 and 11.4.

7. The following example has a determiner which agrees with the numeral, as does the predicate:

(ii) R : *Prošla* (fem sg) *je prva* (fem sg) *stotina   godina . . .*
      Passed   the first   hundred years
      (Andrić, *Na Drini Ćuprija*)

For an outline of the whole cardinal number system see Popović (1979).

8. For example, in Russian up to the fourteenth century, all the numerals from 5 upwards retained the main noun-like qualities: they took agreement in gender and number both of the determiner and of the predicate, and the quantified noun normally stood in the genitive plural (Lomtev, 1956, 442–8; Šerech, 1952, 146). In Modern Russian, as we have seen, *pjat'* '5' takes a noun in the genitive case only when the numeral is in a direct case; *sto* '100' is losing the vestiges of nouniness and *tysjača* '1,000' is under pressure (Ivanova, 1969).

9. For comparable data from a smaller corpus, but differentiated according to textual type, see Mathiassen (1965, 17–51).

In this final chapter, our remaining tasks are to review the types of variation previously examined together with the patterns they revealed, to assess the adequacy of our proposed analysis, to consider the implications of this work beyond the Slavic languages and lastly to explore possible motivations for the agreement universals.

12.1 Variation and Patterns

At several points in our study we have met cases where different languages require different agreement forms in the same grammatical construction. Sometimes the difference is absolute (for example, one language requires the singular while a second has the plural), sometimes it is a question of varying preferences (both forms being available in each language). Diachronic variation has figured prominently, as have differences between standard and dialectal usage, literary and journalistic usage. We have seen examples of stylistic variation and cases where the socioeconomic background, age, education or sex of the speaker can be correlated with a particular choice of agreement form. While variation along these different dimensions is most interesting, the sociolinguistic factors involved do not form the basis for more general patterns. For example, while we observed instances where the semantically justified form has become more frequent with the passage of time (§7.5), there are other cases where it has become less frequent (Table 8.3) or has even advanced and retreated again (Table 11.13). The constant patterns found relate to the agreement targets and controllers. The role of the two Target Hierarchies was established in Chapters 2-4 and the link between them demonstrated in Chapters 5 and 9. From the point of view of the controller, the two major factors are animacy and precedence (Chapters 7 and 8); there are additional, more specific factors, which relate to individual constructions, as discussed in Chapters 10 and 11. Thus the real determiners of agreement, the constraints on variation, are grammatical; our investigation into linguistic variation has led to insights into 'pure' syntax (cf. Sankoff, 1978, xiii).

12.2 Adequacy of the Proposals

We began this investigation with a number of previously proposed
universals and we have been concerned not only to find evidence to
support or refute these claimed universals, but rather to use them in
an attempt to cover the data available and go beyond. And indeed, all
the data which had already been collected and which were sufficiently
detailed were included in our account. Thus the evidence for the
adequacy of our claims is very strong. In the course of the study we
were forced to refine the original proposals: the requirements of the
Agreement Hierarchy were extended to cover differences in agreement
caused by case distinctions; the level of operation of both hierarchies
was clarified; and the traditional opposition between syntactic and
semantic agreement was replaced by the notion of degree of semantic
justification. Detailed investigation of the data also led us to examine
the interaction of target and controller factors. Thus the data available
for the Slavic languages – a limited but taxing area – have been accoun-
ted for, while at the same time the original proposals have been made
more precise. The application of proposed universals to the full range
of data from a restricted language area is a promising way forward for
typological study.

12.3 Implications beyond Slavic

It has been stated at various points that the major factors which influence agreement have been previously identified and postulated as
universals. To be specific, the Agreement Hierarchy was originally
proposed on the basis of data from a variety of languages, only a
minority of which are Slavic languages. It is worth noting that the
Agreement Hierarchy accounts for the distribution of other agreement
phenomena, such as attraction, in addition to the options which have
been our concern in this study. The Predicate Hierarchy was similarly
based on data from a range of languages. The major controller factors,
animacy and precedence, were previously put forward as universals associated with the Agreement Hierarchy. Data on the relationship of the
two factors, as given in §7.3.1, §7.5 and §8.4.3, are also available for
non-Slavic languages (Corbett, forthcoming b), and the same paper
provides a general typology of resolution rules, which puts the Slavic
data into a wider context. Finally, the correlation between noun-like
behaviour and the numerical value of numerals was claimed on the

basis of a survey of over 70 languages (Corbett, 1978b); the link with agreement is clear.

Thus the major factors we have investigated operate in languages beyond the Slavic family. The fact that we have amassed such a large amount of evidence in their favour from Slavic languages gives some further support to their claim to universality. To this extent the study has implications beyond Slavic. More importantly, we have seen that the factors in question together account for a large proportion of all the previously established facts about agreement options in Slavic. We are therefore dealing with a system of universals rather than with isolated universals. The major implication which goes beyond Slavic concerns methodology: by testing universals against all the relevant data in a particular language group, postulated universals can be further justified, the claims they make can be defined more accurately and their modes of interaction can be established – which means that they are then seen as a system rather than as a set of isolated constraints.

12.4 Motivation

Our main concern has been to present a coherent factual account and to show how the data fit into general patterns. We have been able to operate with basic concepts (such as verbal predicate and animate noun) which – in the vast majority of cases – give no major problems of definition and identification. While the goal must be to explain linguistic data, explanation depends on a solid factual foundation, and we have concentrated on the latter. We will now consider the lines along which explanations might be sought, bearing in mind that complete explanations for the universals we have been discussing will probably lie at least in part outside linguistics.

As a first step towards discovering why the distribution of alternative agreement forms is regulated as it is, it is logical to consider why there are alternative possibilities at all. Mismatches between morphology and semantics or syntax and semantics may arise for a variety of reasons: historical, cultural and linguistic. For example, Russian *vrač* 'doctor' was originally masculine as it referred to males. When women began to enter the profession, form and meaning no longer coincided; a new feminine form might have been created by morphological means, but this did not occur and so we get the agreement options described in §2.3. Honorific *vy* 'you' shows a similar mismatch of form and meaning. Its use for a single addressee was probably motivated originally by the idea that the person so addressed represented a power greater than that of one man (though by the time polite forms were borrowed into Slavic this motivation had probably been lost). In ordinary polite address there is a lack of correspondence between plural form and singular referent. Besides historical and cultural examples, there are cases where developments in the categories of number and gender have given rise to alternative agreement possibilities. The loss of the dual number led to the two options for agreement with the numerals 2–4 in Serbo-Croat, described in §2.1.3 and §5.4. An example of a change in gender categories is the move away from the use of the neuter for the young of humans and animals; thus Czech *děvče* 'girl' (§2.1.1) now allows feminine as well as neuter personal pronouns. The same development, together with the coincidence of feminine singular and neuter plural endings, produced the complex agreement possibilities with Serbo-Croat *deca* 'children', analysed in Chapter 5. These alternative possibilities relate to specific lexical items; there may be an agreement choice in one language but not in another closely related language if the combination of contributory factors is not identical.

Other types of alternative agreements occur more frequently; these are based on ambiguities in syntactic structure. For example, if the subject of a given sentence consists of two conjoined noun phrases, then a potential agreement choice arises. A verbal predicate typically agrees with a noun phrase and may therefore agree with one of the two conjoined noun phrases. However, the conjoined structure is in turn a noun phrase and so agreement may be with this larger noun phrase. These are the familiar alternatives presented in §6.2. Similarly in the case of comitative phrases, agreement may be with the noun phrase standing in the nominative or it may be with the complex noun phrase. Quantified expressions include at least two noun phrases – there is a noun phrase with the quantified noun as its head and the whole complex noun phrase. As we saw in §11.1, it is not always clear which element is the head. It is no surprise that there are alternative agreement possibilities in such constructions.

We now turn to the constraints on the alternative agreement possibilities and their motivation. In the case of the Target Hierarchies, the different positions represent successively weaker syntactic links as we move rightwards. Thus, as is well known, the link between noun phrase and verbal predicate is weaker than that between head noun and adjective. As we progress to successively weaker links, in other words to increasing syntactic distance between controller and target, so the scope for interference from semantic factors increases. (Cornish,

1982, 275-6, explains the Agreement Hierarchy in terms of 'the increasingly greater independent reference potential' of the elements as we move rightwards along it.)

In the case of the major controller factors, the picture is less clear, as we observed in §8.1. Animacy may be linked to the notion of individuation: animates are more likely to be viewed separately than are inanimates. Individuation favours semantically justified agreement forms. At the same time, individuated elements are more topic-worthy than are non-individuated elements; topics typically occur pre-verbally in Slavic and so have precedence when predicate agreement is involved. However, the interrelation of these different factors, the role of the related factor of definiteness and especially the notion of topic all require clarification. In contrast, the problems discussed in Chapters 10 and 11 are less general and allow us to get closer to an explanation. In the case of resolution rules, person and number resolution can be explained in semantic terms. Gender resolution, which shows considerable variety, can be understood by reference to semantic and functional factors, the differences between Slavic languages being traceable to differences in the morphology of gender, as we saw in §10.4. In Chapter 11 we found that there is a correlation between the numerical value of a numeral and the likelihood of the quantified expression taking semantically justified agreement: the higher the numeral, the more like a noun it is and the less probable plural agreement becomes. It is not difficult to see why the more noun-like numerals are less likely to take plural agreement. As discussed in §11.3.1, a nounier numeral is more likely to be taken as the head of the quantified expression and so to block access to the features of the quantified noun. It is less easy to see why numerical value should correlate with nouniness, though the beginnings of a solution can be suggested. In the course of history the need has arisen for successively higher numerals; nouns referring to a vague large number have then taken on a specific numerical value, larger than that of the previously largest numeral. Thus the higher numerals are nouns pressed into service as numerals. An example would be Old Church Slavonic *t'ma* 'multitude' which came to mean '10,000'. As in the course of cultural development new numerals are introduced, naturally at the top of the earlier system, the previously highest numeral may be further integrated into the system and lose some noun-like features. One must still ask why the items pressed into service as higher numerals are always nouns. This regularity is linked to the notion of individuation. Nouns such as *t'ma* 'multitude' originally denote a number too large to grasp, conceivable only as an undifferentiated group. It is difficult for us to imagine a time when 10,000 was the normal upper limit for counting. Nevertheless, we recognise that it is easier to view, say, a group of four as individuals than a group of 100. Thus individuation (which favours semantically justified agreement forms) is inversely proportional to numerical value.

Our discussion of motivation has of necessity been speculative. Previous hypothesising in this area has had a rather insecure base, and our main aim in the book has been to provide a more solid factual foundation. Now that the basic patterns of agreement have been established and interrelated as a system, the way is open for more satisfactory explanatory hypotheses.

In the perplexing variety which confronted us at the beginning of this study, we have identified several patterns, notably the hierarchies, which relate to targets, and the controller factors. While these had been postulated before, we have combined them into a system of universals — an approach which has implications for typological studies in general. As more patterns and systems of this type are discovered, in different areas of language, so we will come closer to full explanations for the major regularities we have established.

REFERENCES

This is not a complete bibliography of works on agreement in Slavic; only items referred to in the text are listed.

Apresjan, Ju. D. (1982) 'O vozmožnosti opredelenija lingvističeskih ponjatij', *Russian Linguistics*, 6, 175-96
Atraxovič, K.K., Bulaxaŭ, M.G. and Šuba, P.P. (eds.) (1966) *Hramatyka belaruskaj movy, II, Sintaksis*, Minsk, Navuka i tèxnika
Babić, S. (1973) 'Sročnost (kongruencija) u suvremenom hrvatskom književnom jeziku', *Zbornik Zagrebačke slavističke škole*, I, pt 1, 199-218
Bajec, A. (1955-6) 'Vezanje več osebkov s povedkom', *Jezik in Slovstvo*, 1, 12-14
Bartoš, J. and Gagnaire, J. (1972) *Grammaire de la langue slovaque*, Bratislava, Matica slovenská and Paris, Institut d'études slaves
Bauernöppel, J., Fritsch, H. and Bielefeld, B. (1976) *Kurze tschechische Sprachlehre*, 3rd edn, Berlin, Volk und Wissen
Belić, A. (1924) 'Napomena o jednoj sintaksičko-morfološkoj osobini srpskohrvatskog jezika', *Južnoslovenski filolog*, 4, 24-8.
—— (1932) *O dvojini u slovenskim jezicima*, Belgrade, Srpska kraljevska akademija
Bogdanov, V.N. (1968) 'Osobyj slučaj dialektnogo soglasuemogo s podležaščim po smyslu i kategorija predstavitel'nosti', *Naučnye doklady vysšej školy: filologičeskie nauki*, no. 4, 68-75
Bogusławski, A. (1973) 'Nazwy pospolite przedmiotów konkretnych i niektóre właściwości ich form liczbowych i połączeń z liczebnikami w języku polskim' in Topolińska, Z. and Grochowski, M. (eds.), *Liczba, ilość, miara: materialy konferencji naukowej*, Wrocław, PAN, pp. 7-35
Borkovskij, V.I. (ed.) (1978) *Istoričeskaja grammatika russkogo jazyka: sintaksis: prostoe predloženie*, Moscow, Nauka
Brooks, M.Z. (1973) 'Rola liczby i rodzaju przy zgodzie niektórych podmiotów z orzeczeniem' in Matejka, L. (ed.), *American Contributions to the Seventh International Congress of Slavists: Warsaw, August 21-27, 1973, I, Linguistics and Poetics*, The Hague, Mouton, pp. 59-66
Browne, E.W. (1980) 'Relativna rečenica u hrvatskom ili srpskom jeziku u poređenju s engleskom situacijom', unpublished doctoral dissertation, University of Zagreb
Bukatevič, N.I., Gricjutenko, I.E., Miževskaja, G.M., Pavljuk, N.V., Savickaja, S.A. and Smaglenko, F.P. (1958) *Očerki po sravnitel'noj grammatike vostočnoslavjanskix jazykov*, Odessa, Odesskij gosudarstvennyj universitet im. I.I. Mečnikova. Reprinted as Slavistic Printings and Reprintings no. 137 (1969), The Hague, Mouton
Bulaxovskij, L.A. (1958) 'Mestoimenija kak predmet sintaksičeskogo analiza i škol'nogo usvoenija', *Russkij jazyk v škole*, no. 4, 30-6
Burzan, M. (1981) 'Interferencija u kongruiranju predikata sa subjektom u broju u govornoj produkciji mađarsko-srpskohrvatskih bilingva na srpskohrvatskom jeziku', *Prilozi proučavanju jezika* (Novi Sad), 17, 119-39
Buslaev, F.I. (1959) *Istoričeskaja grammatika russkogo jazyka*, Moscow, Gosudarstvennoe učebno-pedagogičeskoe izdatel'stvo Ministerstva prosveščenija RSFSR

Buttke, K. (1972) 'Zur Kongruenz des Prädikats mit der Numeralfügung als subjekt im modernen Ukrainischen', *Zeitschrift für Slawistik*, 17, 626-35

Buttler, D., Kurkowska, H. and Satkiewicz, H. (1971) *Kultura języka polskiego: zagadnienia poprawności gramatycznej*, Warsaw, PWN

Bylinskij, K.I. (1939) 'Osobye slučai soglasovanija skazuemogo s podležaščim v sovremennom literaturnom jazyke', *Russkij jazyk v škole*, no. 2, 63-73

Chase, C.I. (1967) *Elementary Statistical Procedures*, New York, McGraw-Hill

Comrie, B. (1975) 'Polite Plurals and Predicate Agreement', *Language*, 51, 406-18

— (1981) *Language Universals and Linguistic Typology: Syntax and Morphology*, Oxford, Blackwell

— and Stone, G. (1978) *The Russian Language since the Revolution*, Oxford, Clarendon

Corbett, G.G. (1978a) 'Problems in the Syntax of Slavonic Numerals', *Slavonic and East European Review*, 56, 1-12

— (1978b) 'Universals in the Syntax of Cardinal Numerals', *Lingua*, 46, 355-68

— (1978c) 'Numerous squishes and squishy numerals in Slavonic', *International Review of Slavic Linguistics*, 3 (= Comrie, B. (ed.), *Classification of Grammatical Categories*, Edmonton, Linguistic Research), pp. 43-73.

— (1978d) 'Apposition involving *dva*, *tri*, *četyre* in Russian – a Solution to Worth's Riddle' *Quinquereme – New Studies in Modern Languages*, 1, 258-64

— (1979a) *Predicate Agreement in Russian* (Birmingham Slavonic Monographs, 7), University of Birmingham, Department of Russian Language and Literature

— (1979b) 'The Agreement Hierarchy', *Journal of Linguistics*, 15, 203-24

— (1979c) 'Adjective Movement', *Nottingham Linguistic Circular*, 8, 1-10

— (1980a) 'Neutral Agreement', *Quinquereme – New Studies in Modern Languages*, 3, 164-70

— (1980b) 'Animacy in Russian and Other Slavonic Languages: Where Syntax and Semantics Fail to Match' in Chvany, C.V. and Brecht, R.D. (eds.), *Morphosyntax in Slavic*, Columbus, Slavica, pp. 43-61

— (1981a) 'A Note on Grammatical Agreement in *Šinel'*, *Slavonic and East European Review*, 59, 59-61

— (1981b) 'Syntactic Features', *Journal of Linguistics*, 17, 55-76

— (1981c) 'Agreement with Honorific *vy* in Russian and its Significance for Subject-raising and for the Analysis of Predicative Adjectives', *New Zealand Slavonic Journal*, no. 2, 73-88

— (1982a) 'Resolution Rules for Predicate Agreement in the Slavonic Languages', *Slavonic and East European Review*, 60, 347-78

— (1982b) 'Gender in Russian: an Account of Gender Specification and its Relationship to Declension', *Russian Linguistics*, 8, 197-232

— (forthcoming a) 'The Number of Genders in Polish' (to appear in:) *Papers and Studies in Contrastive Linguistics*, 16

— (forthcoming b) 'Resolution Rules: Agreement in Person, Number and Gender' (to appear in:) Gazdar, G., Klein, E. and Pullum, G.K. (eds), *Order, Concord and Constituency*, Dordrecht, Foris

Cornish, F. (1982) 'Anaphoric Relations in English and French' unpublished DPhil thesis, University of Sussex

Crockett, D.B. (1976) *Agreement in Contemporary Standard Russian*, Cambridge, Mass., Slavica

de Bray, R.G.A. (1980a) *Guide to the South Slavonic Languages* (*Guide to the Slavonic Languages*, 3rd edn, revised and expanded, Part 1), Columbus, Ohio, Slavica

— (1980b) *Guide to the West Slavonic Languages* (*Guide to the Slavonic Languages*, 3rd edn, revised and expanded, Part 2), Columbus, Ohio, Slavica

—— (1980c) *Guide to the East Slavonic Languages* (*Guide to the Slavonic Languages*, 3rd edn, revised and expanded, Part 3), Columbus, Ohio, Slavica

Decaux, É. (1964) 'L'expression de la détermination au pluriel numérique en polonais', *Revue des études slaves*, 40, 61–72

Degtjarev, V.I. (1966) 'Osobennosti soglasovanija skazuemogo s podležaščim – imenem sobiratel'nym v drevnerusskom jazyke', *Naučnye doklady vysšej školy: filologičeskie nauki*, no. 3, 138–46

Dončeva-Mareva, L. (1978) 'Săglasuvaneto na učtivoto *Vie* săs skazuemoto v bălgarskija i ruskija ezik ot kvantitativno gledište', *Săpostavitelno ezikoznanie*, no. 3, 70–5

Doroszewski, W. (1962) *O kulturę słowa: poradnik językowy*, Warszawa, PIW

Drejzin, F.A. (1966) 'Sintaksičeskaja omonimija v russkom jazyke s točki zrenija avtomatičeskogo analiza', unpublished kandidat dissertation, Moscow. Quoted from Crockett (1976)

Drovnikova, L.N. (1962) 'Konstrukcii typa "vstretil pjati čelovek" v XVII veke (k istorii sklonenija čislitel'nyx)', *Naučnye doklady vysšej školy: filologičeskie nauki*, no. 1, 206–9

Elenskij, J. (1978) 'Oduševlennost' pri čislitel'nyx v petrovskuju èpoxu', *Bolgarskaja rusistika*, no. 4, 57–67

Faska, H. (1959) 'Někotre syntaktiske a stilistiske wosebitosće kongruency predikata ze subjektom', *Lětopis Instituta za serbski ludospyt* (Bautzen), rjad A., vol. 6, 48–72

Findreng, Å. (1976) *Zur Kongruenz in Person und Numerus zwischen Subjekt und finitem Verb im modernen Deutsch*, Oslo, Universitetsforlaget

Givón, T. (1970) 'The Resolution of Gender Conflicts in Bantu Conjunction: When Syntax and Semantics Clash', *Papers from the Sixth Regional Meeting, Chicago Linguistic Society*, 250–61

—— (1976) 'Topic, Pronoun and Grammatical Agreement' in Li, C.N. (ed.), *Subject and Topic*, New York, Academic Press, pp. 151–88

Glavan, V. (1927–8) 'Kongruencija u jeziku starih čakavskih pisaca', *Južnoslovenski filolog*, 7, 111–59

Grappin, H. (1950) *Les noms de nombre en polonais*, Kraków, PAU

Graudina, L.K., Ickovič, V.A. and Katlinskaja, L.P. (1976) *Grammatičeskaja pravil'nost' russkoj reči: opyt častotno-stilističeskogo slovarja variantov*, Moscow, Nauka

Gudkov, V. (1965) 'Dodatak pravilima slaganja predikata sa više subjekata', *Književnost i jezik*, 12, 60–1

—— (1969) *Serboxorvatskij jazyk: grammatičeskij očerk, literaturnye teksty s kommentarijami i slovarem*, Moscow, Izdatel'stvo Moskovskogo Universiteta

—— (1974) 'Prilog o pravilima kongruencije', *Kniževnost i jezik*, 21, 58–61

Gustavsson, S. (1976) *Predicative Adjectives with the Copula* byt' *in Modern Russian* (Stockholm Slavic Studies, 10), Stockholm, Almqwist & Wiksell

Gvozdev, A.N. (1973) *Sovremennyj russkij literaturnyj jazyk, II, Sintaksis*, 4th edn, Moscow, Prosveščenie

Hamm, J. (1956–7) 'Promjena brojeva 2, 3 i 4', *Jezik in Slovstvo*, no. 1, 9–14

Herdan, G. (1964) *Quantitative Linguistics*, London, Butterworths

Herrity, P. (1977) 'Problem kongruencije u srpskohrvatskom i drugim slovenskim jezicima' in *Naučni sastanak u vukove dane*, 7, Beograd, Međunarodni slavistički centar SR Srbije, pp. 261–73

Iomdin, L.L. (1979) 'Fragment modeli russkogo poverxnostnogo sintaksisa: opredelitel'nye konstrukcii', *Južnoslovenski filolog*, 25, 19–54

Ivanova, V.F. (1969) 'Čelovek s tysač'ju lic ili čelovek s tysač'ju licami?', *Russkij jazyk v skole*, no. 2, 66–73

Janko-Trinickaja, N.A. (1966) 'Naimenovanie lic ženskogo pola suščestvitel'nymi ženskogo i muskogo roda' in Zemskaja, A.E. and Šmelev, D.N. (eds.), *Razvitie slovoobrazovanija sovremennogo russkogo jazyka*, Moscow, Nauka, pp. 167–210

Ječmenica, A. (1966) 'O Lalićevoj kongruenciji uz imenice na -a koje označavaju muška lica', *Književnost i jezik*, 14, 304–10

Jentsch, H. (1980) *Die sorbische Mundart von Rodewitz/Spree* (Schriftenreihe des Instituts für sorbische Volksforschung in Bautzen no. 47), Bautzen, Domowina

Jesenovec, F. (1958–9) 'Ali ste prišel (prišla)?', *Jezik in Slovstvo*, 4, 30–1

Johnson, D.E. (1977) 'On Relational Constraints on Grammars' in Cole, P. and Sadock, J.M. (eds.) *Syntax and Semantics, 8, Grammatical Relations*, New York, Academic Press, pp. 151–78

Johnson, D.E, and Postal, P.M. (1980) *Arc Pair. Grammar*, Princeton, Princeton University Press

Kallas, K. (1974) 'O zdaniach *Pachniał wiatr i morze., Andrzej i Amelia milczeli.*', *Studia z filologii polskiej i słowiańskiej*, 14, 57–71

Karlsson, G. (1968) 'Eräs suomen inkongruenssi-ilmiö', *Mémoires de la société finno-ougrienne*, 145, 117–26

Keenan, E.L. and Comrie, B. (1977) 'Noun Phrase Accessibility and Universal Grammar', *Linguistic Inquiry*, 8, 63–99

Kitajgorodskaja, M.V. (1976) 'Variativnost' v vyraženii roda suščestvitel'nogo pri oboznačenii ženščin po professii' in Krysin, L.P. and Šmelev, D.N. (eds.), *Social'no-lingvističeskie issledovanija*, Moscow, Nauka, pp. 144–55

Klemensiewicz, Z. (1930) 'Liczebnik główny w polszczyźnie literackiej', *Prace Filologiczne*, 15, 1–130

— (1967) *Studia syntaktyczne* (Prace Komisji Językoznawstwa PAN 15), Wrocław, PAN

Koneski, B. (1967) *Gramatika na makedonskiot literaturen jazik, I & II*, Skopje, Kultura

Kopeliovič, A.B. (1977) 'K voprosu o kodifikacii imen suščestvitel'nyx obščego roda' in Ickovič, V.A., Mis'kevič, G.I. and Skvorcov, L.I. (eds.), *Grammatika i norma*, Moscow, Nauka, pp. 178–92

Krivickij, A.A., Mixnevič, A.E. and Podlužnyj, A.I. (1973) *Belorusskij jazyk dlja nebelorusov*, Minsk, Vyšėjšaja škola

Kulak, J., Łaciak, W. & Żeleskiewicz, I. (1966) *Język polski: skrypt dla cudzoziemców*, 4th edn, Warsaw, PWN

Langacker, R.W. (1969) 'On Pronominalization and the Chain of Command' in Reibel, D.A. and Schane, S.A. (eds.) *Modern Studies in English: Readings in Transformational Grammar*, Englewood Cliffs, Prentice Hall, pp. 160–86

Legiša, L. (1958–9) 'Pripomba k obliki vikanja', *Jezik in Slovstvo*, 4, 127–8

Lenček, R. (1972) 'O zaznamovanosti in nevtralizaciji slovnične kategorije spola v slovenskem knjižnem jeziku', *Slavistična revija*, 20, 55–63

Lomtev, T.P. (1956) *Očerki po istoričeskomu sintaksisu russkogo jazyka*, Moscow, Izdatel'stvo Moskovskogo universiteta

Makarski, W. (1973) 'Konstrukcje *pluralis maiestatis* w gwarach Rzeszowszczyzny', *Poradnik Jezykowy*, 1, 30–4

Maretić, T. (1899) *Gramatika i stilistika hrvatskoga ili srpskoga književnog jezika*, Zagreb, Hartman

Marković, S.V. (1954) 'O kolebljivosti slaganja u rodu kod imenica čiji se prirodni i gramatički rod ne slažu (i o rodu ovih imenica)', *Pitanja književnosti i jezika* (Sarajevo), 1, 87–110

Mathiassen, T. (1965) 'Bidrag til spørsmålet kongruens mellom subjekt og predikat i russisk – særlig henblikk på det nyere språk (ca 1730-1964)', unpublished dissertation, University of Oslo

Mayer, G.L. (1967) *A Comparative Study of the Syntax of the Cardinal Numeral in the Slavic Languages*, PhD dissertation, University of Pennsylvania. Distributed by University Microfilms, Ann Arbor, 67-12, 778

Megaard, J. (1976) 'Predikatets kongruens i serbokroatisk i setninger med koordinerte subjektsnominalfraser', unpublished dissertation, University of Oslo

Miklosich, F. (1868-74) *Vergleichende Grammatik der slavischen Sprachen, IV, Syntax*, Vienna, Braumüller

Moravcsik, E.A. (1978) 'Agreement' in Greenberg, J.H., Ferguson, C.A. and Moravcsik, E.A. (eds.), *Universals of Human Language, IV, Syntax*, Stanford, Stanford University Press, pp. 331-74

Morgan, J.L. (1972) 'Verb Agreement as a Rule of English', *Papers from the Eighth Regional Meeting Chicago Linguistic Society*, pp. 278-86

Mučnik, I.P. (1971) *Grammatičeskie kategorii glagola i imeni v sovremennom russkom literaturnom jazyke*, Moscow, Nauka

Mullen, J. (1967) *Agreement of the Verb-Predicate with a Collective Subject* (Studies in the Modern Russian Language, 5), London, Cambridge University Press

Nichols, J., Rappaport, G. and Timberlake, A. (1980) 'Subject, Topic and Control in Russian', *Proceedings of the Sixth Annual Meeting of the Berkeley Linguistics Society*, 372-86

Nixon, G. (1972) 'Corporate-concord Phenomena in English', *Studia Neophilologica*, 44, 120-6

Orlovský, J. (1965) *Slovenská syntax*, 2nd edn, revised, Bratislava, Obzor

Panov, M.V. (ed.) (1968) *Russkij jazyk i sovetskoe obščestvo, III, Morfologija i sintaksis sovremennogo russkogo jazyka*, Moscow, Nauka

Patton, H. (1969) *A Study of the Agreement of the Predicate with a Quantitative Subject in Contemporary Russian*, PhD dissertation, University of Pennsylvania. Distributed by University Microfilms, Ann Arbor, 70-7839

Pauliny, E., Ružička, J. and Štolc, J. (1968) *Slovenská gramatika*, 5th edn, Bratislava, Slovenské pedagogické nakladatel'stvo

Pavlović, M. (1965) 'Strukturalno-funkcionalne pojave kod zbirnih imenica u srpskohrvatskom jeziku', *Studia z Filologii Polskiej i Słowiańskiej*, 5, 165-73

Peškovskij, A.M. (1956) *Russkij sintaksis v naučnom osveščenii*, 7th edn, Moscow, Učpedgiz

Petik, V.G. (ed.) (1975) *Sučasna ukrajins'ka literaturna mova*, Kiev, Višča škola

Popov, K. (1963) *Săvremenen bălgarski ezik: sintaksis*, 2nd edn, Sofia, Nauka i izkustvo

— (1964) *Sintaktičnoto săglasuvane v bălgarski ezik*, Sofia, Nauka i izkustvo

Popova, Z.D. (1955) 'Soglasovanie po materialam Azovskoj zapisnoj knigi 1698-1699 gg.', *Trudy Voronežskogo universiteta*, 42, vyp. 3, 91-3

Popović, Lj. (1979) 'Upotreba kardinalnih brojeva u srpskohrvatskom jeziku', *Jugoslovenski seminar za strane slaviste*, 30, 3-24

Potapova, N.P. (1960) 'Soglasovanie skazuemogo s podležaščim, vyražennym imenem suščestvitel'nym s sobiratel'nym značeniem, v govorax permskoj oblasti', *Učenye zapiski Permskogo gosudarstvennogo universiteta*, 16, vyp. 1, 29-40

— (1962) 'Soglasovanie skazuemogo s odnorodnymi podležaščimi v govorax permskoj oblasti', *Učenye zapiski Permskogo Gosudarstvennogo Universiteta imeni A. M. Gor'kogo*, 22, vyp. 1, 59-68

Prokopovič, N.N. (1974) *Voprosy sintaksisa russkogo jazyka*, Moscow, Vysšaja škola

Protčenko, I.F. (1961) 'Formy glagola i prilagatel'nogo v sočetanii s nazvanijami lic ženskogo pola', *Voprosy kul'tury reči*, 3, 116-26

Ransom, E.N. (1977) 'Definiteness, Animacy and NP Ordering', *Proceedings of the Third Annual Meeting of the Berkeley Linguistics Society*, 418-29

Rezvin, I.I. (1970) 'O specifike soglasovanija po čislu v russkom jazyke' in *Jazyk i čelovek: sbornik statej pamjati professora Petra Savviča Kuznecova (1899-1968)*, Moscow, Izdatel'stvo Moskovskogo universiteta, pp. 230-8

Rogić, P. (1955) 'Deklinacija brojeva dva, oba (obadva), tri, četiri', *Jezik*, no. 5, 9-14

Ross, J.R. (1972) 'The Category Squish: Endstation Hauptwort', *Papers from the Eighth Regional Meeting Chicago Linguistic Society*, 316-28

— (1973a) 'Nouniness' in Fujimura O. (ed.), *Three Dimensions of Linguistic Theory*, Tokyo, TEC, pp. 137-257

— (1973b) 'A Fake NP Squish' in Bailey, C.-J. and Shuy, R. (eds.) *New Ways of Analyzing Variation in English*, Washington, DC, Georgetown University Press, pp. 97-140

— (1975) 'Clausematiness' in Keenan, E.L. (ed.), *Formal Semantics of Natural Language*, London, Cambridge University Press, pp. 422-75

Rothstein, R.A. (1973) 'O roli kategorii gramatycznych w ogólnej teorii języka: kategoria rodzaju' in Matejka, L. (ed.), *American Contributions to the Seventh International Congress of Slavists: Warsaw, August 21-27, 1973, I, Linguistics and Poetics*, The Hague, Mouton, pp. 307-14.

— (1976) 'Uwagi o rodzaju gramatycznym i cechach semantycznych wyrazów', *Język polski*, 56, 241-53

— (1980) 'Gender and Reference in Polish and Russian' in Chvany, C.V. and Brecht, R.D. (eds.), *Morphosyntax in Slavic*, Columbus, Slavica, pp. 79-97

Rozental', D.È. (1971) *Spravočnik po pravopisaniju i literaturnoj pravke dlja rabotnikov pečati*, 2nd edn, revised, Moscow, Kniga

— (1974) *Praktičeskaja stilistika russkogo jazyka*, 3rd edn, Moscow, Vysšaja škola

— and Telenkova, M.A. (1972) *Praktičeskaja stilistika russkogo jazyka*, Moscow, Progress

Rudnev, A.G. (1968) *Sintaksis sovremennogo russkogo jazyka*, 2nd edn, Moscow, Vysšaja škola

Sand, D.E.Z. (1971) *Agreement of the Predicate with Quantitative Subjects in Serbo-Croatian*, PhD dissertation, University of Pennsylvania. Distributed by University Microfilms, Ann Arbor, 72-17, 420

Sankoff, D. (1978) *Linguistic Variation: Models and Methods*, New York, Academic Press

Schane, S.A. (1970) 'Phonological and Morphological Markedness' in Bierwisch, M. and Heidolph, K.E. (eds.), *Progress in Linguistics*, The Hague, Mouton, pp. 286-94

Schenker, A.M. (1971) 'Some Remarks on Polish Quantifiers', *Slavic and East European Journal*, 15, 54-60

Šerech, J. [Shevelov, G.] (1952) *Probleme der Bildung des Zahlwortes als Redeteil in den Slavischen Sprachen* (Lunds Universitets Årsskrift, N.F. Avd. 1, Bd 48, Nr 2), Lund, Lund University

Šewc-Schuster, H. (1976) *Gramatika hornjoserbskeje rěče: 2. zwjazk-syntaksa*, Bautzen, Domowina

Shevelov, G.Y. (1963) *The Syntax of Modern Literary Ukrainian: The Simple Sentence*, The Hague, Mouton

Širokova, A.G. (1977) 'Češskij jazyk' in Širokova, A.G. and Gudkov, V.P. (eds.), *Slavjanskie jazyki (očerki grammatiki zapadnoslavjanskix i južnoslavjanskix jazykov)*, Moscow, Izdatel'stvo Moskovskogo Universiteta, pp. 64-118

Skoblikova, E.S. (1971) *Soglasovanie i upravlenie v russkom jazyke*, Moscow, Prosveščenie

Sobinnikova, V.I. (1969) *Konstrukcii s odnorodnymi členami, leksičeskim toždestvom i parallelizmom v narodnyx govorax*, Voronež, Izdatel'stvo Voronežskogo universiteta

Stanislav, J. (1977) *Slowakische Grammatik*, Bratislava, Slovenské pedagogické nakladel'stvo

Stanojčić, Z.S. (1967) *Jezik i stil Iva Andricá (funcije sinonimskih odnosa)*, Belgrade, Filološki fakultet Beogradskog universiteta

Stevanović, M. (1974) *Savremeni srpskohrvatski jezik (gramatički sistemi i književnojezička norma), II, Sintaksa*, 2nd edn, Belgrade, Naučna knjiga

Stone, G. (1976) 'Pronominal Address in Sorbian', *Lětopis Instituta za serbski ludospyt*, Rjad A, 23/2, 182–91

— (1977) 'Address in the Slavonic Languages', *Slavonic and East European Review*, 55, 491–505

Suprun, A.E. (1959) *O russkix čislitel'nyx*, Frunze, Kirghiz State University

— (1961) *Staroslavjanskie čislitel'nye*, Frunze, Kirghiz State University

— (1963a) 'O soglasovanii skazuemogo s podležaščim, vključajuščim količestvennye čislitel'nye v serbo-lužickix jazykax', *Serbo-lužickij lingvističeskij sbornik*, Moscow, pp. 138–53

— (1963b) 'Zametki po sintaksisu pol'skix čislitel'nyx' *Pytannja slovjans'koho movoznavstva* (L'vov), 7–8, 135–45

— (1969) *Slavjanskie čislitel'nye (stanovlenie čislitel'nyx kak osoboj časti reči)*, Minsk, Belorussian State University

Sussex, R.D. (forthcoming) *The Slavonic Languages*, Cambridge, Cambridge University Press

Švedova, N.Ju. (ed.) (1970) *Grammatika sovremennogo russkogo literaturnogo jazyka*, Moscow, Nauka

Titova, R.F. (1964) 'Imja čislitel'noe v delovyx dokumentax konca XVII veka (Dela Azovskoj prikaznoj palaty): količestvennye čislitel'nye' in Sobinnikova, V.I., Popova, Z.D. and Čižik-Polejko, A.I. (eds.), *Materialy konferencii po izučeniju južnorusskix govorov i pamjatnikov pis'mennosti (6–8 dekabrja 1962 goda)*, Voronež, Izdatel'stvo Voronežskogo universiteta, pp. 33–44

Toporišič, J. (1972) *Slovenski knjižni jezik, III*, Maribor, Založba Obzorja

Trávníček, F. (1949) *Mluvnice spisovné češtiny, II, Skladba*, Prague, Melantrich

Vaillant, A. (1977) *Grammaire comparée des langues slaves, V, La syntaxe*, Paris, Klincksieck

Vanek, A.L. (1970) *Aspects of Subject-Verb Agreement (Studies in Slavic Linguistics*, 1), Edmonton, Department of Slavic Languages, University of Alberta. Republished in the series *Current Inquiry into Language and Linguistics*, 23 (1977), Edmonton, Linguistic Research

Večerka, R. (1960) 'K sintaksisu imen čislitel'nyx v staroslavjanskom jazyke' in Georgiev, V. (ed.) *Ezikovedsko-etnografski izsledvanija v pamet na akademik Stojan Romanski*, Sofia, Bulgarian Academy of Sciences, pp. 195–208

Vincenot, C. (1975) *Essai de grammarie slovène*, Ljubljana, Mladinska knjiga

Vinogradov, V.V. and Istrina, E.S. (eds.) (1954) *Grammatika russkogo jazyka, II, Sintaksis, čast' pervaja*, Moscow, AN SSSR

Vinogradov, V.V., Barxudarov, S.G., Blagoj, D.D. and Tomaševskij, B.V. (eds.) (1956) *Slovar' jazyka Puškina, I*, Moscow, Gosudarstvennoe izdatel'stvo inostrannyx i nacional'nyx slovarej

Vondrák, W. (1928) *Vergleichende Slavische Grammatik, II, Formenlehre und Syntax*, 2nd edn, prepared by O. Grünenthal, Göttingen, Vandenhoeck & Ruprecht

Wood, R. (1980) 'Morfologičeskie varianty slov', unpublished undergraduate dissertation, University of Aston

Xaburgaev, G.A. (1974) *Staroslavjanskij jazyk, Moscow*, Prosveščenie

Xitrova, V.I. (1964) 'Ošibki učaščixsja v soglasovanii v uslovijax sel'skoj mestnosti (po materialam Borovskoj školy Novo-Usmanskogo rajona Voroneškoj oblasti)' in Sobinnikova V.I., Popova, Z.D. and Čižik-Polejko, A.I. (eds.), *Materialy konferencii po izučeniju južnorusskix govorov i pamjatnikov pis'-mennosti (6-8 dekabrja 1962 goda)*, Voronež, Izdatel'stvo Voronežskogo universiteta, pp. 122-8

Zahrods'kyj, A.O. (1954) *Hramatyka ukrajins'koji movi, II, Sintaksis*, 9th edn, revised, Kiev, Radjans'ka škola

Zaliznjak, A.A. and Padučeva, E.V. (1979) 'Sintaksičeskie svojstva mestoimenija *kotoryj*' in Nikolaeva, T.M. (ed.), *Kategorija opredelennosti-neopredelennosti v slavjanskix i balkanskix jazykax*, Moscow, Nauka, pp. 289-329

Zdaniukiewicz, A.A. (1973) *Z zagadnień kultury języka: teoria, praktyka, szkoła*, Warsaw, PWN

Zemskaja, E.A. and Kapanadze, L.A. (eds.) (1978) *Russkaja razgovornaja reč': teksty*, Moscow, Nauka

Zieniukowa, J. (1979) 'Składnia zgody w zdaniach z podmiotem szeregowym we współczesnej polszczyźnie', *Slavia Occidentalis*, 36, 117-29

Zwicky, A.M. (1977) 'Hierarchies of Person', *Papers from the Thirteenth Regional Meeting, Chicago Linguistic Society*, 714-33

INDEX

When there are three or more co-authors, only the first appears in the text. All are given in the index; the entries for those subsumed under *et al.* are followed by the name of the first author in parentheses. Scholars are distinguished from literary authors by the inclusion of initials, thus Chomsky, N. but Dostoevskij.